Forces

Belief, Difference,
and Power in
Contemporary
Works by
Ethnic Women

Bonnie Winsbro

The University of
Massachusetts Press
Amherst

Copyright © 1993 by
The University of Massachusetts Press
All rights reserved
Printed in the United States of America
LC 93–4237
ISBN 0–87023–879–5 (cloth); 880–9 (paper)

Designed by Rebecca S. Neimark
Set in Goudy Old Style by Keystone Typesetting, Inc.
Printed and bound by Thomson-Shore, Inc.

Library of Congress Cataloging-in-Publication Data
Winsbro, Bonnie C.
    Supernatural forces : belief, difference, and power in
contemporary works by ethnic women / Bonnie Winsbro.
        p.   cm.
    Includes bibliographical references and index.
    ISBN 0–87023–879–5 (cloth : alk. paper). — ISBN 0–87023–880–9
(pbk. : alk. paper)
    1. American literature—Women authors—History and criticism.
    2. Women and literature—United States—History—20th century.
    3. American literature—20th century—History and criticism.
    4. Ethnic groups in literature.   5. Supernatural in literature.   I. Title.
    PS151.W46   1993
    810.9'37—dc20   93–4237
                                                          CIP

British Library Cataloguing in Publication data are available.

To Vic, Sandy, and Ruth,
with love and deepest gratitude

Contents

Acknowledgments

Acknowledgments for help in completing this book are due to four groups of people: those writers and critics whose previous publications have shaped and inspired my own work; those scholars who guided me in the preparation of the dissertation on which this book is based; those readers and editors who helped me transform the dissertation into a publishable book; and those friends and family who have encouraged me throughout the writing of both dissertation and book.

I wish, first of all, to acknowledge the influence, both conscious and subconscious, of the vast number of writers and critics who have shared their ideas about the authors and their works through previous publications. Several of these writers, because they share the cultural background of the author or have spent many years studying the culture, provided an understanding and insights that would not otherwise have been available to me. The idea of multiple, colliding worlds separated by divisive boundaries, which I have developed as one theme in this book, was suggested by the multiplicity of works—of poetry, fiction, autobiography, literary criticism, ethnography, sociology, psychology—that have used these metaphors to describe the intersection between ethnic groups as well as between an individual and his or her family or community. I especially want to thank Bettina Aptheker, whose book *Tapestries of Life: Women's Work, Women's Consciousness, and the Meaning of Daily Experience* introduced me to several writers and works that I have cited in chapter 1 and whose fifth condition for writing that book served as a goal and an inspiration for me throughout my own work.

I wish to thank the members of my dissertation committee, all from the University of Tennessee, both for their interest in and support of my study and for the considerable time they devoted to review, discussion, and criticism. I am particularly indebted to my major professor, George Hutchinson, whose comments and suggestions—which were invariably relevant, thought-provoking, and challenging—have helped me to write a far more sophisticated work than I could have written otherwise. I am also grateful to Mary Papke, Charles Maland, and John Hodges for their close, insightful, and prompt readings. In addition, Mary has my unending gratitude for believing in both me and my project—and backing up that belief with action—at a time when such support seemed lacking.

Acknowledgments and gratitude are also extended to those who helped me prepare the dissertation manuscript for publication. Roberta Rubenstein, author of *Boundaries of the Self: Gender, Culture, Fiction*, which was at the time of my research the only existing book of criticism offering a multicultural view of women's contemporary literature, read the manuscript and offered valuable comments on ways in which to improve it. Hertha D. Wong, author of *Sending My Heart Back Across the Years: Tradition and Innovation in Native American Autobiography*, also read the manuscript. I am especially grateful to her for her close reading, which revealed several of the types of culturally based misrepresentations often made by a person writing from the outside looking in, as well as for her generous support of my work. I also want to thank Clark Dougan of the University of Massachusetts Press, both for his enthusiastic response to the manuscript and for his assistance in helping me move through the stages of manuscript review with far less effort and pain than I would have believed possible. Thanks are also extended to Dawn Potter, whose meticulous care in copyediting the manuscript revealed errors that had gone undetected through more readings than I care to admit.

I also wish to thank four colleagues and friends who have from the very beginning of this project listened to my ideas, concerns, and fears and have always responded with interest, enthusiasm, and support: Vickie Reddick, Beth Giddens, Lisa Crafton, and Judith Slagle. Suzin Eiselstein, in addition to listening to semiannual progress reports, took precious time from her summer vacation to proof pages. My gratitude to three other friends—Victor Cain, Sandra Ballard, and Ruth Gat—knows no bounds; without their love and support and belief in my abilities, I would not have completed my dissertation and degree, much less this book. Finally, I thank my parents, Robert Berkeley Winsbro and Ella Melvin Winsbro, for having instilled in me as a child the belief that I could accomplish any goal I set for myself.

Supernatural Forces

1 Belief, Ethnicity, and Self-Definition

I . . . want my work to capture the vast imagination of black people. That is, I want my books to reflect the imaginative combination of the real world, the very practical, shrewd, day to day functioning that black people must do, while at the same time they encompass some great supernatural element. We know that it does not bother them one bit to do something practical and have visions at the same time. So all the parts of living are on an equal footing. Birds talk and butterflies cry, and it is not surprising or upsetting to them. These things make the world larger for them. Some young people don't want to acknowledge this as a way of life. They don't want to hark back to those embarrassing days when we were associated with "haints" and superstitions. They want to get as far as possible into the scientific world. It makes me wonder, in such cases, if the knowledge we ignore is discredited because we have discredited it. —Toni Morrison[1]

The relationship between humans and their gods has always been a primary theme in literature. The American literary canon, like that of other nations, traces the history of the religious beliefs of the country, beginning with the early Puritanism of Edward Taylor and Anne Bradstreet and continuing through the Calvinism of Jonathan Edwards, the transcendentalism of Ralph Waldo Emerson and Henry David Thoreau, the pantheism and religious ecstasy of Walt Whitman, and the rebellion of Nathaniel Hawthorne, Herman Melville, and Emily Dickinson against a restrictive religion and a stern and bullying god. Finally, twentieth-century modernists, confronted with a godless universe and deprived of a living mythology, either denied the need for mythology, turned to ancient or Eastern mythologies, or sought to create new mythologies with which to fill the gap. Despite the changes and variety over time in the depiction by American writers of their relationship to the supernatural, those works included in the American canon have almost universally focused on the Judaeo-Christian god, praising, fearing, rebelling against, or denying his power. What has rarely been treated seriously in American literature until recently, or at least rarely published, are human relationships with deities other than the Judaeo-Christian god, with the spirits of the deceased, and with those men and women who draw on the powers of such deities and spirits to extend their own mortal power—powers referred to as supernatural, religious, mythological, or magical.

The five novels and one autobiography discussed here reflect a view of reality that differs significantly from that presented by the previously established literary canon. According to the reality represented by these works, the world is inhabited by a host of spirits and deities, all of whom possess the power to influence or control events that affect humans. Motivated by fear, loneliness, reverence, or gratitude, the humans in this world maintain a continuous and intimate communication with its many nonhuman inhabitants. This world is also inhabited by sorcerers and witches who, manipulating supernatural powers to advance the forces of evil and destruction, are responsible for such phenomena as sudden illness or death, failed crops and dying livestock, flood and drought. To counteract the powers of evil, however, humans can call on conjurors, shamans, and healers, who apply magic and ritual to restore health, fecundity, and balance to the universe. Thus, the works discussed here represent an alternative reality to that represented by those American authors who have written and are continuing to write out of a Judaeo-Christian tradition. They also, of course, represent a view of reality that has been "disproved" by science.

Although science has methodically disproved the objective reality of spirits, deities, and supernatural forces, it has failed to destroy belief in the supernatural because that belief provides a logical answer to questions that have plagued humans since the awakening of their cognitive powers. Many cultures, for example, believe that the soul leaves the body during dreaming and that during these dream periods one's soul is threatened by evil spirits who wish to steal it or to take its place in the deserted body. This belief is validated for such cultures not only by the phenomenon of dreaming itself but also by the perception that an ailing individual is cured when his or her soul is returned or when a foreign spirit is ousted from the individual's body by the resident healer. "An Iban *knows* his theories are correct," writes research psychiatrist

E. Fuller Torrey about a group of people living in Borneo, "because his subjective experiences during dreaming prove it and because when the *manang* captures a lost soul during treatment, the sufferer usually gets well."[2] The Iban's beliefs are not just the product of an overactive imagination; they are both suggested and validated by the experiential evidence of their dreams and of their culture's healing process. The Iban have constructed a reality that serves them in time of need as effectively as a scientific or Judaeo-Christian reality serves others.

This book, then, examines a few of the different world views that constitute different realities for different people. It recognizes that today's world is not defined by one reality but by many realities and that, while these realities sometimes overlap or coexist amicably, they often intrude on or clash with each other. Although multiple realities have always existed, dominant cultures have historically sought to unify reality by imposing their own version on those around them. As a result, the realities, or beliefs, of marginal cultures have frequently been destroyed; when not totally destroyed, they have been carefully hidden from view and passed on through secret ritual and ceremony, or they have been transformed and modified to merge with or incorporate other realities. Within the United States, the beliefs of those ethnic groups that have been rendered powerless through decimation of their numbers, through enslavement, through an externally imposed silence and invisibility, and through a process of colonization that has denied them the right to construct and represent their own reality are the beliefs that have been most at risk. Since the 1960s, however, a renewed interest in ethnicity has motivated members of such groups to assert their differences, to revitalize and reconstruct their own realities and world views, and to represent and validate these alternative beliefs through literature that, although often written primarily for their own people, asserts to audiences from all cultures that multiple realities do exist.

This new body of ethnic literature, in addition to celebrating the differences among groups, is also concerned with the individual, with his or her daily concerns both within the group and at the boundary that separates the group from the society at large. The writers discussed here are particularly concerned with the responses by ethnic individuals to the collision of worlds, realities, and beliefs when the boundary separating the marginal community from the dominant society is crossed, violated, or destroyed. Frequently, individuals caught between cultures are confronted with a multiplicity of realities, an experience that is confusing at best and potentially both physically and psychically destructive. Taken together, these works argue that the survival and growth of ethnic individuals depend on effective self-definition, the process by which they define who they are and what they believe in relation to surrounding social units—family, community/tribe, and society at large. Such an experience of individuation, if completed successfully, instills personal power, a power that in some cases is supplemented by a belief in an alternative reality, one that acknowledges the existence of those spirits, deities, and empowered humans who are celebrated and remembered in culturally specific folklore, myths, and religion.

In chapters 2 through 7, then, I examine five novels and one autobiography—Lee Smith's *Oral History* (1983), Louise Erdrich's *Tracks* (1988), Leslie Marmon Silko's *Ceremony* (1977), Gloria Naylor's *Mama Day* (1988), Toni Morrison's *Beloved* (1987), and Maxine Hong Kingston's *The Woman Warrior: Memoirs of a Girlhood Among Ghosts* (1976)— and their depiction of different responses by ethnic individuals to the crossing, violation, or destruction of geographical or sociocultural boundaries. My own focus in examining these different responses is to determine the role of the individual's belief in supernatural forces in his or her individuation. How is the process of self-definition affected by one's personal beliefs, by the community's beliefs, and by the outside world's beliefs? When are such beliefs—or conflicts between beliefs— constructive, and when are they destructive? When is a partial or total reconstruction of such beliefs called for? Ultimately, all the works argue for power through self-definition, for the construction of one's own world and one's own identity, for the location and claiming of one's own center.

Smith's *Oral History*, for example, clearly demonstrates the devastating consequences of being defined from without. The failure of Red Emmy, labeled by Granny Younger and the community as a witch, to redefine her identity in her own terms serves to highlight the powerlessness of many Appalachian women to break out of their socioculturally defined identities. The curse Red Emmy passes on to succeeding generations is the curse of being hopelessly confined within both geographical and sociocultural boundaries. As *Oral History* demonstrates, belief in the supernatural is double-edged: it serves both to entrap women and to offer them their only means of escape. Because of this double-edged nature of Appalachian belief, the reader, at the novel's end, is both dismayed and relieved by what Rosalind B. Reilly sees as "the end of a great era of belief."[3]

Erdrich's *Tracks* also tells the story of a witch, but that witch—Fleur Pillager—differs from Red Emmy in being defined from within as well as from without. Fleur receives her identity as a witch in several ways: she is born into a family known for its power in dealing with supernatural forces; she alone survives the consumption that kills the rest of her family; and she survives two drownings before the age of fifteen, a clear indication to both her and the community that she has been befriended by Misshepeshu, the Chippewa water god. Because Chippewa culture allows for and respects the role of the witch, or evil shaman, within the community, Fleur's identity as a witch enhances her power both in her own eyes and in those of the community. With the increasing intrusion of whites into the Chippewa community, however, Fleur discovers that her own supernaturally endowed powers are insufficient to stop both their intrusion and their destruction. In her characterization of Fleur, Pauline Puyat, and old man Nanapush, Erdrich suggests three possible responses of the Chippewa to the intrusion of whites into their world, an intrusion that threatens to destroy them by destroying their belief in the powers of the Chippewa gods and spirits.

Whereas *Tracks* suggests that Native American beliefs in the supernatural cannot survive white contact, Silko's *Ceremony* suggests that such beliefs not only survive but remain essential to the health and well-being of the modern Pueblo. *Ceremony* suggests that a Pueblo who wanders too far from home, crossing an invisible boundary that separates the Pueblo world from the white world, risks being both physically and psychically transformed by that experience. Simply returning home in body, recrossing the geographical boundary, is ineffective unless one can return home spiritually, healing the internal division arising from an inability to reconcile conflicting world views. Returning home to Laguna after World War II, Tayo must reconcile his Pueblo beliefs, as related in old Grandma's stories, with European-American beliefs, as related by white teachers and doctors, in order to cure himself and, by extension, the tribe and the universe. Unlike Red Emmy, entrapped by Appalachian beliefs in the supernatural, Tayo has the freedom to define himself, and through a painful but healing process of individuation, he succeeds in locating what Paula Gunn Allen refers to as one's "right relationship to earth and society."[4]

Naylor's *Mama Day* is similar to *Ceremony* in that it dramatizes a confrontation between two worlds and world views. The world of New York is characterized by its emphasis on culture, alienation, and science, whereas the world of Willow Springs is characterized by its emphasis on nature, community, and supernatural forces. Thus, George, born and raised in New York, relies on the power of the self to accomplish goals while Bernice, born and raised in Willow Springs, relies on the power of external forces to accomplish miracles. Miranda suggests that both sources of belief are valuable, each supplementing and extending the power of the other. Her grandniece, Cocoa, however, finds herself caught between the two worlds and their opposing approaches to accomplishment and self-empowerment. Cocoa, recognizing that life in New York threatens to transform her into "a total stranger,"[5] returns home once a year, home being a place where she knows herself because she is known by others. Her movement between two worlds, however, without a firm identity to sustain her results in a constant struggle. Until she learns, as she does at the novel's end, to draw on strengths from both worlds to construct a personal world and personal identity, she can know no peace.

Morrison's *Beloved* also depicts characters searching for peace—and power—through self-definition. Self-definition becomes possible for the characters in *Beloved* only through a painful confrontation with the past, as incarnated in Beloved, Sethe's deceased daughter. Only by confronting Beloved, an egoless ghost who mirrors their own fear, guilt, desire, and loneliness, can Sethe, Denver, Paul D, and the community come to know themselves and restore the connections among them that were originally severed by Sethe's actions eighteen years earlier. In *Beloved* the belief in ghosts—in the return of the spirits of the beloved dead to their families, homes, and communities—is consoling. When, however, the return of a spirit becomes, as Ella describes it, an "invasion,"[6] it can become potentially destructive. Morrison suggests, nevertheless, that only by confronting, knowing, and exorcising one's ghosts—the past—can one move forward toward health and power.

Kingston's autobiography, *The Woman Warrior*, makes a similar argument: only by knowing one's ghosts, giving them life and substance, can one know oneself. By imagining her ghosts' lives, by filling in the details of those lives, Maxine[7] transforms them from "forever wandering,"[8] forever haunting ghosts into people—fully fleshed and permanently grounded—who no longer threaten her. By understanding her relationship to these ghosts, the ways in which she resembles and differs from them, Kingston defines herself in relation not only to the ghosts but also to the sociocultural heritage she shares with them. Through a process of self-definition, she learns how to do battle against anyone—her parents, the community of emigrant villagers, and the larger world of white bigots and bosses—who would attempt to entrap her in a predetermined identity. Eventually, Maxine creates for herself an identity and a voice that transcend the sociocultural barriers that threaten to enclose or, alternatively, to exclude her.

The types and consequences of belief in the supernatural differ among these works, as do the relationships between the protagonists and their surrounding social units. All begin with cultural difference, portraying the spoken and unspoken conflicts of being ethnic in the United States, but they present different types of conflicts arising from their ethnicity and different types of resolutions. Some of the protagonists, raised without mothers, suffer from the lack of a mother's nurturing and socializing influence; others suffer from a dual heritage, rejected by both parental groups or confused by conflicting loyalties to two cultures; others are second-generation children, born and raised in the United States by immigrant parents who cling to a homeland their children know only in abstraction; and still others are so Americanized that they have never fully recognized or acknowledged the contribution of their ethnicity to their personality and behavior. In each work, the individuals suffer the consequences of being different not only from the society at large but also from their families or communities. Their individuation in relation to those sociocultural units is either helped or hindered by beliefs in the supernatural—sometimes by their own beliefs and sometimes by those of the surrounding community. These works suggest that such beliefs are extremely powerful, capable of destroying a fragmented individual and a fragmented community or of healing them. The experience of examining, rejecting, renewing, or modifying the beliefs of several cultures is both liberating and empowering; it liberates individuals from a reality constructed and imposed by others and empowers them with the strength to find substance and voice in a world that until recently has rendered them both invisible and silent.

Early in the planning for this book, I recognized that the great extent and variety of ethnic works dealing with empowerment through self-definition in relation to one's beliefs in the supernatural would require that I make certain decisions to help guide the selection of writers to be included. My primary objective was to examine the works of writers from several different ethnic groups within the United States to demonstrate that the trend is a cross-cultural one; extending this examination across cultures, however, meant that I would need to limit the book in other ways. The two limitations that I chose to impose—works written since 1970 and works written by women—were in some ways dictated by the subject matter itself. The current interest of American ethnic writers in self-definition, for example, can be seen as a direct outgrowth of the renewed desire since the 1960s by ethnic groups of the United States to assert their differences from, rather than similarities to, the dominant culture. One difference recognized by many ethnic writers as distinguishing their group from the dominant culture is the difference in beliefs about the supernatural. The interest in and representation of alternative belief systems by ethnic writers is certainly not new, as demonstrated by the novels and stories of Zora Neale Hurston, Charles Chesnutt, and Margaret Walker dealing with voodoo, conjuration, and herbal healing. Nevertheless, I chose to limit the book to works written since 1970 so that I could focus on the reasons for and the strengths of the more recent post-1960s appeal.

Although the renewed interest in and desire to represent alternative belief systems in literature cannot be denied, the beliefs described by the writers included here—in witches, healers, and ghosts—cannot be considered as representative of the beliefs held by most members of any of these groups. Indeed, many African Americans, Native Americans, Chinese Americans, and Appalachians hold strong Protestant or Catholic as well as scientific beliefs and thus may be somewhat dismayed by this tendency of contemporary writers to return to what they, along with many members of the dominant culture, think of as "primitive" beliefs. Many African Americans and Native Americans, for example, have chosen Christianity over the traditional religions of their ancestors because they have witnessed and experienced its power and found it self-affirming. Others, having been raised within Christianity, naturally consider it—whether adopted directly or reshaped to fit their individual needs—to be their traditional and authentic religion. For still other, more sociopolitically minded ethnics, the renewal of interest in ancient beliefs and alternative realities threatens to undo past efforts and hard-won successes in stressing similarities to, rather than differences from, the dominant culture. Because racial equality and the consequent social, economic, and educational gains have been so long denied to subordinate groups on the basis of perceived differences, many ethnics continue to see cultural differences as needing to be smoothed over and diminished rather than preserved and accentuated.

Similarly, although male ethnic writers are interested in asserting difference and in redefining group and individual identity, they tend to be less concerned with examining, preserving, and representing cultural traditions, including belief systems, than are women. Dexter Fisher, for example, notes that among African-American writers, males "tend to focus their literature on the confrontation between the black and white worlds" while women "concentrate more intensely on the black community alone and the human relationships within that community."[9] Thus, despite the existence of works dealing with alternative belief systems by such male writers as Alex Haley, N. Scott Momaday, and Rudolfo Anaya, my interest in examining the influences of belief on individuation seemed to suggest primarily women writers, whose desire to represent the community fully and accurately demands that they deal with such topics. Somewhat contrary to Fisher's statement, however, the works of the ethnic women writers discussed here are similar to works by male African-American writers in that they are clearly concerned with the confrontation between the ethnic world and that of the dominant culture. Nevertheless, these works do differ from those by male African-American writers in that they shift emphasis from the confrontation itself to the effect of that confrontation on the individual and on his or her relationships to and within the community.

For male ethnic writers, one might say, power often derives from *participating in* and perhaps even *furthering* the confrontation, whereas for female ethnic writers power derives from *overcoming* the effects of that confrontation as one moves toward a unity of self and a reconciliation with others.

Although the women writers I have selected—Smith, Erdrich, Silko, Naylor, Morrison, and Kingston—do not necessarily express ideas and views that can be considered representative of their respective ethnic groups, they are certainly representative of a growing desire among women of different racial and cultural backgrounds to, in Bettina Aptheker's words, "make connections . . ., while recognizing and respecting . . . differences, as an integral way of knowing."[10] In fact, for women, this scrutiny and celebration of cultural differences often goes hand in hand with their scrutiny and celebration of gender differences. In chapters 2 through 7, I discuss the six works individually, emphasizing the different responses to similar multicultural situations and conflicts. In the final chapter I briefly discuss the role that beliefs play in the creation of boundaries both between and within ethnic groups. Before looking at the individual works, however, I devote the remainder of this chapter to an examination of ethnicity and ethnicization and of the importance of cultural and individual self-definition in attaining power.

Ethnicity, Ethnicization, and the Ethnic Writer

Werner Sollors, in his book *Beyond Ethnicity,* defines ethnic literature as fiction and nonfiction works that have been "written by, about, or for persons who perceived themselves, or were perceived by others, as members of ethnic groups."[11] Although this definition appears reasonable, difficulties begin to arise, as Sollors demonstrates in his first chapter, when one attempts to define "ethnic group" and "ethnicity." Both Sollors and social scientist William Petersen attempt to gain a better understanding of the concept of ethnicity by reviewing the etymological roots of the word, but such a review threatens to add to rather than alleviate the confusion. On the one hand, the Greek word *ethnikos,* meaning "particular to a race or nation," points to the inheritance of certain sociobiological characteristics—that is, the inheritance of racial or national characteristics through biology (genetic makeup) or through cultural socialization (language, religion, subsistence patterns, family organization). In this sense, all people are ethnics because all people have distinct, although often mixed, racial and national origins. On the other hand, when the word "ethnic" was first incorporated into the English language in the nineteenth century, it was used to mean "not Christian or Jewish, pagan, heathen,"[12] a definition that strongly emphasizes otherness, or difference from the dominant culture. Thus, although all Americans are, in one sense, ethnics, the term is commonly used today to mean "nonstandard . . . or not fully American."[13] From this definition comes the idea that an ethnic group is synonymous with a minority or marginal group, which is not necessarily true if one accepts that members of majority or culturally dominant groups are also ethnics.

The common denominator between both definitions of ethnicity—difference as constituted by race or nationality and difference from a politically, economically, and socially dominant group—is their emphasis on differences among groups of people. Ethnicity implies that one group is separated from another by perceived differences, differences that are accentuated, minimized, or modified through the interactive processes of ethnicization, assimilation, and acculturation. The persistence of ethnic differences within multi-ethnic nations, despite the mixing of groups through intermarriage, social interaction, and the common pursuit of certain national goals, has been explained in two ways. One theory holds that ethnicity is a response to a sociobiological force, or a psycho-physical inheritance, that necessarily separates one ethnic from another. The other holds that ethnics create and maintain artificial boundaries in the absence of true cultural differences to ensure continued separation from the mass.

Horace Kallen, who studied the assimilation of U.S. immigrants in the early part of the century, believed that each human being was separated from another by the inheritance of certain intrinsic psycho-physical features: "Behind him in time and tremendously in him in quality, are his ancestors; around him in space are his relatives and kin, carrying in common with him the inherited organic set from a remoter common ancestry. In all these he lives and moves and has his being. They constitute his, literally, *natio*, the inwardness of his nativity."[14] Similar to Kallen's view that one's ethnicity is, to a large degree, genetically or biologically determined is social scientist Michael Novak's belief that ethnicity is the result of the cultural conditioning that begins at infancy. "How often children are held in the arms, by whom, and in which emotional patterns may establish the rhythm of their own future emotional expectations," Novak writes. "How many voices surround them and with what qualities of passion, what is encouraged in their behavior and what is inhibited, the repertoire of facial expressions and gesture and information that they absorb—all these are communicated, most often, without theory and apart from conscious decision."[15] An unconscious victim of cultural and familial experience and conditioning, the individual has very little control over his or her development.

Although Novak and Kallen differ in their opinions about how ethnic differences are inherited, with Kallen emphasizing genetics and Novak emphasizing cultural and familial conditioning, both agree that ethnic groups are distinguished by distinctly different ways of perceiving and responding to their physical and social environment. In opposition to Kallen, Novak, and others who emphasize sociobiological differences among cultures, Fredrik Barth argues that in fact very little in the actual content of cultures serves to distinguish one group from another. Rather, through a process of self-ascription and ascription by others, groups select from a large group of available alternatives those cultural features that are to be used as "signals and emblems of difference," ignoring others and in some cases minimizing or denying those major differences that do exist. This emphasis on ascription of group characteristics in defining group identity means that the continuity of ethnic groups depends not on a naturally occurring, sociobiological force but on the artificial construction and maintenance of ethnic boundaries. To understand ethnic continuity, then, according to Barth, one must study "the ethnic *boundary* that defines the group, not the cultural stuff that it encloses." In fact, the cultural features that signal membership and exclusion tend to change over time, with a consequent change in the cultural features of the group itself. What remains, however, despite such change is the boundary, the "continuing dichotomization between members and outsiders," and this persistence of the dichotomizing boundary, rather than nonchanging cultural features, is responsible for the persistence of a distinct cultural identity.[16]

Barth's theory that ethnicity is constructed rather than inherited, particularly as it has been represented by Sollors in *Beyond Ethnicity,* has understandably met with strong opposition from some ethnic Americans. One cannot deny, however, that the construction and maintenance of boundaries have long been used by all cultures as a means of asserting difference and establishing and maintaining social, economic, and political barriers. What falls within the boundaries is superior, privileged, and dominant; what falls without is inferior, deprived, and subordinate. Implicit in boundary construction is the power of definition—the power to define the ideal identity in terms of the values, beliefs, and attitudes held; the power to define others in relation to that ideal; and the power to include or exclude potential members accordingly. The maintenance of boundaries is, however, an interactive process between members and nonmembers. Ethnic groups that choose not to be absorbed by the dominant culture often construct and maintain ethnic boundaries to resist homogenization and to affirm their difference from others, particularly from what threatens to be an increasingly amorphous and all-encompassing American identity. Since the civil rights movement of the 1960s, African Americans, Native Americans, and Chicanos have displayed and acted on a renewed desire to emphasize their differences from European Americans, partly to distinguish their own beliefs, values, and life-styles, partly to instill group pride, and partly to seek political power and economic benefits. The success with which such groups have emphasized differences to achieve group solidarity clearly demonstrates the way in which boundary creation and maintenance can be used to promote ethnicization.

The ethnic women writers discussed here also emphasize difference by focusing their attention on those boundaries that set their groups apart from the dominant culture. Movement across those boundaries, whether it involves an invasion of the dominant culture inward or the passage of an ethnic individual outward, causes conflict—an internal division or disunity—that the individual must resolve to regain psychic and sometimes physical health. As a group, the works suggest that individuals of multi-ethnic origin or of an ethnic origin differing from that of the dominant culture are faced with a choice of identity. As Morrison points out, "Now people choose their identities. Now people choose to be Black. They used to be *born* Black. . . . You can be Black genetically and choose not to be."[17] Thus, ethnic Americans have the choice of asserting their ethnic origins, maintaining boundaries by differentiating themselves from all other cultures; of acculturating to one of the available cultures, denying or minimizing difference; or of creating a new cultural identity by merging aspects of two or more cultures. Indeed, this choice is not only a right, these works argue, but a necessity; to define oneself, one must define one's beliefs and one's relation to surrounding groups, thus choosing or creating one's own center and one's own boundaries.

In fact, as I discuss more fully in chapter 8, these works suggest that the boundary separating one ethnic group from another, as well as an individual from the community, is often created and maintained by beliefs instilled by cultural and familial conditioning. Adherence to the beliefs strengthens the boundary, whereas rejection or modification of the beliefs weakens, or perhaps reconfigures, the boundary. Whether the decision to maintain, reject, or modify one's beliefs, and consequently the boundary created by those beliefs, is the "correct" one— that is, whether it is empowering or destructive—depends on whether the boundary itself contributes to or limits one's survival and growth. In all instances, however, the individual's psychic and physical health depends on an examination and evaluation of the beliefs inherited from his or her family and community.

The emphasis on the conflict between one's culturally inherited beliefs and those of other groups is exactly what makes the writers included here "ethnic writers." An ethnic writer is any writer who chooses to emphasize racial or national differences from others, whether those differences are indeed real or only perceived to be real. Although ethnicity is not synonymous with marginality, ethnic literature, like feminist literature, incorporates a consciousness of marginality; both ethnic literature and feminist literature depend on the writer's consciousness and expression of differences from a normative world view, value system, and/or literary style. The motivation for emphasizing difference varies among ethnic writers. It may be to instill group pride and to foster group solidarity; it may be to obtain sociopolitical power and economic benefits; or it may be to preserve traditions and beliefs of the past, either to prevent their total loss from memory or to inspire present and future generations who feel alienated in the modern world. An ethnic writer, like a feminist writer, acknowledges that differences and boundaries do exist and examines the options for and consequences of preserving, modifying, or eliminating those differences and boundaries.

Power through Cultural Self-Definition

Julia Kristeva argues in "Women's Time" that the feminist struggle for power, both collective and individual, passes through three phases, each distinguished by the way in which women relate female power to male power. During the first phase, women seek power by attaining rights similar and equal to those enjoyed by men; during the second phase, they seek power by rejecting male ideas and structures of power, replacing them with female ideas and structures. Kristeva expresses the belief, and the hope, that women will move on to a third phase in their search for power in which "the very dichotomy man/woman as an opposition between two rival entities may be understood as belonging to *metaphysics*. What can 'identity,' even 'sexual identity,' mean in a new theoretical and scientific space where the very notion of identity is challenged?"[18]

This dismissal of both the "notion of identity" and the concept of difference by contemporary theorists disturbs both feminists and ethnics. Linda Hutcheon, for example, argues that neither feminists nor ethnics—"ex-centrics"—are willing to give up notions of identity because they have not yet had the freedom to experience their own subjectivity: "unlike the male, white, Eurocentered poststructuralist discourse that has forcefully challenged humanism's whole, integrated ideal of subjectivity, . . . these more ex-centric personalities know that they cannot reject the subject wholesale, mainly because they have never really been allowed it."[19] Similarly, Henry Louis Gates, Jr., in discussing the current demand to dissolve the subject, says that

the Western male subject has long been constituted historically for himself and in himself. And, while we readily accept, acknowledge, and partake of the critique of *this* subject as transcendent, to deny us the process of exploring and reclaiming our subjectivity before we critique it is the critical version of the grandfather clause, the double privileging of categories that happen to be *preconstituted*. Such a position leaves us nowhere, invisible and voiceless in the republic of Western letters. Consider the irony: precisely when we (and other third world peoples) obtain the complex wherewithal to define our black subjectivity in the republic of Western letters, our theoretical colleagues declare that there ain't no such thing as a subject, so why should we be bothered with that?[20]

Members of ethnic groups, Hutcheon and Gates remind us, are speaking and writing from a reality and experience that differ significantly from those of many contemporary theorists.

Members of ethnic groups, because they have already experienced both cultural annihilation and individual alienation, must recover or construct an identity if they are to survive. The Native American population has been decimated from a precontact number estimated at twelve to twenty million to a current population of about one million, with a low point early in this century of only about two hundred and fifty thousand.[21] "Many Native American cultures," writes Erdrich, "were annihilated more thoroughly than even a nuclear disaster might destroy ours, and others live on with the fallout of that destruction, effects as persistent as radiation—poverty, fetal alcohol syndrome, chronic despair."[22] African Americans were forcibly uprooted from their homeland, transported across the ocean in murderous conditions, enslaved for three hundred years, and perceived and treated as animals and children. An estimated sixty million Africans died either in captivity in Africa or during transportation on slave ships.[23] As for Asian Americans, Jeffery Paul Chan and others state that racism in the United States has robbed them of an identity, alienating them from both European Americans and Asians. Furthermore, Asian Americans "live in and accept a state of euphemized self-contempt" that is "nothing more than the subjects' acceptance of white standards of objectivity, behavior, and achievement as being morally absolute and their acknowledgment that, because they are not white, they can never fully measure up to white standards."[24] Similarly, Allen states that for those Native Americans who survived white contact, the "compulsory indoctrination" to European-American values, world views, scientific facts, and thinking processes has resulted in "thousands of Native people [who] suffer the ravages of despair brought on by too much shame, too much grief, and too much irrepressible and helpless fury."[25]

To understand the degree to which the dominant culture of the United States has alienated marginal groups, rendering them powerless by erasing ethnic differences and destroying group identity under the guise of promoting American unity and homogeneity, one need only consider the effects of cultural dominance on the language and religion of Native Americans. Irene Mack Pyawasit, of the Menominee in Wisconsin, tells of how her grandmother prepared her as a child for the attempts by whites to deny Pyawasit her own language and religion: "My grandmother knew they were going to whitewash us [at the mission school]. She knew the methods they employ, and she knew that we were going to have to learn to speak nothing but English because they were not going to let us speak our own language, and they would try to take our religion away. She said, 'You have to keep your religion inside you, in your heart.' They wouldn't let us practice our religion because to the government employees, we were just a bunch of pagans, uncivilized savages. So I had to keep within me all that I had learned from her."[26] To survive the experience of "compulsory indoctrination" to European-American standards of civilization, ethnics like Pyawasit learned from their grandmothers how to protect within themselves the remnants of their own culture, sustained by the fact that they could periodically return for renewal to a group sharing their own world view.

Similarly, John Big Bluff Tosamah, a fictitious character in N. Scott Momaday's novel *House Made of Dawn*, tells of the last time the Kiowas gathered as a living Sun Dance culture: "They could find no buffalo; they had to hang an old hide from the sacred tree. . . . Before the dance could begin, a company of armed soldiers rode out from Fort Sill under orders to disperse the tribe. Forbidden without cause the essential act of their faith, having seen the wild herds slaughtered and left to rot upon the ground, the Kiowas backed away forever from the tree. That was July 20, 1890, at the great bend of the Washita. My grandmother was there. Without bitterness, and for as long as she lived, she bore a vision of deicide."[27] The destruction by one group of another group's gods, of its living mythology, is one of the most effective, even if unintended, means of achieving group disintegration and disorientation and the consequent psychic alienation of its members. When the European Americans destroyed the buffalo, Joseph Campbell writes, they destroyed the "binding symbol" of the Plains tribes in North America, for whom the relationship between humans and the animals on which they relied for food had been the "central, pivotal concern of the religiously maintained social order," and within a few years the religion of the tribes became archaic and nearly died.[28]

The emphasis by contemporary ethnic writers on the threat posed to individuals who have been denied the right to a strong, empowering group identity suggests that the primary danger of the cultural dominance of one group by another is not, then, that one group obtains and maintains political and economic power over the other. The real threat is that it robs a group of its psychological and spiritual power. Aptheker explains that the process by which women are colonized by men "involves an internal corrosion, a loss of esteem, a loss of confidence in one's knowledge, an inability to give expression to experience. To understand the colonization of women is to understand its interior dimensions, its psychological consequences, its hold on the imagination, and the enormity of effort, individual and collective, which is required to break its cycle. At the heart of the colonization is a belief in the superiority of men; in the superiority of male judgment and authority; and in the absolute priority given to achieving male approval and validation."[29] Colonization, whether it entails the oppression of women, classes, or other cultures, always involves the imposition by only one race, one class, or one sex (or one subset cutting across these categories) of its values, traditions, beliefs, and world view—its "reality"—on a society that is actually composed of multiple races, classes, and genders. As colonization progresses, the way of life of the dominant society is gradually believed to represent a "natural" or "given" order when in reality it represents the perspectives of only a single subset of that society.

Eventually, the maintenance of the way of life desired by the dominant culture depends on the continued silencing of marginalized groups and their internalization of the dominant culture's beliefs, values, attitudes, opinions, and style. Elizabeth Janeway, exploring power relationships among humans in her book *Powers of the Weak*, believes that the "power to disbelieve, the first power of the weak, begins . . . with the refusal to accept the definition of oneself that is put forward by the powerful. . . . By disbelieving, one will be led toward doubting prescribed codes of behavior, and as one begins to act in ways that can deviate from the norm in any degree, it becomes clear that in fact there is *not* just one right way to handle or understand events."[30] Attitudes, then, follow behavior; by first disbelieving and then rebelling against the prescribed order, acting in new and different ways, one begins to develop a new sense of self. As part of the movement toward cultural self-definition, many ethnics are rejecting the order prescribed by the dominant culture and are returning to the stories, the representations of reality, of their ancestors as a basis for creating new, empowering identities.

The ethnics of the United States, having already experienced the destruction and dissolution of identity and subjectivity, are now in the process of reclaiming and, in many cases, reconstructing both group identity and individual subjectivity. Because they have been defined and reconstructed from without, some ethnics, like contemporary theorists, have come to realize that both group identity and individual identity are sociocultural constructs. In defining themselves, then, not all ethnics are merely returning to old identities; some prefer to construct new identities. Thus, while working within their own culturally specific and sometimes ancient traditions, contemporary ethnic writers, in depicting their characters' efforts to define themselves, demonstrate their understanding of the need for change rather than simple regression. They also recognize that, just as group power derives from the construction of a group identity, individual power derives from the construction of an individual identity. Despite the tremendous influence of cultural conditioning on human development, the individuality of each ethnic must be recognized no matter how close his or her ties to the group. The variety of responses to marginality, the different ways in which ethnics define themselves in relation to the multiple cultures that influence them, either positively or negatively, is emphasized by contemporary ethnic writers, who demonstrate that the process of individuation differs significantly among their protagonists.

Power through Individual Self-Definition

When we think of oppression, we normally think of the oppression of one culture, class, or gender by another. Not all ethnic individuals, however, experience the dominant culture as the most damaging source of oppression. Some suffer more from oppression within their own families and communities, which insist on conformity to group values to assure group cohesion, strength, and continuity. Like all oppressive groups, families and communities maintain the status quo through a process of social reward and punishment. Those individuals who most closely meet established familial and community mores and goals are praised and rewarded while those who do not are punished, usually through exclusion and ostracism. As a result, those ethnics whose individuality is stifled or whose difference is cause for ostracism by the community may actually welcome contact with other cultures, finding such contact both liberating and invigorating. Novak, in studying the adaptation of emigrants to the American identity, noted that they "sometimes experience a release in the new culture, which rewards in them qualities of mind, heart, or action that may have been repressed in their culture of origin."[31]

The narrator of Ursula Le Guin's novel *Always Coming Home,* in describing her development from childhood to maturity, comments at one point, "As a kitten does what all other kittens do, so a child wants to do what other children do, with a wanting that is as powerful as it is mindless. Since we human beings have to learn what to do, we have to start out that way, but human mindfulness begins where that wish to be the same leaves off."[32] The process by which children stop imitating and patterning themselves after others and begin thinking and choosing rather than blindly following the path they have been trained and conditioned to follow is what psychologists refer to as maturation, individuation, self-realization, self-definition. "The aim of individuation," Campbell writes, "requires that one should find and then learn to live out of one's own center, in control of one's for and against."[33] To develop that sense of self that is necessary for achieving one's full potential, psychologists Dennis A. Bagarozzi and Stephen A. Anderson write, one "must reconcile those aspects of the self that are in conflict and those aspects of the self which act as internal censors. . . . It does not matter whether these internal censoring agents are called conditions of worth or referred to as the superego—some harmonious integration must be achieved among all conflicting components if full maturity is to be attained."[34] Achieving this goal of "harmonious integration" is difficult and thus, according to Bagarozzi and Anderson, rarely achieved.[35] If such integration is difficult for those born into the dominant culture and to parents of a single heritage, it becomes a formidable task for members of subordinate cultures or individuals of mixed heritage, torn on the one hand by the self-hatred that comes from discrimination and colonization by a dominant culture and on the other by the confusion caused by conflicting cultural loyalties or the alienation caused by exclusion from one or both parental cultures.

Many ethnics suffer from a sense of being caught in the middle, not knowing whether to attain personal power by adhering to traditional values and life-styles or by fighting the enemy on its own ground, by asserting one's difference or one's similarity. Trinh T. Minh-ha expresses her own angry confusion resulting from the conflicting attitudes about whether members of ethnic groups should strive for "authenticity," for ethnicity and difference from the dominant culture:

Every notion in vogue, including the retrieval of "roots" values, is necessarily exploited and recuperated. . . . To persuade you that your past and cultural heritage are doomed to eventual extinction and thereby keeping you occupied with the Savior's concern, inauthenticity is condemned as a *loss of origins* and a whitening (or faking) of non-Western values. Being easily offended in your elusive identity and reviving readily an old, racial charge, you immediately react when such guilt-instilling accusations are leveled at you and are thus led to stand in need of defending that very ethnic part of yourself that for years has made you and your ancestors the objects of execration. Today, planned authenticity is rife; as a product of hegemony and a remarkable counterpart of universal standardization, it constitutes an efficacious means of silencing the cry of racial oppression. We no longer wish to erase your difference. We demand, on the contrary, that you remember and assert it. At least, to a certain extent. Every path I/i take is edged with thorns. On the one hand, i play into the Savior's hands by concentrating on authenticity, for my attention is numbed by it and diverted from other, important issues; on the other hand, i do feel the necessity to return to my so-called roots, since they are the fount of my strength, the guiding arrow to which i constantly refer before heading for a new direction.[36]

The problem for Minh-ha and others is that to privilege one identity over the other—that is, to assert one's "authentic," different self at the expense of the "inauthentic," assimilated self or vice versa—is to risk losing one's identity entirely. This constant pull between difference and similarity, combined with the insistence that one must find and assert one's "true" identity to attain and maintain personal health, results in an increasingly self-conscious, and thus increasingly futile, search for identity.

Inherent in such a search for identity, Rita Felski writes, is the belief in the existence of "a 'good' inner self, beneath the layers of oppressive social conditioning, which needs only to be liberated." However, like Minh-ha, Felski warns that "the 'authentic self' is itself very much a social product"; there is no pure inner self that is untouched by cultural conditioning, whether by an affirming culture of origin or by an alienating dominant culture.[37] Nevertheless, the pervasive and persistent belief that an authentic inner self does exist, defining and delineating each person, forms the basis of much autobiographical literature, including that of ethnics. Indeed, the fear of having betrayed one's authentic self is the central focus of several early ethnic novels that pose as autobiographies. In writing about two of these works— James Weldon Johnson's *The Autobiography of an Ex-Colored Man* and Abraham Cahan's *The Rise of David Levinsky*—Werner Sollors suggests that both protagonists believe at the end of their lives that they are guilty of having sacrificed some "lost potential of childhood" in order to achieve success in the world of "practical" men.[38] Sollors believes that choosing one identity over the other, ethnic over American or vice versa, is doomed to failure; the only possible success lies in a synthesis of the two. To develop a workable identity, he argues, bicultural individuals must merge both identities available to them to create and authenticate new identities that simultaneously represent both ethnic individuality and an Americanized identity. This creation of new bicultural identities results in a continuous revitalization of American culture, particularly its music, art, and literature.[39]

Anthropologist Michael M. J. Fischer, in his review of recent ethnic autobiographies, suggests that development of a contemporary ethnic identity involves "finding a voice or style that does not violate one's several components of identity." The resulting voice is more vital for its "inter-references," its echoes of several different cultural traditions.[40] The Chicana writer and poet Gloria Anzaldúa, although not mentioned by Fischer, is an example of the type of writer who actively seeks to create a new voice from multiple traditions, both cultural— Mexican, Indian, and Anglo—and religious—Aztec and Catholic. Anzaldúa, who refers to her existence among these various traditions as life in the Borderlands, "la Frontera," describes the way in which Chicanos have developed both a language and a religion that mediate between multiple cultures. Chicano Spanish, she says, grew out of the Chicanos' need to identify themselves as a people distinct from both Spanish and Anglo cultures, just as the Chicano allegiance to *La Virgen de Guadelupe* mediates between the serpent goddess *Coatlicue* and the Virgin Mary. Caught between Spanish, Indian, and Anglo worlds, the

Chicano, Anzaldúa says, is constantly torn between opposing forces, which result in "a cultural collision." Out of this collision, which is painful but transformative, comes a new consciousness, the "consciousness of the Borderlands."[41] Anzaldúa has used her own "cultural collison" to create not only a new consciousness but also a personal mythology and an individual culture. "Don't give me your tenets and your laws," she writes. "Don't give me your lukewarm gods. What I want is an accounting of all three cultures—white, Mexican, Indian. I want the freedom to carve and chisel my own face, to staunch the bleeding with ashes, to fashion my own gods out of my entrails. . . . I will . . . stand and claim my space, making a new culture." Furthermore, Anzaldúa says, "I will have my voice: Indian, Spanish, white. I will have my serpent's tongue—my woman's voice, my sexual voice, my poet's voice. I will overcome the tradition of silence."[42] The right to develop a uniquely individual mythology, culture, and voice is one Anzaldúa claims as essential to her self-definition both as a person and as a poet and to the self-definition of every person who is torn between two or more cultures.

The works discussed in the following chapters portray through fiction and autobiography the existence of a multicultural universe, one in which individual worlds continuously collide, intersect, or exist side by side and in which boundaries, both geographical and sociocultural, are violated daily. Ethnic individuals, who must frequently cross the boundaries separating one world from another, are forced to determine where they stand, and thus who they are, in relation to those worlds. If, as contemporary theorists suggest, individuals can never locate an essential or unified self, they can nevertheless construct or adopt an identity that serves them for the present time. All individuals have the option of positioning themselves on one side of a boundary or the other or of creating, as Anzaldúa does, a zone or borderlands, a new space situated at the boundary itself. From this new space, one can draw beliefs from both sides to construct an individual world view, reality, and identity that constitute one's center—a center that may or may not ever coincide with that of another person. What the works included here ultimately offer readers is the knowledge that all worlds are possible and that defining one's own world is the first step toward creating it.

2 A Witch and Her Curse: External Definition and Uncrossable Boundaries in Lee Smith's *Oral History*

I intend for this journal to be a valid record of what I regard as essentially a pilgrimage, a simple geographical pilgrimage, yes, but also a pilgrimage back through time, a pilgrimage to a simpler era, back—dare I hope it—to the very roots of consciousness and belief. —Lee Smith[1]

As early as the 1870s, travelers passing through Southern Appalachia[2] began to report that the people living in the mountains, despite having an Anglo-Celtic background similar to the travelers' own, seemed different from those living in other parts of the country. The inhabitants of the mountain communities, isolated from each other as well as from the economic and technological progress that was transforming the rest of the United States from a pioneer wilderness into a thriving, industrialized society, continued to follow the primitive, frontier life-style of 1750. Today, the people of Appalachia continue to maintain a life-style as well as a system of values, beliefs, and attitudes that tend to separate them from the dominant European-American culture of the United States. One trait of the Appalachians, inherited from those ancestors who first settled in the region, is an especially strong spirit of independence, self-sufficiency, and individualism. Although bonding and loyalty among families and within communities are also quite strong, many homesteads and communities are still located in isolated pockets and hollows, separated from each other by miles of undeveloped mountainside and poorly maintained roads. The people of Appalachia seem unable to band together to form a single, cohesive group and to find a strong, unified voice with which to demand economic assistance. This aim is further hampered by the people's insistence on self-sufficiency and independence, which would prohibit them from asking for aid even if they could locate a unified voice. As a result, the people of Southern Appalachia constitute what is perhaps the least recognized marginal group in the United States.

Historian Henry D. Shapiro, in his book *Appalachia on Our Mind*, argues that the Appalachian region, as a geographically and culturally discrete entity, is not natural but was instead "invented" between 1870 and 1890 by two movements prevalent at the time—the local-color movement and the home missionary movement.[3] Other sociologists believe, however, that Appalachians constitute a distinct ethnic group because they are separated from other Anglo-Celtics by a boundary, defined from both within and without, that has effectively included and excluded membership in both groups since late in the nineteenth century. Today, however, continuing industrialization and modernization of the Appalachian region threaten to dissolve the differences that define that boundary, erasing still another marginal group. Writers such as Lee Smith, Bobbie Ann Mason, Denise Giardina, Fred Chappell, John Ehle, and Cormac McCarthy, following the earlier examples set by Wilma Dykeman, Harriet Arnow, James Still, and Mildred Haun, attempt in their novels to capture and preserve the peculiarities that define Appalachians as a unique sociocultural group. In *Oral History* Smith succeeds in portraying not only those characteristics that continue to distinguish many Appalachians today but also the degree to which Appalachians have over the past hundred years become increasingly acculturated to the dominant life-style of the United States. By the time *Oral History* ends in the 1970s, the novel's characters are assuming a life-style—attending college, selling Amway products, and transforming the old homestead into Ghostland—that cheapens even as it enriches. Thus, Smith poignantly captures the loss experienced by so many marginal groups in the United States: as one way of life is gained, another is irretrievably lost. Despite her regret for the inevitable dilution that comes with homogeneity, however, Smith warns against sentimentalizing and romanticizing Appalachia. She sees the changes and the exploitation that have accompanied economic progress as perhaps regrettable but inevitable. Furthermore, life in Appalachia, particularly in its mountain communities, can be unbearably hard, in a way and to a degree largely unimaginable by outsiders, and any lightening of that hardship must be considered as good.[4]

Of the works discussed in this book, *Oral History* is the least positive in its treatment of the power of belief and of one's ability to define oneself and to cross sociocultural boundaries. The novel demonstrates the way in which beliefs that empower and sustain the group necessarily victimize those who stand outside its boundaries. The power that springs from deep conviction is always double-edged: it can kill as well as cure; it can inhibit as well as foster self-definition and growth. Granny Younger, empowered and ennobled by her belief in supernatural forces and revered by the community, is nevertheless guilty of denying another woman the right to define and change herself. By defining Red Emmy as a witch, Granny Younger prohibits Emmy not only from defining herself but also from crossing the sociocultural boundary that separates and excludes her from the community. Even after Emmy attempts to conform, modifying her behavior to meet the standards of civilization held by the community's dominant society, she remains an outsider. The curse of being defined from without and of being barred from or unable to adapt to the dominant society is not limited to Emmy alone. The same curse falls on all those who attempt to cross the boundary that separates the mountains of Appalachia from mainstream America, whether they are attempting to move inward or outward.

Appalachian Women and Belief
Emma Bell Miles, in her book *The Spirit of the Mountains,* which was published in 1905, suggests that the supernatural beliefs of her people—both their continuing belief in witches and ghosts and their belief in God and the devil—are related to the strategies they have developed to confront and cope with the hardships under which they live. About the typical beliefs in omens and haunting spirits held by Appalachian women in the early 1900s, Miles writes:

> early in childhood she grows into dim consciousness of the vastness of human experience and the nobility of it. . . . She gains the courage of the fatalist;

the surety that nothing can happen which has not happened before; that, whatever she may be called upon to endure, she will know that others have undergone its like over and over again. . . . To her mind nothing is trivial, all things being great with a meaning of divine purpose. And if as a corollary of this belief she is given to an absurd faith in petty signs and omens, who is to laugh at her?

She has heard the stories of everything in the house, from the brown and cracked old cups and bowls to the roof-beams themselves, until they have become her literature. From them she borrows a sublime silent courage and patience in the hour of trial. From their tragedies, too, a sense of the immanent supernatural. It is almost as if they were haunted by audible and visible ghosts. Who would not fear to sit alone with old furniture that bears the marks of blows, stains of blood and tears? They are friendly, too. They stand about her with the sympathy of like experience in times of distress and grief.[5]

The women living in the mountains of Appalachia find the strength to endure because they see themselves as a part of the continuous flow of history. The knowledge that one's mother and one's mother's mother and one's mother's mother's mother have all experienced and survived similar trials transforms the past into a living entity continuous with the present, empowering the mothers of the past to speak through present omens and investing the artifacts of the past with life. The voices of the past, both haunting and empowering, impinge on the present.

Although the ability to hear the voices of the past murmuring from the corners of one's house and to see the future in signs and omens is shared by many of the women of Appalachia, certain women, such as Granny Younger and Ora Mae Cantrell, seem to have a special gift. Granny is highly regarded by those who have witnessed the truth of her predictions, the effectiveness of her healing techniques, and her assumption of a nobility that derives from her total confidence in her power to know and her ability to act on that knowledge to save others. Ora Mae, too, despite her refusal to apply her gift as a healer, occasionally seems to take on mythic proportions. When Ora Mae throws Pricey Jane's cursed golden earrings into a river gorge, Sally watches the woman rise to a level of almost divine presence: "she stood there with her arms flung out, like a big black statue in a church or something, for the longest time" (p. 283). Although Ora Mae is ennobled and Granny Younger is empowered by a belief in signs, ghosts, witches, and curses, the same beliefs can also produce a Ludie Davenport. Ludie's experience with the supernatural is limited to the ludicrous: the devil enters the body of her chow dog, causing it to bite her grandfather's knee, and the witch Red Emmy chases Ludie down a mountain path, causing her to lose her wart poultice. Granny Younger and Ora Mae, however, see, hear, feel the existence of powerful forces around them, and they witness the effects of those forces in the illnesses, deaths, and misfortunes—and occasional miraculous recoveries—of their neighbors.

Despite the differences, however, in the ways in which the three women experience the supernatural, the *consequences* of their belief can be equally constructive or destructive for them all. Ora Mae's belief that the curse is carried in the earrings, which she then hurls into a river gorge, brings an end to the curse. Granny's belief in her ability to heal others gets her out of bed, forestalling death until she has tried to help Almarine's family. Ludie's belief in the power of reciting the Lord's Prayer saves her from Red Emmy's spirit and the ghost-dog that consorts with her. By the same token, however, both Ludie and Granny go to bed, stricken by pain caused by unexpected encounters with Red Emmy. Ora Mae moves from the family homestead because, for her, it is and always will be haunted. Worst of all, Granny's belief—her unquestionable certainty—that Red Emmy is a witch destroys the life of an innocent woman. Red Emmy is the victim of a system of belief that is ennobling, empowering, but also endangering.

Granny Younger as Storyteller

By 1898, when Almarine Cantrell is looking for a wife, opinions about witchcraft among the inhabitants of the tiny Appalachian community of Tug and the three mountains encircling it—Hoot Owl, Hurricane, and Snowman—are mixed. Some believe while others scoff. Even the scoffers, however, find themselves reverting to belief when they experience some phenomenon they cannot explain in any other way. Among those who do not believe are the master storytellers who still delight, as does Parrot Blankenship, in entertaining their neighbors with the witch stories they have created or have heard repeated by other storytellers over the years. Among those who do believe, however, is Granny Younger, who is a storyteller in her own right.

Granny's power as a storyteller is so great that she succeeds in convincing those who know better, including both Almarine Cantrell and the reader, that Red Emmy is indeed a witch. Granny's power, and the respect and trust accorded to her by the reader, derive in part from her own conviction in her beliefs, a conviction born of years of experience validating her own perceptions of the world: "I been here a long time. Years. I know what I know. I know moren most folks and that's a fact, you can ask anybody. I know moren I want to tell you, and moren you want to know" (p. 17). Right from the beginning, then, Granny Younger asserts that she knows what she tells is true, but the listener (or reader) has the freedom to believe or to disbelieve, to stay and listen to a story that is told in her own mode and style of telling, or to go on along his or her way. "The way I tell a story is the way I want to," she says, "and iffen you mislike it, you don't have to hear" (p. 28). The more Granny tells, the more the reader does begin to believe, partly because Granny's years in the mountains and her close relationship with Almarine make her the most reliable source to impart this particular history and partly because she earns the respect of the reader just as she has earned the respect of the community.

Granny grew up on Hurricane Mountain long before most of the other members of the community were born or had migrated to the area. She knows and is known by all because she has served as midwife at the birth of most, has applied healing herbs, poultices, chants, and charms to cure everything from childhood disease to broken limbs, and has laid out many of their dead. In times of crisis—birth, illness, and death— the community turns to Granny Younger, and they express their gratitude for her services throughout the year by dropping off gifts of whatever they have most recently harvested, canned, or butchered. The community's regard for Granny Younger is similar to the regard for older women expressed by Miles in 1905: "I have learned to enjoy the company of these old prophetesses almost more than any other. The range of their experience is wonderful; they are, moreover, repositories of tribal lore—tradition and song, medical and religious learning. They are the nurses, the teachers of practical arts, the priestesses, and their wisdom commands the respect of all."[6] One indication of the community's regard for Granny is that nothing told by any other narrator raises any doubts about the veracity of Granny's story; such corroboration is unusual in this kaleidoscopic work, in which each narration not only contributes to the whole but also colors and distorts the truth of the other speakers' perceptions and ordering of events.[7]

This community regard for Granny encourages the reader's trust in her as a reliable narrator. More important, however, is the strength of Granny's confidence in herself. As critic Frank Soos notes, "Granny is asking [the reader] to trust her version of events. . . . She is demanding belief, a belief that stands outside logic, language, or words."[8] In fact, the confidence Granny inspires in all those who listen to her, the confidence that what she knows and tells is unquestionably true, validates and makes real stories that would not normally be accepted from other speakers. Ultimately, Granny's own self-confidence in what she knows misleads both Almarine and the reader. In telling what she knows of Red Emmy, both before and after Emmy first encounters Almarine, Granny invents for her readers the apparition of a witch where no witch exists. Although Granny herself does not tell Almarine the stories about Red Emmy that she relates to us, her responses to Almarine's questions about Emmy validate the stories he hears from the community. If Almarine had not trusted Granny as much as he did, he would not later have given credence to the gossip, thus leading him to interpret certain events as signs of Red Emmy's witchery. When he does begin to suspect Emmy of being a witch, Granny's confirmation of his suspicions and her advice to drive Emmy away persuade him to banish his lover, who is pregnant, from his home.

One tends to forgive or perhaps even to overlook Granny's culpability because she is clearly motivated by a belief that is often both ennobling and empowering. This belief empowers her to perceive and guard against dangers unrecognized by others. Granny Younger is, in Miles's terms, a repository of the tradition, medical knowledge, and religious learning of Southern Appalachia at the turn of the century. If she errs in her judgment of Red Emmy, she does so out of a sincere belief in her own perception of reality and her desire to protect Almarine from dangers he does not see. She stands apart, then, from Rose Hibbitts, whose malicious storytelling about Red Emmy's curse is motivated by jealousy, repressed sexual desire, and revenge for Almarine's curt dismissal of her advances, and from Ludie Davenport, whose superstitious fancies are brought on, as the Rev. Aldous Rife suggests, by the unfortunate situation of being "a still-healthy woman saddled with a sick husband" (p. 186). Despite her good intentions and the sincerity of her belief, however, Granny Younger, respected by community and reader alike, is guilty along with others in the community of inventing a witch out of a woman who is merely different. In warning Almarine to avoid Emmy and in advising him to drive her away, she creates a witch for him, and in presenting her oral history of their story, she creates a witch for the reader. This, then, is the power wielded by a master storyteller: the power not only to create reality but to demand that others accept, at least temporarily, that reality.

The Making of a Witch

Red Emmy's true history has always been a mystery to the community. They know that she lives among the caves high up on Snowman Mountain with old man Isom Charles. Although Isom grew up on Hurricane Mountain, he left the mountains after his mother died and after he killed a brother and beat the father who had beat him as a child. When he returned many years later, he had Emmy—then just a child—with him. Although Granny claims to know Isom as well as anybody does, she says that nobody knew where Emmy came from. Because Red Emmy's origins are suspect and because Isom himself leads such a wild, isolated life, only occasionally descending into town for supplies, Granny believes, as do other members of the community, that "old Isom's red-headed Emmy . . . could never have a mortal man in all her days. She belonged to the devil is why. Her daddy had done pledged her years before" (p. 35). As consort to the devil, Emmy is naturally believed to be a witch empowered through him to leave her own body at night, entering the bodies of other humans or of animals to satisfy her own desires or those of the devil.

Exactly how or why the story that Isom pledged Emmy to the devil originated is unclear, but the story had apparently been incorporated into the local mythology long before Almarine first saw and fell in love with Red Emmy. Granny tells of how a singing redbird enticed Almarine off the well-worn trace over Snowman Mountain into wild, unknown territory where he discovered Red Emmy bathing in a mountain pool. She tells of Almarine's instant longing and desire for Red Emmy, of the way in which Emmy suddenly disappeared without a sign, and of the way Almarine's dog responded first to the redbird and then to

Emmy, growling, whimpering, the hair on his body standing on end. All these signs—gleaned from Almarine's account rather than witnessed firsthand—strengthen Granny Younger's conviction that Emmy is a witch and thus not a proper match for Almarine. Granny herself knows from her years of searching for healing herbs that "what you want the most, you find offen the beaten path. I never find nothing I need on the trace" (p. 28). Despite her knowledge that what one needs most is found only "offen the beaten path," Granny refuses to tell Almarine anything that will help him find Emmy, telling him instead to look for "a sweet God-fearing town girl" (p. 37).

After Emmy comes to Almarine, appearing without warning beside his bed one night, the lovers spend two full days in bed before resuming some semblance of real life, turning their attention to tending the house and the fields. Granny, however, refuses to acknowledge the months that follow as real. She refers to this honeymoon period in which the two are totally immersed in each other, in their own sexual experimentation and fulfillment, as a period of "froze-time" in which Emmy, she says, is merely playing house, playing at being a good wife before her true nature emerges: "Now what was Emmy up to a-cooking beans? It was like she was a little child with a new play-pretty, and that play-pretty was Almarine. She was just a-playing house, is all, until her true nature come out" (p. 40). According to Granny, this "froze-time" during which Almarine and Emmy were so happy "tweren't natural, no moren a snow in July" (p. 41).

Why, one might ask, does Granny react so negatively to what are actually two very common aspects of the first six months spent together by many young couples? Why does she view two very natural responses—sexual indulgence and the "play-acting" aspect of assuming a new role—as so unnatural in this situation? In fact, Granny describes the initial enthusiasm for housekeeping displayed by Emmy, of whom she disapproves, and that of Almarine's subsequent wife, Pricey Jane, of whom she approves, in much the same way. About Red Emmy she says, "Lord, she was a-dusting, and a-sweeping, and a-cooking and milking the cow. As I said she was playing house. She looked real young and real pretty—her red hair just a-bouncing all down her back as she walked" (p. 41). Similarly, she says that Pricey Jane "was a girl like a summer day. And work! Lord, she turned that cabin upside down and sideways cleaning it, she was a-drying apples on the shed roof, she churned butter so light it'd melt in your mouth" (p. 56). Whereas Pricey Jane, according to Granny, is appropriately displaying her skill as a young housewife, Red Emmy is only "a-playing house." In reality, the only difference between the housekeeping displayed by the two women is the difference in Granny Younger's own expectations: she expects Pricey Jane to act like a new housewife, but she expects Red Emmy to act like a witch. She is, in essence, waiting for Red Emmy to show her "true nature"; thus, this "froze time" is actually time frozen not for Emmy and Almarine but for Granny, who is herself entrapped as she waits for her own expectations to be fulfilled. In fact, Granny is so certain that eventually Red Emmy's true nature will come out that she proves what she once said about Almarine: "Iffen a body searches for so long, he's bound to find something, that's a fact" (p. 38). Thus, when Granny gets caught "spying on a witch and her business" (p. 44), she succeeds in experiencing firsthand the power of Emmy's witchery; experience validates belief.

Crossing the foot of Hoot Owl Holler on her way to care for a baby suffering from "thrash," Granny decides to visit Almarine. When she first arrives at his cabin, she says, "It all seemed natural to me right then, I couldn't feel no witchery in the air, nor nothing wrong atall on the trace nor around that cabin when I got to it. Almarine's chickens come a-running and a-scratching, and that witch had her wash strung out on the line like anybody. Can you feature a witch a-washing? She must of wanted so bad to be natural, what I think. She must of tried hard for a while" (p. 42). Granny's conviction, then, that Red Emmy is a witch is so great that she is unable to accept that what looks natural is natural. Although she gives Emmy credit for trying hard, she insists that Emmy is trying hard to overcome her "true" identity—that of witch—rather than that Emmy is trying hard to construct a new identity for herself—that of wifely companion to Almarine—an identity for which, after living alone in the caves with Isom, she has had neither role model nor training.

When Granny finally locates Almarine, he is plowing the garden while Emmy walks behind him, dropping corn in the furrows. Despite the naturalness of the scene, however, Granny remains hidden, watching the couple from where she stands in a clump of cedars. Even when a thunderstorm that has quickly arisen breaks loose around her, Granny continues to watch from the cedars as Almarine and Emmy abruptly stop their work and begin kissing in the open field amid the lightning and thunder. As Granny continues to watch from the trees, reliving sexual sensations that have long lain dormant, the two lovers race to the house and to bed. As they pass, however, Emmy turns and looks straight at Granny where she hides in the trees, spitting once in her direction. Granny immediately feels a pain in her side that bends her double, she says, and keeps her in bed for seven days. Because she fails to recognize that guilt and dismay at being discovered as a sexual voyeur have caused her own psychosomatic pain, this experience confirms Granny's belief that Emmy is a witch and that "spying on a witch and her business" is dangerous.

In the same way that Granny distinguishes between Emmy's housekeeping and Pricey Jane's, she also distinguishes between the two women's relationships with Almarine. While living with Pricey Jane, she says, Almarine had "a clear-eyed look," whereas with Emmy he had "moved like a man set under a spell, which is what he was" (pp. 57, 41). Again, the difference is primarily one of expectations. Granny is looking for signs indicating that Emmy is a witch; and when Almarine begins to walk around in a daze and then loses weight and energy, he fulfills her expectations: "I knowed what was happening, of course. A witch will ride a man in the night while he sleeps, she'll ride him to death if she can. She can't holp it, it is her nature to do so" (p. 45). Granny is once again misled by her expectations, seeing in Red Emmy and Almarine's relationship exactly what she expects of a witch.

Despite the misinterpretation caused by Granny's expectations, however, certain differences do distinguish Pricey Jane from Red Emmy in terms of their sexuality and of Almarine's response to that sexuality. Pricey Jane, sixteen years old, is clearly infatuated with Almarine: "Pricey Jane loves Almarine so much," says the omniscient, third-person narrator of Pricey Jane's segment, "it's like she made him up out of her own head, the perfect only man for her to love" (p. 61). She is still young enough to hold romantic illusions about love; "all the time mooning" about love as a child, "Pricey Jane's still mooning," says the narrator (pp. 61, 62). Furthermore, she is tiny and dainty and doll-like, eliciting in Almarine a desire to indulge her by bringing her gifts from town and to protect her from harm. Pricey Jane seems to inspire love, indulgence, and protection, feelings that are apparently less threatening to Almarine than the overwhelming sexual desire he felt for Emmy.

Emmy, on the other hand, is a red-haired, red-blooded woman of forty living with a big, blond twenty-two-year-old man.[9] At the height of her own sexual desire, she may be experiencing sex for the first time in her life—and with a young man near his own sexual peak. Alternatively, as Smith has herself suggested, Red Emmy may have been sexually abused as a young child.[10] In any case, Emmy was raised in the wild by a man reputed to be both crazy and violent, without benefit of the nurture or socializing influence of a loving mother or father. What she knows about sex she has learned through observation of animals or, possibly, through sexual abuse—neither of which would have offered any lessons about sexual modesty, coyness, or inhibition. As John C. Campbell and Cratis Dearl Williams report, however, and as the experience of several characters in the novel who bear illegitimate children demonstrates, girls and women living in Appalachia around the turn of the century often displayed an open, uninhibited sexuality. Although not encouraged, sexual intercourse and even pregnancy before marriage were rarely impugned to such a degree that a girl was cast out by either family or community.[11] This attitude of Appalachians toward sexual indiscretion is demonstrated by the competition among Luther Wade and the other young men of Tug who court the pregnant Dory Cantrell, despite the general consensus that she has been "ruint" by Richard Burlage. One can conclude, then, that Emmy's sexuality in itself is not inappropriate but that it violates some unspoken code defining acceptable sexual behavior. Possibly she is sexually aggressive, initiating sex herself rather than waiting for Almarine to take the lead; possibly she has excessive desires that Almarine's own sexual energies cannot match. The excessiveness of Emmy's desire is suggested by Granny's belief that Emmy is riding Almarine to death, with no loss or depletion of her own energies, as if she were feeding off him. A third explanation, however, is suggested at various points in the novel and in varying contexts by Granny, Pricey Jane, and the men at the town store.

Granny tells the reader that Almarine wants Emmy so much that his wanting has become a consuming fire. "If you're bound and determined to play with fire," Granny says, "you'll do it whether or no—you'll play till it burns you up, or the other one up, or the both of you, or mought be till it burns out" (p. 40). Later Pricey Jane, sitting on her porch and musing about the past, thinks about the songs she has heard all her life, some describing love "as a game, with dosey-do and curtsy and funny responses" but others describing it "like a sickness upon death" (p. 61). While the love between Almarine and Pricey Jane may be seen as a "game," that between Almarine and Emmy is more like a "sickness"; their love is based on a sexual passion that becomes a consuming fire, threatening to burn one or both up. The two are obsessed with each other, mutually possessed with a passion and desire that affects both equally; as Granny herself admits, Emmy is just as bewitched as Almarine is. In Almarine's case, however, the passion, "like a sickness upon death," seems to deplete him whereas Emmy seems to thrive, growing stronger.

Almarine's wasting away can perhaps be explained by his fear of and even embarrassment about what he perceives as Emmy's power over his body and, consequently, over his mind and will. Despite Appalachia's many ballads and stories about killing love, such a consuming love is not really deemed appropriate or manly by the people, particularly the men, of the mountains. A man marries, first and foremost, because he needs sons to help him farm his land and because he needs a woman to tend the house and work the garden. He does not marry for love or even for passion, although he does expect his wife to fulfill his sexual needs as they arise. Horace Kephart, describing male-female relations in Appalachia in the early 1900s, explains that

> the man of the house is lord. He takes no orders from anybody at home or abroad. Whether he shall work or visit or roam the woods with dog and gun is nobody's affair but his own. About family matters he consults with his wife, but in the end his word is law.
>
> The mountain farmer's wife is not only a household drudge, but a field-hand as well. She helps to plant, hoes corn, gathers fodder, sometimes even plows or splits rails. . . . To him she is little more than a sort of superior domestic animal. . . .
>
> And yet it is seldom that a highland woman complains of her lot. She knows no other. . . . Indeed she would scarce respect her husband if he did not lord it over her and cast upon her the menial tasks.[12]

In his relationship with Red Emmy, Almarine is clearly master of neither his home nor the situation. As he grows weaker, lying abed,

Emmy grows stronger, continuing to work the fields alone. Drained by his passion for Emmy, Almarine loses his will and, consequently, his manliness (as Appalachians conceive of manliness).[13]

That this tendency to excessive passion is a characteristic of Almarine's own nature, however, rather than proof of Emmy's supernatural powers is demonstrated by the passion he later feels for Pricey Jane, which is similar in intensity if not in kind. One night during his marriage to Pricey Jane, Almarine hesitates to stay from home an extra night to play poker with the guys. Harve Justice, noticing Almarine's hesitation, jeers, asking whether "his gypsy-girl [Pricey Jane] had put him on a leash or maybe under a spell, or maybe he was still under a spell from the first one" (p. 67). To Harve Justice, unlike Granny, Almarine is equally bewitched, and equally unmanned, by both women. Thus, Almarine differs from the other men of Appalachia, just as he differed from other boys when he was, in Granny Younger's words, "a sweet moony child," who spent nights alone on Black Rock Mountain where he would "scream in the night like a painter until the painters all around were screaming back" (p. 18).

The differences that set Almarine apart as a child, then, are the same that distinguish him as a young man. He loves the mountains, living close to nature and isolated from other humans, but is constantly dreaming about something beyond those mountains. As Granny explains, "Almarine allus wanted something—who knows what?—and that's why he kept staring out beyond them hills" (p. 21). He is at once too independent and too sweet to get along well with the other mountain people, and he is a little too wild, a little too dark, as a result of his frequent visits to the perfect circle atop Hurricane Mountain and his many years growing up on Hoot Owl Mountain, a mountain Granny Younger describes as "dark" and worrisome. Whereas Pricey Jane elicits the full measure of Almarine's sweetness and perhaps that wanting that seems to entice him away from the mountains, Red Emmy draws out what seems to be a desire to merge with the wildness of the mountains, eliminating the difference that separates him from the screaming "painters," from the bubbling, snorting mountain springs, from the rocky cliffs, and from herself—a woman whose childhood was darker and more wild than his own. Despite the differences between the two women and in the responses they elicit from Almarine, in both cases he responds with an intensity and excessiveness that sets him apart from the typically stolid and stoic men of the mountains. Only after Pricey Jane's death, when Almarine empties himself of all feeling and desire, does he become a man like other men, taking his brother's widow Vashti as his wife—without love or passion—to bear the sons he needs to work his land.

Thus, Almarine's inherent tendency toward excessive passion is elicited by both Pricey Jane and Emmy in their different ways, one appropriately and one inappropriately in Granny's eyes. When, however, Almarine recognizes the degree to which his sexual passion for Emmy is depleting his will and his energy, he begins to fear her and what appears to be her power over his body. He remembers the witch stories he has heard all his life, the more recently told stories about Emmy's arrangement with the devil, and Granny's warnings about Emmy, and he begins to project on Emmy his own feelings of difference: it is Emmy rather than himself whom he perceives as different; it is Emmy's true nature rather than his own that emerges after a few months of marriage. Almarine makes the mistake, as so many of us do, of projecting onto another person the source of a disturbance within himself. Eventually, his fear that Emmy is a witch overpowers his ability to reason until, following Granny's advice, he drives Emmy from his home despite his continuing passion for her.

Caught up by Granny's story, by her conviction that Emmy is truly a witch and Almarine a blameless victim of her bewitchment, the reader may overlook the cruelty with which Emmy is treated. Through no fault of her own, having committed no crime other than indulging her sexual desires, she is victimized by beliefs passed down through generations. Guided by Granny's timeless wisdom—a wisdom that includes an age-old belief that strange, single women tend to be consorts of the devil—Almarine deprives Emmy of her one chance for a husband, a home, a family—for an existence that, hard though it may be, is normative for the time and environment in which she lives.

An interesting side note about the tendency of a community to see witches where only strange and different women exist is that Granny Younger herself, whether she recognizes it or not, is highly vulnerable to the charge of witchcraft. Granny is a single woman, never married, living alone in her home on Hurricane Mountain. She boasts at one point in her story, "Now, I've got my own holler, mind. Nobody ever lived in it but me and mama, and mama's dead. . . . I'd not put up with a regular man if you paid me" (p. 25). Granny is old and eccentric and outspoken. Furthermore, she is known to have special powers, both of foresight and of healing, and most cultures that believe in the supernatural powers of gifted humans believe that the powers for good can be easily subverted to perform evil when the need or desire arises.[14] Only one hint of Granny's own vulnerability appears in *Oral History,* and that occurs when she is laying out Almarine and Pricey Jane's son, Eli, for burial. The third-person, omniscient narrator of this section remarks that while Granny was in the lean-to laying out Eli, some of the other neighbors who have come to help "heard her murmuring voice out there, and looked quickly away from each other's faces. Who knew what Granny was saying, or worse yet, what-all she did?" (p. 73). Wielding words, both to heal and to create fictions, Granny, rather than Emmy, is the one who possesses potentially threatening powers. If the community had not had Red Emmy, Granny herself could quite possibly have come under suspicion for the many ensuing deaths and catastrophes in Hoot Owl Holler that are later attributed to Red Emmy and her curse on Almarine Cantrell.

The Making of a Curse

Although no one knows, or at least no one tells, how the story about old Isom's pledging Red Emmy to the devil originated, we do learn how the story about Red Emmy's curse on Almarine Cantrell and Hoot Owl Holler begins. Rose Hibbitts is at the Cantrell homestead the night that Pricey Jane dies and, along with other neighbors, watches as Almarine runs up into the mountains, screaming as if he were crazy or, she says, "bewitched" (p. 75). Rose is still there when Almarine, torn and bloody, returns home in the morning, explaining his appearance by telling Rose and her sister that his dog was killed in a fight. Rose, however, believes that Almarine has not told the full story: "We knowed the truth of course, that he had gone to that witch and kilt her" (p. 77). When, a little later that morning, the other neighbors begin to leave the Cantrell homestead, Rose's mother, Rhoda Hibbitts, insists that her daughter stay at Almarine's cabin to tend to his needs and to care for his baby daughter, Dory. Rose claims that, because she knew that her mother was just trying to marry off an ugly daughter who was quickly passing the age of eligibility, she begged her mother not to make her stay. Despite her protest, however, Rose is clearly smitten by Almarine, feeling that she will die if he looks at her and die if he fails to (p. 76).

Denying or perhaps not even fully comprehending her own sexual desire, Rose becomes increasingly nervous during her stay with Almarine and Dory, crying easily and suffering periods of weakness. One night Rose awakens in the one-room cabin she shares with them, and believing she has heard Almarine speak, she calls his name twice in the dark. From this time—these long, silent moments spent lying in the dark with her heart "a-beating, beating to beat the band" and the blood rushing to her head while Almarine "slept on and on"—Rose begins to see him as "hateful" and "awful" (p. 76). She believes that he is deliberately and callously rejecting her attempts to care for and to love him and his child. As Almarine continues to ignore Rose, responding curtly and abruptly if at all, she becomes so obsessed with what she perceives as his rejection of her that she forgets that she is dealing with a man still grieving over the loss of his wife and son. Rose is so focused on her desire for love, her need for sexual satisfaction, and her expectation of rejection that she is unable to allow for that grief. Out of an accumulation of frustrated desire, need, and expectation, supplemented by a "fanciful nature" (p. 74), Rose conceives and nurtures the curse that follows Almarine and his descendants through the coming generations.

Rose invents the curse spontaneously, involuntarily, when she returns home to her mother after having been dismissed by Almarine when Vashti appears on his doorstep. Rose, realizing instantly that her mother is angry with her for having failed to catch Almarine, attempts to exonerate herself by insisting that Almarine asked her to stay but that she refused. "Hit ain't my fault," she tells her mother. "Hit ain't my fault atall. He ast me to stay but I won't. . . . He ast me to get married and I turned him down. Hit's a curse on the whole holler, . . . and I ain't having any part of it. Almarine has done tole me hisself. That witch, she put it on him before he kilt her, and I ain't staying there, Mama, you couldn't pay me to stay" (p. 81). Rose is surprised, she says, at how easily the words slip out of her mouth, "smooth as glass," and she "liked to have died" when she heard them: "I have never knowed what I would say till I opened my mouth" (p. 81). Rose's mother, dumbfounded and dismayed, puts her arm around Rose's waist, drawing her in out of a cold October rain, saying "Oh Rose" in the "funniest voice" so that Rose cannot tell, she says, "if she credited me or not" (p. 82).

Soon Rose's tales of murder, curses, and the Cantrells' haunted "holler" begin to pop up throughout the region. With each passing year, Rose grows increasingly unstable, telling her stories to anyone who will listen—as well as those who will not—until many of the people in the community begin to attribute all the misfortunes that befall the Cantrells to Red Emmy's curse. The list of violent and seemingly needless deaths that strike the Cantrell family is a formidable one and could easily suggest to those who hold such beliefs that Almarine and his descendants are indeed cursed. However, as Rev. Aldous Rife suggests to Justine Poole during an afternoon tryst (one of many in what has been a long and companionable sexual relationship), "Look, Justine. You could make up something about anybody up in those hollers, and you know it. Take the Skeens, and that fire they had last Christmas and three of the children burned up, or the way Mavis Rife had two babies to die in a row, just up and died in the cribs with no reason Doc Story could find to ascribe to it" (p. 186). According to Aldous, life in the mountains is extremely difficult for everyone, with sudden violence, inexplicable death, and undeserved misfortune the rule rather than the exception. To Justine, however, all the other occurrences cited by Aldous are natural, whereas the afflictions of the Cantrells are unnatural. She believes in the curse and cannot understand why Aldous, who also believes in spirits, insists on denying the evidence of that curse. Surprised, Aldous asks, "What spirits?" She responds, "Father, Son, and Holy Ghost, I reckon. . . . The big three. I reckon they're spirits too" (p. 186).

Although Justine's response silences Aldous momentarily, he soon bursts forth in somewhat of a tirade, insisting that Rose Hibbitts is solely responsible for starting the stories about the Cantrells, then expressing his disgust for the type of ignorance that breeds such belief in supernatural occurrences, a belief that he equates with the literal belief in the existence of heaven and hell held by the local Free Will Baptists: "Somebody could have started up a tale about her [Rose]—this is the point—only she started up a tale about Almarine instead. And once it starts, it just goes on by itself, it takes on a life of its own no matter who may be hurt in the process. It's ignorance, is what it is, and by God I see no end to it, to ignorance and darkness. I can't see that it does any good to preach false hope or promise some kind of golden hereafter, some happy heaven that people believe in only because the things of this world are so goddamn bleak they can't stand it if they don't have that to fall back on, or that to look forward to, some spurious golden robe" (p. 187). After listening to Aldous complain for several minutes, Justine interrupts to remind him that people go to church because it makes them feel good.

This exchange between Aldous Rife and Justine Poole is interesting for several reasons. First, Aldous's description of how Rose started the story about the curse on Almarine, when anybody could have started a similar story to explain any of the unfortunate events that occur in the mountains, provides a clue about the way in which the original story about Red Emmy's being pledged to the devil was started and passed on over the years. Thirty or forty years after the fact, no one—at least none of the history's narrators—knows who told the first tale about Isom, Red Emmy, and the devil. What the reader does know from having read *Oral History* is that these people are born storytellers, and they love both telling and hearing a good story, whether it is Ludie Davenport's story about being chased off Hoot Owl Mountain by Red Emmy and Almarine's ghost-dog, presented "as the Gospel" (p. 176), or Parrot Blankenship's elaborately developed and artfully refined story about the "widder lady reputed to be a witch," also presented as a truthful account up until the point at which he delivers the killing punch line (p. 205). "When Parrot tells a story," Jink Cantrell says, "you can't help believing it's every word true, like the way he'll throw off on hisself instead of building hisself bigger, and look you in the eye, and grin at how dumb he was" (pp. 205–6).

This inability of so many listeners to distinguish between fact and fiction, which Jink recognizes and admires as the sign of a master storyteller, is exactly what disturbs Aldous Rife. He sees the people's belief in Rose's story and their belief in the literal existence of heaven and hell as one and the same, as "ignorance and darkness." Similarly, but more positively, Justine sees her own belief in the powers wielded by the spirit of Red Emmy and Aldous's belief in the powers residing in the Father, Son, and Holy Ghost as one and the same thing, a comprehension of the formidable powers of the supernatural. Whereas Aldous believes in God (despite the doubts that have plagued him for some years) but not witches, Justine, like many of the people in the community, believes in both: if spirits exist in one context, why not in the other? Furthermore, people believe in the things they do, Justine suggests, because it makes them feel good to renew their hope for and belief in their personal salvation. The people born and raised in the mountains around Tug seek not truth, as Aldous does, but rather an escape from the hardships of this world, particularly the death and violence and loss they experience daily. Belief—in both God and witchcraft— empowers the people of Appalachia by providing them with both an explanation and a hope for eventual escape from a seemingly inescapable existence of hardship and misery.

Uncrossable Boundaries

Aldous, despite having spent most of his life in Appalachia, is an outsider; he settled in Tug after having been educated at the University of Virginia and having served as a Methodist circuit rider. Although he understands and accepts many of the Appalachians' peculiarities, he does not understand the benefits they receive from a style of worship that he dismisses, even condemns, as mere "carnival emotionalism." The boundary separating his own "dry and somber" ministry from the emotional and participatory religion of the mountains is one that Aldous is unable to cross and, to his disappointment, one that the people of Tug show no desire to cross in the opposite direction. Despite the differences in religious practice that separate Aldous from the people of Appalachia, he generally tolerates and is tolerated by the community.

Less successful in his attempt to cross the boundary separating the mountains of Appalachia from the region's "civilized" towns and cities is Richard Burlage, the privileged son of a wealthy businessman in Richmond, Virginia, who journeys to the mountains in 1923 to serve as a schoolteacher. Uninspired by the sterility of his own Episcopalian upbringing and his "gentlemen's education" at Charlottesville, Richard believes that he can find in the mountains a "system of belief" that is more vital, more emotionally powerful than his own (p. 93). What he discovers, deep in the mountains of Appalachia, is life being lived rather than cataloged and dissected. He finds the Free Will Baptists, who handle snakes, speak in tongues, seek salvation, and immerse themselves in the icy mountain waters; he finds Almarine Cantrell and his sons, who will kill with no compunction any man who interferes in their lives and their business; and he finds Dory, whose open sexuality is responsible for, as he says, bringing him to his senses (p. 155). Finally, as he falls victim to a passion that is a "sickness upon death," lapsing into fever and delirium, he even finds himself infected by old Rose Hibbitts's "nonsense," her mutterings "to the effect that Hoot Owl Holler is haunted, and . . . that Dory, too, was cursed, and that a 'witch-woman' walks up and down Grassy Creek from Hoot Owl to Tug and over to Snowman Mountain" (p. 160).

Ultimately, Richard rejects the life of the mountains, a life that is more than he can stand, more than he can control. He returns home after serving only five months as a teacher to fall back into the type of life originally laid out for him, marrying the daughter of an Episcopalian bishop. His life with this woman is utterly controlled, a still life that is disturbed only when, ten years after his departure from the mountains, he makes a one-day visit back to Tug to capture on film the remnants of the only life he ever really experienced. He finds himself being shot at, not this time for ravaging a young girl but for epitomizing the external world of progress and development that, having recently discovered the value of Appalachia's coal and timber, has ravaged its mountains, its solitude, and its way of life. Richard, with his fancy car and photographer's distanced view of the world, is clearly recognized by the people of the mountain communities as one of "them," as much an outsider in 1933 as he was in 1923. For those Appalachians living in the mountains, the boundary separating "us" from "them," insiders from outsiders, is real; it is clearly demarcated by an incongruence in attitude, deportment, and economic level, not to mention belief.

Although an outsider, Richard, in his inability to cross the boundary separating two worlds, experiences the same curse that has plagued many of the Cantrells, a curse going back not only to Almarine but also to Red Emmy, the woman accused unjustly of perpetrating it. The curse of so many of the characters in Oral History is the curse of desiring an alternative way of life that, because of a failure of their own or of a person they love, they are powerless to attain. Unfulfilled, the desire becomes destructive, a wasting and consuming fire. As Sally says about her family, "People say they're haunted and they are—every one of them all eat up with wanting something they haven't got" (p. 239).[15] What each of Almarine's descendants seems to want, as Richard also wants, is an escape from his or her own circumscribed existence. Their sexual passion, like their religious passion, is not an end in itself but a means to an end, an escape from the violence, barrenness, and futility of life in the mountains.

The first time Red Emmy saw Almarine, when he first came upon her bathing in the spring, "a shadow crossed her face. She looked sadder for a minute than a body has ever looked. . . . It was like she knew for the first time what it was she couldn't have" (p. 35). Just as Emmy desires something that is withheld from her by an invisible but all too real boundary, so does Almarine seem to need or want something that exists far beyond the mountains encircling Hoot Owl Holler. Both his daughter Dory and his youngest son, Jink, inheriting Almarine's attraction to the world outside Appalachia, are strongly drawn to Richard Burlage because he offers to both, albeit in different ways, the same hope—the hope of an escape from the mountains, their hardship, their isolation, their "ignorance and darkness" through travel, cultivation, and education. Like the Free Will Baptists, they seek salvation, but they want it now, not in some distant future. Dory is enchanted by Richard's tales of how it will be when they leave the mountains together. "Tell me about the train," she says, and Richard describes again the journey they will take. "I tell it again," he says, "how we will board the spur line at Claypool Hill, and how she will wear a hat, and how we shall disembark at Marion, and spend the night in a fine hotel and eat in the dining room, . . . and I tell her that there will be a rose in a silver bud vase on our linen-topped table in the dining car, and a little silver pitcher to hold the cream" (p. 157). Richard knows, of course, that this journey will never occur. He has recognized from the beginning the reasons for not becoming involved with Dory, going so far as to prepare a list comparing the reasons for pursuing and for forgetting "Miss Cantrell." Among the reasons for forgetting Dory are "she is not of the same social class" and "she is ignorant and largely uneducated; such a gap exists between us that it could never be truly bridged, not even by any attempt on my part to educate her" (p. 134). When Richard does leave Appalachia, Dory remains behind, pregnant with twin daughters and irremediably infected with his tales of the train and the towns along its route.

Dory's younger brother Jink is also infatuated with Richard Burlage. He loves him for the stories he reads, the books he loans to him, the promise he seems to offer of a different life outside the mountains. Jink inherits both his father's dreaminess and his sweetness, as shown by his tender care for his epileptic sister, Mary. For Jink, the orange Richard Burlage gave him at Christmas, now old and hardened, symbolizes the wide world that exists outside the mountains: "I knowed—knew—it had come from Florida in the South, and in the dark I made like it was still bright orange . . . and . . . as round as the whole big globe of the earth he had, and I thought to myself how I'd up and leave here after while, me and Mary we'd up and leave and strike out walking as far as we could get acrost the big round world" (p. 212). Thus, when Richard Burlage leaves on the train to Richmond after only five months in Tug, he leaves two of Almarine's children dreaming of a world beyond the mountains. Although Dory never succeeds in crossing into that world, Jink, Ora Mae later reveals in her narrative, leaves Hoot Owl Holler soon after his sister Mary dies, and he never returns.

One of Dory's twin daughters, Pearl, also dreams of life beyond the mountains; in fact, she seems to receive a double dose of desire, inherited on one side from her father, Richard Burlage, and on the other from her mother, Dory, and her grandfather, Almarine. Pearl, according to her sister Sally, wants so much she will never be fully satisfied. "What I keep thinking," Pearl tells Sally, "is that there's something else, you know, something that Mama knew about and never told us, something she was going to tell us when we got old enough, she said that one time, but then she died, and everything that comes up, I think well is this it?" (p. 271). Pearl's sense that her mother had intended to tell her daughters something—something, she thinks, about love—recalls the time Pearl's grandmother Pricey Jane sat on her porch nursing Dory and thinking back about her own mother: "Her mama's face was white and thin and grainy, and she never said a word about love. . . . And then she was always so tired. If you asked her about love, her eyes would glaze over like she couldn't remember how it felt or what it meant or even recognize the word spoken right out loud like that, in air. . . . In any case, Pricey Jane's mother had died before she ever gave any answer, if she had any answer to give" (p. 61). These memories recollected by Pricey Jane the afternoon before she dies suggest that the answer her mother would have given, had she ever decided to speak, is that love and passion, if they are felt at all, wear out after the almost yearly bearing of children, the toil of surviving in the mountains, and the frequent loss of those who are loved. What Dory would have told her daughters, surely, is that Luther is not Maggie and Pearl's father, that their father is a schoolteacher from Richmond who spent only five months in the mountains.[16] What else Dory might have told her daughters—about men and love and passion and wanting—one can only guess, just as one can only guess about what all the mothers who died young might have told their daughters if they had lived to speak. What would Red Emmy's mother have told her about love and passion? What would Pricey Jane have told Dory? What would Pearl have told her daughter, Jennifer? The deaths of the mothers ensure that the curse will continue to be inflicted on the daughters because those deaths leave the daughters wanting, questing, struggling to forge a new way of living only to fail, dying young and unfulfilled just as their mothers did.

Harriette C. Buchanan, in discussing the passivity of Smith's characters, says that the women Smith writes about are "faced with a world for which they are unprepared. These women . . . have little idea of where to look for guidance, because their families and communities provide so little in the way of honest or genuinely nurturing support. The families are broken, with key members either physically or mentally absent. These characters are so frequently lost and spiritually impoverished that they see no solution to their problems."[17] The passivity that characterizes so many of these women can be traced to the absence of guidance, as Buchanan suggests, to the early deaths of the mothers, and to the hesitancy of the mothers to speak while they are alive. The passivity can also be traced, however, to the women's acceptance of a way of life that they have never thought of as open to change. As Kephart says, "It is seldom that a highland woman complains of her lot" because "she knows no other." The passivity of the Appalachian woman can also be traced to the very belief that, according to Miles, gives her the strength to survive—the belief "that nothing can happen which has not happened before; that, whatever she may be called upon to endure, she will know that others have undergone its like over and over again." For several hundred years the women of the mountains have seen no escape from a continuous cycle of physical hardship, endless childbearing, and early death.

Oral History dramatically demonstrates the power of boundaries—cultural differences—to separate one person or group from another. Set in the Appalachian Mountains during a hundred-year span extending from the 1870s to the 1970s, the novel depicts the gradual encroachment of "civilized" America into the deepest recesses of the mountains. To the inhabitants of Tug, Red Emmy and old Isom represent the depth of depravity, wildness, and primitive existence, and they are shunned as consorts of the devil because of their difference, their failure to conform to the codes of behavior set by the community. To Richard Burlage, however, the inhabitants of Tug appear just as depraved and primitive as Red Emmy appears to them. For Richard, who feels himself "a sojourner . . . between places" (p. 141), the gap between Tug and Richmond and thus between Dory and himself is unbridgeable. For Almarine the gap between Red Emmy and himself is equally unbridgeable. Both men—who, unlike the women, hold the power to decide and to act—choose sweetness and control over wildness and passion. In so doing, they retain their freedom and power to define themselves, but they also deprive themselves of a life-giving passion, and, perhaps more important, they deprive the women—Emmy and Dory—of the opportunity to re-vision and redirect *their* lives through a redefinition of self.

Oral History demonstrates, on several levels, the consequences of being defined from without. Red Emmy is defined by Granny Younger, the community, and eventually Almarine as a witch; Rose Hibbitts is defined by the community and eventually herself as ugly; Dory is defined by Richard Burlage as a mountain girl; the typical Appalachian woman is defined by her husband as "a sort of superior domestic animal." Entrapped in the definitions imposed, these women find personal growth, development, and modification impossible. Instead, they derive what consolation they can from their belief in the supernatural: they explain inexplicable losses through witchcraft; they feel the presence of their mothers in the objects around them; they experience momentary escape in the "carnival emotionalism" of their religious sects; and they look toward death and the "golden hereafter" as a final, liberating escape. The times, however, are changing, and the beliefs that ennobled and empowered Granny Younger and sustained the mountain women in 1900 are no longer sufficient a hundred years later. Without new, successful, empowering examples, Smith seems to say, the daughters of Appalachia are destined to repeat the lives of their mothers, enduring but not truly living. One of the greatest strengths of *Oral History* is its ability to portray the double-edged nature of belief in a world controlled by supernatural forces: the strengthening, liberating sustenance it provides and the suffocating, binding oppressiveness it imposes.

3 Predator, Scavenger, and Trickster-Transformer: Survival and the Visionary Experience in Louise Erdrich's *Tracks*

I pressed charcoal into her hand one day. "Go down to the shore," I told her. "Make your face black and cry out until your helpers listen."

But she would not. "I'm tired, old Uncle." The sound of her complaint was bright and hollow. She crept toward the bed and when she thought I was not looking, she eased herself under the blankets and lay with her face to the wall. I smoked a pipe, and I thought of what I'd say to her if only she would listen.
—Louise Erdrich[1]

Like Smith's *Oral History*, Louise Erdrich's novel *Tracks* also tells the story of a witch. Unlike Red Emmy, however, Fleur Pillager accepts, takes pride in, and works to enhance her identity as a witch. Where Emmy's development is stymied by the community definition of her as a witch, Fleur's is enhanced; where Emmy is destroyed, Fleur is empowered. The experiences of the two women are similar, however, in that their sense of identity is radically altered by an intrusion by outside forces: in Emmy's case, Granny Younger and the community intrude, destroying her belief in her ability to construct a new identity for herself; in Fleur's case, the whites intrude, undermining her belief in her ability to draw on her existing identity as a witch to stop them. Although Fleur's life as a witch is as irremediably destroyed as is Emmy's short-term life as a housewife, Fleur survives because she recognizes that, although deprived of the identity that has always empowered her, she still possesses the power of a woman who refuses to be defeated by those who have destroyed that identity.

52

According to ethnographers of traditional Chippewa culture, the Chippewa believed that each individual gains personal identity through an adolescent visionary experience in which he or she is visited by a spirit—usually an animal spirit—who not only bestows an identity but also serves as a guardian, appearing and offering assistance in times of need throughout the individual's life. To lose belief in the existence of such spirits would necessarily result in the loss of identity and of the source of one's power. Such a loss of belief, followed by the consequent loss of identity and power, occurs when the whites invade the Chippewa world, stealing the land, killing the game, destroying the trees, infecting the people with white diseases, and imposing their own language and religious beliefs. Whereas the boundary separating the mountains of Appalachia from the rest of the United States appears impassable in Smith's *Oral History*, the boundary separating and once protecting the Chippewa from the whites appears, in Erdrich's *Tracks*, to be steadily eroding. A survivor, Fleur Pillager exhibits one response to the collapse of the boundary and the ensuing threat to Chippewa beliefs in supernatural beings and to the personal power springing from those beliefs; Pauline Puyat and Nanapush, who are also survivors, exhibit two alternative responses.

Survival and the Visionary Experience

For the Chippewa, or Ojibwa, success in hunting, and thus survival, depended on the hunter's ability to persuade a Manitou—that is, the spirit prototype of some animal, plant, or elemental force—to assist him in time of need.[2] "Ojibwa tradition created its intensest religious expression," anthropologist Ruth Landes writes, "through this pursuit of a guardian spirit who revealed (or yielded) himself in 'dreams' or visions to a boy or man undergoing ritual fasts and other privations, ritual or not."[3] In the era described by Erdrich in *Tracks*—1912 to 1924—ritual fasting is rarely necessary; the scarcity of game during the long, bitterly cold winters of northern North Dakota ensures enforced fasting through starvation. Such is the case in the winter of 1917 when Nanapush hands nineteen-year-old Eli his gun, sends him north to find food, and then lies down on his bed to call on his "helpers" to guide Eli. "In my fist I had a lump of charcoal, with which I blackened my face," Nanapush remembers. "I placed my otter bag upon my chest, my rattle near. I began to sing slowly, calling on my helpers until the words came from my mouth but were not mine, until the rattle started, the song sang itself, and there, in the deep bright drifts, I saw the tracks of Eli's snowshoes clearly" (p. 101). In this trancelike state, Nanapush serves as a conduit through which the voices of his spiritual helpers guide and direct the young hunter. Eli, when Nanapush first sees him in his vision, is somewhat dazed; weak from hunger, he is so unattuned to his environment that he is uncertain about what type of game and thus what type of signs he should be looking for. As Nanapush's song reaches him, however, Eli becomes aware that the conditions are excellent for killing moose. From this point, Nanapush's song—which is actually no longer his song but that of his helpers—guides Eli in tracking, shooting, and butchering the moose and, eventually, guiding him home. As a partial reward for his assistance, Nanapush receives a portion of the moose's liver, which Eli has carefully divided into three pieces: one piece goes to Nanapush, one is eaten by Eli, and the third is sprinkled with tobacco, wrapped in cloth, and buried in the snow where the moose was shot, thereby feeding and expressing gratitude to the spirit of the moose for having given his body to the hunter. In this instance, credit for the success of the hunting expedition is equally divided among shaman, hunter, and Manitou.

The shaman differs from the ordinary Chippewa hunter-visionary in that he or she develops the visionary experience to the level of art or profession. Whereas the hunter's vision is almost always intended to satisfy individual needs, a shaman's vision frequently affects other members of the community, either beneficially or adversely. Among the Chippewa, the shaman normally specializes in only one of three types of visions—hunting, curing, or warfare—but occasionally participates in all three. Nanapush's shamanistic powers are directed toward hunting and curing. Fleur, the other recognized shaman in *Tracks*, focuses her talents on warfare; her powers are almost always used to drive off or destroy those whites and Indians who are taking or collecting fee allotments for Chippewa—and particularly Pillager—land.[4] Because of the many deaths attributed to Fleur, she is both respected and feared by the community as an evil shaman or witch. The third person displaying extraordinary visionary powers in *Tracks* is Pauline Puyat.[5] Pauline, too, focuses her powers on matters of warfare; unlike Fleur, however, Pauline's battle is internal, pitting one half of her identity against the other. Although her visions do affect the external world, she is not viewed by the community as possessing any special power because no one other than herself is ever aware of her vision-directed actions. Although the reader may view Pauline's visions, which depict an ongoing battle between Christ and Misshepeshu, as manifestations of madness, they are nevertheless just as self-empowering as those of Fleur and Nanapush.

In writing *Tracks*, Erdrich herself displays the art of a Chippewa hunter-visionary. Nanapush, in describing his success as a hunter, says, "I think like animals, have perfect understanding for where they hide, and in my time I have tracked a deer back through time and brush and cleared field to the place it was born" (p. 40). Guided by stories told by her Chippewa relatives, her study of Native American history and culture, her own experiences as a woman of Chippewa-German heritage, and her tremendous powers of vision and imagination, Erdrich has honed her ability to think like a Chippewa, tracking her ancestors—or perhaps more accurately, the characters of her first novel, *Love Medicine*—back through time and space to their birthplace. The novel that she creates in the process, *Tracks*, is an elegy for what has been lost—human life, land and game, a way of life originally founded on kinship and community, and, finally, religion. Survival, in the face of so many losses, often places a burden of responsibility on the survivor. Erdrich herself feels such a burden and attributes her impetus as a writer to her recognition of that burden. "One looks back," she says, "and sees that of the 12 million to 20 million Native Americans who were here at one time there was a low point when there were only 250,000 left—now there's a little more than a million. And one wonders in looking down through one's own background and heritage, 'Why me? Why am I one of the survivors?' And the role of the survivors is to tell the stories of those who haven't survived, and of those who can't tell them on their own, and of those who are still suffering the effects of that long and immensely arduous history."[6] Thus, Erdrich tells her story to those who will listen, as Nanapush tells his story to Lulu, to remember both those who have died and those who, in surviving, have injured themselves, their neighbors, or their loved ones.

Tracks dramatically portrays the costs and betrayals inherent in survival. All the Chippewa are survivors in the sense that they have survived the killing, dislocation, starvation, and disease that have decimated the Native American population since the arrival of Europeans in America. Unfortunately, the drive to survive sometimes leads to the desire to prosper at the expense of one's neighbors, thus dividing tribes among those who, like the Lazarres and Morrisseys, assist the colonizers to benefit themselves and those who, like the Kashpaws and Pillagers, attempt to hold on to a Chippewa way of life. The division among the two groups often leads to more violence and more "dead Indians." Against this backdrop of tribal conflict and rivalry among the surviving Chippewa living on the Turtle Mountain Reservation, Erdrich focuses on the lives of three special survivors. Nanapush, Fleur, and Pauline are special because, in addition to having extraordinary visionary powers, each is the sole survivor of a Chippewa family totally decimated by smallpox and consumption.

Fleur, Pauline, and Nanapush undergo a process of defining—and redefining—themselves in relation to the tribe, Chippewa beliefs in the supernatural, and the power exhibited by the encroaching whites. All three survive, locating sources of personal power through, respectively, predation, scavenging, and self-transformation. Survival, however, is not won without cost. Although Fleur and Pauline survive, for example, both must sacrifice their connection to family and community. Paradoxically, their respective daughters, Lulu Lamartine and Marie Kashpaw, both of whom are raised by other members of the tribe, not only become matriarchs of large families but also incorporate the unfulfilled visions of their respective mothers. Lulu wins the battle to hold on to a piece of reservation land, and Marie becomes a saint in the eyes of the community if not in the eyes of her mother, who is now known as Sister Leopolda. The lives of the daughters, however, belong to a different story; *Tracks* focuses on the lives of the mothers, demonstrating that the story of the Turtle Mountain Chippewa has "no beginning," just as *Love Medicine* demonstrates that it "has no ending" (p. 31).

Fleur as Predator

In the winter of 1918, Father Damien visits Fleur's cabin at Lake Matchimanito, bringing a map distinguishing among those homesteads for which the government fees have been paid, those that have been sold and are now lost to the tribe, and those that are questionable. Confronted with the map, Margaret, Nanapush, and Fleur all react differently to what they see. Margaret is angry about the amount of land that has been taken over by such families as the Morrisseys and Lazarres, those Chippewa who have worked with the government agents, the bankers, and the lumber companies, selling out their neighbors to pay for their own land. "It was like her," Nanapush says, "to notice only the enemies that she could fight, those that shared her blood however faintly" (p. 173). Nanapush, on the other hand, is much more concerned about the land lost to the outsiders, "the land we would never walk or hunt, from which our children would be barred" (p. 174). Unlike both Margaret and Nanapush, however, Fleur regards the map with contempt, claiming that it has "no bearing or sense, as no one would be reckless enough to try collecting for land where Pillagers were buried" (p. 174). Briefly closing his eyes, however, Nanapush glimpses the world to come: "I saw . . . leaves covering the place where I buried Pillagers, mosses softening the boards of their grave houses, once so gently weeded and tended by Fleur. I saw the clan markers she had oiled with the sweat of her hands, blown over by wind, curiosities now, a white child's toy" (p. 174). Both Margaret and Nanapush, whose greater age and experience allow them to see more clearly than Fleur the changes that threaten tribal life, no longer believe that either respect for or fear of the Pillagers can overcome the desire for money. Furthermore, although Nanapush knows that "Pillager land was not ordinary land to buy or sell," he recognizes that something, although he is unsure what, has weakened the Pillagers' power (p. 175).

Perhaps the primary indication of the diminishment of the Pillagers' power is that they, like so many other Chippewa, have succumbed to the deadly diseases introduced by the whites. None of the Pillager magic, or "medicine," whether "good" or "bad," was sufficiently powerful to protect them from the consumption that swept through the Turtle Mountain Reservation during the winter of 1912. By the spring of 1913, all that remains of the once-formidable power of the Pillager clan resides in its sole survivor, seventeen-year-old Fleur.[7] The stories told by Nanapush and Pauline trace Fleur's efforts to assume the burden of being the family's only survivor, her rising reputation as a witch, and, ultimately, the decline of her supernatural powers.

A Pillager by birth, Fleur naturally inherits a potential for power. "Power travels in the bloodlines, handed out before birth," Pauline says of Fleur (p. 31). As a descendant of the Pillagers, then, Fleur possesses several potential sources of power—those of the gambler, the bear, the wolf, the water monster, and the spirits of the Pillager dead. Despite these potentialities, the personal identity of a Chippewa is not determined, ethnographer Christopher Vecsey says, until he or she undergoes an initial visionary experience: "A human did not begin life with power and full identity; those came . . . from the vision acquired through the puberty fast when an Ojibwa gained the aid of a manito." Although an individual's new identity and subsequent power may not be immediately recognized, Vecsey continues, they are revealed over time through his or her success in hunting and other endeavors.[8] Thus, although Fleur, in keeping with Chippewa tradition, would not have revealed the nature of her puberty vision or the identity of her guardian spirits to the community, both are eventually recognized by her neighbors as they witness and experience the effects of her powers.

Although Fleur's power seems to derive from several sources, then, the powers most frequently witnessed by her neighbors are those deriving from Old Man Pillager's connection with Misshepeshu, the water monster living in Lake Matchimanito.[9] In Chippewa myth, water monsters come in various forms—water lions, water serpents, water bears, mermaids, mermen, and the Great Fish, a monstrous sturgeon sometimes referred to as a whale or shark.[10] Pauline imagines the water monster as a glittering deity made of copper, brass, mica, and gold.[11] Ultimately, however, she knows that Misshepeshu, horned, fanged, clawed, and finned, is a thing of water, of "beach moss," "dry foam," and "death by drowning" (p. 11). Dying in the arms of the water monster is particularly feared because, according to Chippewa belief, drowning and burning are the two types of death that cannot be "survived." Victims of all other types of death continue to live; that is, their spirits journey west to what Ruth Landes calls the "village of souls," where they continue to live a life similar to that of the living. Victims of burning continue burning, however, while the drowned remain drowned forever.[12] By surviving two near drownings by the age of fifteen, then, Fleur Pillager clearly exhibits her special relationship with Misshepeshu.

Because of these two early instances in which Fleur nearly drowns and the men who intervened to save her later died or disappeared, the men on the reservation avoid her. "Even though she was good-looking," Pauline says, "nobody dared to court her because it was clear that Misshepeshu, the water man, the monster, wanted her for himself" (p. 11). The people believe that Jean Hat and George Many Women die for having challenged Misshepeshu's claim on Fleur. The two men die, however, not for having challenged Misshepeshu but for having participated in the surveying, measuring, mapping, and selling of tribal land. Before their deaths, both Hat and Many Women were guides working for the government. They and the man who disappeared are the first of Fleur's victims drawn from among those who attempt to buy or to collect fees on Pillager land.

During the spring after her family dies, Fleur goes back to the cabin by the lake, living there alone despite Nanapush's request that she live with him. Nanapush fears that Fleur's shamanistic powers, drawn from Pillager "bloodlines" and from her connection with the spirits of the Pillager dead, can become self-destructive without the experience of age to temper that power. Fleur at seventeen "was too young and had no stories or depth of life to rely upon. All she had was raw power, and the names of the dead that filled her" (p. 7). Carried to an extreme, the visionary experience leads to madness and alienation from society. During those first months following her family's death, however, Fleur not only survives the initial danger of being filled with "the names of the dead"—that is, the danger of being enticed by Pillager spirits into following them on their journey west—but also learns to use those spirits as accomplices. Nanapush says that the Agent who went out to Fleur's cabin to collect fee money on the Pillager land "got lost, spent a whole night following the moving lights and lamps of people who would not answer him, but talked and laughed among themselves. . . . Yet he asked Fleur again for money, and the next thing we heard he was living in the woods and eating roots, gambling with ghosts" (p. 9). Instead of luring Fleur into madness or death, then, the spirits of the deceased direct their energies against Fleur's enemies, who gamble, trading their sanity or their lives in an attempt to take Pillager land.

After her family's death, then, as more and more trespassers on Pillager land disappear, lose their minds, or die in unusual circumstances, Fleur develops within the community the reputation of a witch. Stories of her eccentricity, her nightly hunting, her transformation into other bodily forms abound. According to Pauline, Fleur, living "alone out there,"

> went haywire, out of control. She messed with evil, laughed at the old women's advice and dressed like a man. She got herself into some half-forgotten medicine, studied ways we shouldn't talk about. Some say she kept the finger of a child in her pocket and a powder of unborn rabbits in a leather thong around her neck. She laid the heart of an owl on her tongue so she could see at night, went out, hunting, not even in her body. We know for sure because the next morning, in the snow or dust, we followed the tracks of her bare feet and saw where they changed, where the claws sprang out, the pad broadened and pressed into the dirt. By night we heard her chuffing cough, the bear cough. By day her silence and the wide grin she threw to bring down our guard made us frightened. Some thought that Fleur Pillager should be driven from the reservation, but not a single person who spoke like that had the nerve. (P. 12)

Like many women designated as witches, Fleur disturbs the community by her refusal to conform to its unspoken codes. She lives alone at the cabin, which even Nanapush notes as unusual behavior, she dresses "like a man," and she refuses to listen to "the old women's advice." These eccentricities, added to her descendance from the "Pillagers, who knew the secret ways to cure or kill" (p. 2), her survival of two near drownings by the time she was fifteen, and the misfortunes befalling the men who had trespassed on Pillager land, encourage the people's belief in Fleur's supernatural powers. According to Vecsey, the Chippewa were particularly afraid of "witches who posed as bears, either by wearing the skins of bears or by metamorphosing into bears. These bear-walkers owed their powers to their personal manito, the bear, and traveled in disguise at night, causing disease among their victims."[13]

Determining which signs are true indications of the sources of Fleur's power, gained through her puberty fast, and which are reflections of the community's fears is sometimes difficult. Nanapush believes that the community's fear of Fleur arises, in part at least, from the tendency of people to believe their own lies—or their own versions of truth—if they repeat them often enough (p. 9). The distinction between the powers Fleur knows she possesses and those powers that others attribute to her is perhaps meaningless, however, because in either case her reputation increases; as her reputation increases, so do her powers, and vice versa.

All deaths, insanities, illnesses, and disappearances in the community are attributed to Fleur; even when she is not responsible, as in the death of Napoleon Morrissey, she receives the blame. However, because Fleur knows that her continuing power—at least over her neighbors—depends on their continuing belief in her, she is willing to accept responsibility for all the community's misfortunes. Jean Hat and George Many Women would not have died if they had not believed that Fleur derived special powers from her connection with Misshepeshu; their belief, combined perhaps with guilt for having betrayed their neighbors, is sufficient to kill them. Similarly, the Agent who demands the payment of fees on Pillager land would not have gone insane had he not believed the stories about ghosts inhabiting the woods around Fleur's cabin. The Agent and the other whites who attempt to take Pillager land may not believe in Misshepeshu or the Manitous, but they do believe in ghosts.

Although those people who fear Fleur's power would like to drive her from the reservation, they also depend on her to control Misshepeshu. During the summer that Fleur was in Argus, Misshepeshu was particularly troublesome. With her return, however, "the lake man retreated to the deepest rocks. The fish struck hungrily dawn and dusk, and no boats were lost" (p. 35). But is Misshepeshu's retreat in the fall of 1913 a sign of Fleur's control, or is it a sign of his withdrawal from the lake and from the people who live there or, perhaps, of his demise?[14] Pauline says that in the spring of 1915, "Misshepeshu went under and wasn't seen much in the waves of the lake anymore. He cracked no boats to splinters and drowned no more girls, but watched us, eyes hollow and gold" (pp. 69–70). Although Pauline continues to believe over the next six years that Misshepeshu presents a threat to Christ, just as she imagines that Fleur poses some threat to her, both Misshepeshu and Fleur appear to be losing power. Fleur's last successful act of sorcery, which is only half-successful, occurs in the spring of 1918, when she avenges Margaret's shame for having her braids cut and her head shaved by Boy Lazarre and Clarence Morrissey. To show her sympathy and alliance with Margaret in what has developed into a war between the two groups of families, Fleur shaves her own head. "Then," Nanapush says, "she went out, hunting, didn't even bother to wait for night to cover her tracks" (p. 117). In this instance, Fleur wants the community to *know* that she is responsible. Fleur goes first to town, displaying her bare head to the community before following Lazarre and Clarence to the Morrissey farm, where she collects clippings of hair, nails, and eyelashes from the two men. Two days after Nanapush ensnares Clarence, accomplishing his own revenge, Fleur encounters Lazarre in a reservation store. As soon as he sees her, Lazarre points to his infected arm and collapses dead on the floor. Those who witness this event draw their own conclusions: "All the whispers were true. She had scratched Lazarre's figure into a piece of birchbark, drawn his insides, and rubbed a bit of vermilion up his arm until the red stain reached his heart" (p. 125).

Despite the success of Fleur's medicine on Lazarre, however, it has little effect on Clarence. Clarence does end up with a twisted mouth, but that deformity results from Nanapush's vengeance rather than Fleur's.[15] Although Clarence recognizes that Fleur deals in "bad medicine" (p. 119), he is not overwhelmed by fear as Lazarre is. Similarly, Pauline explains that despite experiencing real fear when forced to confront Fleur's anger over her part in Sophie and Eli's sexual encounter in the slough, "the weight of my danger gave me courage. . . . I don't believe the Pillagers could harm that easily" (pp. 88–89). If Pauline had believed that "the Pillagers could harm that easily," as Lazarre obviously did, she would certainly have died from that concentration of Fleur's "raw power" on her defenseless body. Instead, Pauline takes courage, as perhaps Clarence does, defusing and deflecting Fleur's power. Thus, the extent of Fleur's power over the community reflects the extent of their belief in her power. Pauline and Clarence fear Fleur, but they do not necessarily believe she possesses the magnitude or variety of powers attributed to her.

Regardless of what the community believes, however, by the winter of 1919 Fleur herself recognizes that her power has greatly dissipated. She is unable to save her second child, either by preparing her own curative teas or by journeying to the land of the dead to gamble for his life. In the months that follow the infant's death, Fleur exerts her powers to keep the family—Eli, Lulu, Nanapush, Margaret, and Nector—from starving. She dreams of deer tracks in the snow, but Eli, sent out with directions, returns empty-handed. She cuts a hole in the ice to fish, but Misshepeshu offers only one "weak runt perch." She sings words that Nanapush has never heard before, "chilling and cold as the dead, restless and sharp as the wind of the month when the trees crack" (p. 171). The family is saved, ultimately, not by Fleur's dreams or her connection to Misshepeshu or her songs but by government supplies sent to the reservation from outside. Although the receipt of the supplies breaks the "back of the famine," Nanapush says, "there was something lost. . . . [Fleur] had failed too many times, both to rescue us and save her youngest child, who now slept in the branches of bitter oaks. Her dreams lied, her vision was obscured, her helper slept deep in the lake." The loss of her child, followed by her inability to feed her family, destroys Fleur's belief in her own powers. "Fleur was a different person than the young woman I had known," Nanapush says. "She was hesitant in speaking, false in her gestures, anxious to cover her fear" (pp. 176–77).

Hoping to console Fleur for the loss of her power, Nanapush explains to her that "power dies out, power goes under and gutters out, ungrasp-able. It is momentary, quick of flight and liable to deceive. As soon as you rely on the possession it is gone. Forget that it ever existed, and it returns" (p. 177). Nanapush tells Fleur that he has never viewed himself as a god or even a possessor of supernatural powers. He sees himself only as a conduit through which the supernaturals work; thus, if they choose not to work through him, he cannot be held responsible for failure. To have believed otherwise, to have believed that the power lay only in his own hands, would have long since destroyed Nanapush, who has tried to save and has lost so many loved ones. Such understanding of the ways of power comes only with the collection of stories and a "depth of life." Fleur, whose power has never failed her until the recent death of her child, is still weak because she has not yet accumulated enough stories and thus is unprepared to accept the possibility of her own powerless-ness. Perhaps even more difficult is the transference of responsibility, and blame, from herself to the Manitous, who have apparently deserted her. Nanapush tells Lulu that Fleur, seeing herself as a sort of all-powerful god, "huge" and "endless," believes that she differs from Nanapush or other lesser shamans, who often succeed but sometimes fail. Such a belief in oneself, in one's powers, places a tremendous burden and responsibility on one who is, ultimately, only human, no matter how greatly empowered. Added to that responsibility is the knowledge that, "as the lone survivor of the Pillagers" and "the funnel of [Chippewa] history," she carries the burden of deserving the gift of life (p. 178). The historical powers and deeds of the Pillagers, once mighty and prolific, have dwindled to those of a single surviving daughter. The continuity of the family and, by extension, the tribe depends on her ability to hold on to the land, to protect its trees, to keep the waters of the lake from receding, to maintain the connection with Misshepeshu, and, like any mother, to save and nurture the children of her womb.

Vecsey explains that a traditional Chippewa hunter, whose survival depended on his ability to track and kill animals, was totally dependent on his relationship with his guardian spirit: "He knew that he was powerless to find and kill animals unless the manitos granted him success. They allowed him to live; his existence depended on them. His continuation as a person relied on his continued relations with the manitos." Thus, Vecsey continues, "in the nineteenth century when game was scarce and many Ojibwas starved, belief in the manitos did not waver, but their own self-confidence did. . . . Traditionally, they had relied on their relations with the manitos for their identity; now these assumed relations were failing them."[16] When, a year after the death of her child, Fleur learns that Margaret and Nector have applied all the money they had earned to Kashpaw land, allowing the Pillager land to go to the lumber company, Fleur knows that her Manitous have deserted her. Filling her pockets with stones and clutching a boulder to her chest, Fleur walks into the lake, nearly drowning for the third time. Life without the aid of the Manitous seems impossible because without their aid she possesses neither power nor identity—an identity that, over the years, has become one not only of mother, hunter, and warrior but also of witch. Thus, Nanapush believes that as the lumber crews steadily eat into her land, Fleur will now give up and be forced to move from her cabin to Kashpaw land. "Instead," Nanapush says, "she took strength" (p. 218).

Fleur's strength, ultimately, is that of a woman who refuses to give in, to compromise, to allow the lumber crews to take the land with no fight, no loss of life, and no destruction of property. To accomplish her final act of sorcery, Fleur relies on her own muscle and wits, borrowing Nanapush's favorite hunting technique: "When I hunt," Nanapush says, "I prefer to let my game catch itself" (p. 118). When the lumber crews surround her cabin, they find themselves entrapped in a truly haunted forest, one that is "suspended, lightly held. The fingered lobes of leaves floated on nothing. The powerful throats, the columns of trunks and splayed twigs, all substance was illusion. Nothing was solid. Each green crown was held in the air by no more than splinters of bark" (p. 223). All that remains is to call one last time on one of her helpers, the wind Manitou. As the wind builds, the trees topple, crashing down on the loggers, their carts, and their horses. Once again, the men who have gambled their lives for a piece of Pillager land have lost.

In many ways, however, Fleur, too, is a loser. Despite her final, fierce, victorious display of power, the woods are destroyed, thus signaling the final departure of the spirits who have lingered there, the dispersal of the animals and the Manitous whose spirits they represent, and the retreat of Misshepeshu from the lake. Bereft of her helpers, the supernaturals who have aided her in the past, Fleur is also separated from her land, her home, and her family. Despite all these losses, any one of which would threaten the survival of a Chippewa, whose strength derives from his or her connection to family, home, land, and spirits, the reader's final view of Fleur is of a woman who has regained confidence in her own inner power, the power that "travels in the bloodlines, handed out before birth." Furthermore, despite killing losses, she has held out against the pressure by the whites to submit, to vanish, to become white. Sustained by Pillager blood and by the stories and "depth of life" gained from her life to date, Fleur survives, changing over time to become, as readers of Erdrich's The Beet Queen know, nomadic rather than sedentary, peddler rather than predator, healer rather than witch.

Pauline as Scavenger

When Napoleon Morrissey's body is found in the bushes near Lake Matchimanito, the community is quick to believe the story told by the Morrisseys and Lazarres. "Not two days and that story was on every tongue. . . . Fleur had killed Napoleon by drowning, just another in her line of men. She had discarded him, stolen his tongue. Wrapped in a fishskin and worn in her belt, it enabled her to walk now without leaving tracks. No one else knew what else she did to him, or why, but the remains of her medicine were scattered everywhere—piled rocks, acorns, the screech owl's feathers" (p. 215). The story, as created and refined by the community, makes sense to those who know both Fleur's history and the ways of sorcery. The Chippewa, Landes says, believed that "a death-dealing shaman gloatingly cut out the tongue of the corpse, to use in love and other bad medicine, and to keep a tally of victims."[17] Thus, the death by drowning, the missing tongue, and the scattered remains of the sorcerer's medicine all point to Fleur. After all, who else on the reservation possesses such power?

The death of Napoleon is the second instance in which deaths attributed to Fleur are actually the work of Pauline. The first instance—the death of the men at Argus—plunges Pauline into insanity, whereas the second—the death of Napoleon—makes her whole again, healing the cleft left by the "sin of those days in Argus" (p. 195). Pauline suffers for years from her guilt and her fear of punishment for having locked the men in the freezer, reenacting the scene each night in her dreams. Pauline feels no guilt, however, for killing Napoleon: "There was no guilt in this matter, no fault. How could I have known what body the devil would assume?" (p. 203). Pauline feels no guilt, partly because she has become adept by this time in transferring blame to others but also because she believes that in killing Napoleon, whom she mistakes for Misshepeshu, she has served Christ: she has tamed Christ's rival, the devil who lives in Lake Matchimanito. Standing exhausted and victorious over the dead body of Napoleon, preparatory to taking her vows as a nun, Pauline sees the end of several struggles. In taming Misshepeshu, who manifests himself in the body of Napoleon, Pauline tames, controls, denies one half of her identity: celibacy wins out over sexuality; the family of the Church replaces the family of the tribe; the strictness of life wins over release through death. All of these struggles, however, can be seen as part of a much larger one: her struggle between Christian and Chippewa beliefs and, by extension, between her identity as a white versus that as an Indian.

Nanapush, in describing Pauline, says that she "schemed to gain attention by telling odd tales" and that as time passed, "she got peculiar, blacked out and couldn't sleep, saw things that weren't in her room" (p. 39). As the novel progresses, the reader becomes increasingly aware of the truth of this description. Pauline creates fantastic tales, and she frequently sees things—for example, Christ—that are not actually present. Both types of behavior, however, grow out of tendencies that are natural to and even encouraged among the Chippewa—storytelling and vision seeking. Because she separates herself spiritually, emotionally, and physically from the Chippewa, repressing her cultural heritage, Pauline denies herself the outlet that would likely have guided her to an identity as a Chippewa shaman similar to Nanapush or Fleur. Instead, as she attempts to gain acceptance within the white world, her natural inclination toward the visionary experience leads her to the outlet provided by Catholicism—the role of martyr and nun. As critic Catherine Rainwater, speaking of Pauline's confusion of two cosmologies, notes, "despite her scorn for Native American upbringing, Pauline . . . cannot quite escape her old ways of constructing."[18]

Pauline, despite her desire to deny her Chippewa heritage, demonstrates it dramatically when, after returning to the reservation after her time in Argus, she undergoes a puberty vision while attending the death of a schoolmate, Mary Pepewas. Sitting at Mary's bedside in a half-dreaming, half-waking state, Pauline participates in Mary's death, which she envisions as the pulling away of a boat from shore. Pauline's response to this experience is extraordinary: "A cool blackness lifted me, out the room and through the door. I leapt, spun, landed along the edge of the clearing. My body rippled. . . . And that is when, twirling dizzily, my wings raked the air, and I rose in three powerful beats, and saw what lay below." From her vantage point in the trees, Pauline looks down on Mary's mourners, seeing them as "stupid and small." "Even Bernadette," she says, "who would teach me what I needed to know, appeared simply tired, as though this were no joy. I alone, watching, filled with breath, knew death as a form of grace" (p. 68). In this visionary experience Pauline discovers and experiences mystic identification with her guardian spirit, the crow Manitou. As Fleur was transformed into a bear, Pauline is transformed into a crow.

Although the identity that Pauline discovers during her first vision would most likely be discarded as inappropriate by most Chippewa, whose goal in the vision quest is skill in *hunting*, not scavenging, Pauline is pleased, recognizing that her identity as a crow clearly distinguishes her from the tribe: "After that, although I kept my knowledge close, I knew I was different. I had the merciful scavenger's heart. I became devious and holy, dangerously meek and mild. I wore the nuns' castoffs, followed in Bernadette's tracks, entered each house where death was about to come, and then made death welcome" (p. 69). Pauline's satisfaction with her new identity as a crow—and with the associated role she plays in the community—derives from her experience of death during her initial vision as a "joy," a release, "a form of grace." Pauline experiences pleasure—a mystical identification with another's death that temporarily fulfills her own death wish—each time she helps release another soul from its body. Attracted as she is to death, however, Pauline soon discovers that "death would pass me over just as men did, and I would live a long, strict life" (p. 75). Thus, Pauline is forced to feed on the death of others just as she feeds during this period on the sexuality of others; she becomes a voyeur both of death and of sex.

Pauline's visions of Christ are a natural extension of her first vision, in which she received her identity as a crow. The first time that Pauline—prepared by the starvation and self-inflicted pain of the martyr—sees Christ, she says, "He . . . told me I was chosen to serve" (p. 137). Guided by a series of visions in which Christ appears to her, Pauline understands that as a crow attending at the deaths of her neighbors, her mission is to scavenge for Indian souls, delivering them to Christ and thereby helping to undermine the power of his rival, Misshepeshu. In performing this mission for Christ, Pauline further removes herself from the Chippewa view of the world because her mission emphasizes a Christian yearning for death that is not shared by the Chippewa. "The Ojibwas did not yearn for death as the missionary did," Christopher Vecsey says. The missionary "sought unity with God in heaven; the Ojibwas sought unity with the living world and the manitos in this life."[19] Thus, Pauline's identity as a crow, gained through her initial vision and strengthened through subsequent visions of Christ, and her attraction to death are characteristics that emphasize her move toward a new identity. In her attempt to repress her Chippewa identity and to acquire a white, Christian one, she ultimately combines both Chippewa and Christian identities in a uniquely—and terrifyingly— destructive form. As Rainwater notes, Pauline's "notion[s] of evil and the supernatural," drawn from two opposing world views, merge to yield an aberrant form of Christianity: "Twisted and deformed away from their shamanic matrix, and grafted into a Christian cosmology, such notions mark her sadomasochistic Christianity as marginal and aberrant, even within the conventions of martyrology."[20]

Pauline's adoption of an aberrant world view and identity arises, however, not so much from an attraction to the Christian world view as from a desire to deny her Chippewa blood. The young Pauline, who is three-quarters Chippewa and one-quarter white, chooses to go to Argus, she says, because "I wanted to be like my mother, who showed her half-white. I wanted to be like my grandfather, pure Canadian. That was because even as a child I saw that to hang back was to perish. I saw through the eyes of the world outside of us" (p. 14). A few years later, after the birth of an illegitimate and unwanted child drives her into the convent, Pauline is visited by Christ, who sits on the stove and tells her that she is not Indian but white: "He said I was not whom I had supposed. I was an orphan and my parents had died in grace, and also, despite my deceptive features, I was not one speck of Indian but wholly white" (p. 137). Soon after this visitation, Pauline begins referring to the Chippewa as " 'them.' Never *neenawind* or us." When Pauline learns that the convent does not accept Indians, she hastens to inform the mother superior of her "true background" as revealed by Christ (p. 138).

The Pauline who goes to Argus has no vocation or desire to be a nun; she simply wants to be white, and to her, acceptance within the world of the convent signifies acceptance within the world of the whites. As the events of her life unfold, however, Pauline begins to see her world as divided between good and evil: whites, Christianity, Christ, celibacy, pain, and death are good, and Indians, Chippewa beliefs, Misshepeshu, sexuality, pleasure, and life are evil. As this faulty polarization and compartmentalization of the world intensify, she begins to see any temptation by or attraction to those "evil" aspects of the world as sinful; thus, a denial of those aspects of life appears to her to be the only avenue by which she can rid her life of sin.

Many of Pauline's problems arise from her confused sexuality. Warring against her natural feelings of desire are her conviction of her own undesirability, her witnessing at age fifteen of Fleur's rape, her Chippewa belief that sexuality is associated with Misshepeshu and death by drowning, and her Catholic belief that feelings of lust are the work of the devil. The strength of Pauline's own sexual desire, however, is undeniable when she is around Fleur and Eli: "I could not pass between the two of them—the air was busy, filled with sparks and glowing needles, shimmering. . . . They made my head hurt. A heaviness spread between my legs and ached. The tips of my breasts chafed and wore themselves to points and a yawning eagerness gripped me" (pp. 71–72). She concludes that she must get married.

Finding a husband is not easy for Pauline. Her body is sharp and angular, she says, and her face is wrinkled, marked with the strain of attempting to blot out memory, not only the memory of her own hand lowering the lock on the freezer at Argus but also her memory of Fleur's rape (p. 71). Each night in her dreams, Pauline says, "I was witness when the men slapped Fleur's mouth, beat her, entered and rode her. I felt all. My shrieks poured from her mouth and my blood from her wounds" (p. 66). Pauline does not merely witness Fleur's rape; through an act of mystic identification she actually enters Fleur's body, becomes one with her, and experiences the rape. Fleur's pain, Fleur's humiliation, Fleur's mortification are her own. The horror of witnessing the rape, combined with her guilt for having failed to intervene, for having held back to watch from a safe distance, later emerges as a primary impetus for Pauline's self-inflicted punishment after she enters the convent.

Pauline experiences a similar identification when she spies on Sophie and Eli's lovemaking. This time, however, the experience is one of pleasure rather than pain: "as I crouched in the cove of leaves, I turned my thoughts on the girl and entered her and made her do what she could never have dreamed of herself. I stood in the broken straws and she stepped over Eli, one leg on either side of his chest. . . . He moved his hands up her thighs, beneath the tucked billow of her skirt. She shivered and I dug my fingers through the tough claws of sumac, through the wood-sod, clutched bark, shrank backward into her pleasure" (p. 83). Pauline's identification with Sophie, entering Sophie's body both to guide her and to experience her pleasure, is remarkably similar to her identification with Fleur when she is raped. Both recall the mystic identification of a visionary with his or her guardian spirit—the identification, for example, between Fleur and the bear Manitou or between Nanapush and his helpers.

Soon after this incident, Pauline begins sleeping with Napoleon to satisfy her sexual desire. When she discovers she is pregnant, she is overcome by the horror of her sin, and she sees Napoleon as Satan and the fetus growing in her womb as the offspring of Satan. At the moment of birth, Pauline tries to withhold Marie from life not only because she believes that there will be "no taint or original sin on her unless she breathe[s] air" but also because she fears that having a bastard child will make her more of an outcast from the human community of the reservation than she already is (p. 135). No longer recognized as a Chippewa nor accepted as a white, Pauline is a lonely woman. Although she knows that she is not welcome, she continues to visit Fleur's cabin, seeking to find there a substitute for the mother and sisters she lost to consumption. The only other companion and mother-figure in Pauline's life is Bernadette, who first introduces Pauline to the task of attending the dying and laying out the dead. Although this function is important in the community, Pauline's association with death tends to separate her even further from other people. As a "midwife" who delivers her clients into death rather than life, Pauline is avoided as much as possible (p. 75). As Nanapush says, "A man needs no reminding of his mortality"; Pauline "was the crow of the reservation, she lived off our scraps" (pp. 53, 54).

Pauline's identity as a crow and scavenger, feeding off the scraps of her dying neighbors, recalls Windigo, the giant, cannibalistic skeleton of ice. Although Pauline's guardian spirits are the crow Manitou and Christ, those Chippewa who attempt to guess the identity of her guardian by observing her actions might believe that she is actually guided by Windigo and is herself a windigo. The windigos, Vecsey explains, "appeared as skeletons of ice, or as people whose insides were ice. . . . A human could become a windigo through possession by the Windigo, by the acquisition of the Windigo as a guardian, by witchcraft, or by winter starvation. . . . A windigo developed an insatiable craving for human flesh, sometimes eating family members."[21] Nanapush describes the way in which after the death of the Pillagers, he and Fleur, weakened by grief and starvation, felt "the names of their dead" swell inside them, filling them "with the water of the drowned, cold and black," which in the freezing temperatures of a North Dakota winter turns to ice: "Within us, like ice shards, their names bobbed and shifted. Then the slivers began to collect and cover us. We became so heavy, weighted down with the lead gray frost, that we could not move. . . . We had gone half windigo" (p. 6). Although Nanapush uses the term "windigo" in its now common usage to indicate any psychic disorder, its derivation from Windigo, the skeleton of ice, is clear from his description of his and Fleur's condition. The windigo Nanapush and Fleur experience, however, manifests itself through a suicidal starvation inspired by grief rather than through cannibalism.

Pauline's tendency to feed on the "scraps" of her dead neighbors clearly links her to Windigo, and the fact that she becomes increasingly unbalanced with time suggests that she has gone windigo. In fact, excessive fasts and visions—carried, for example, to the extent that Pauline carries them—are believed to lead to windigo disorders, which, Landes says, "involved projection of the sufferer's fears and vindictiveness."[22] Thus, Pauline projects her own internal battle, which incorporates all her sexual-spiritual "fears and vindictiveness," outward in such a way that she imagines herself and Fleur locked in battle, with herself serving as an emissary of Christ and the white world and Fleur serving as an emissary of Misshepeshu and the Chippewa world. Guided by her visions of Christ, Pauline waits for "instruction by His lips, as to what I should do about Fleur":

> She was the one who closed the door or swung it open. Between the people and the gold-eyed creature in the lake, the spirit which they said was neither good nor bad but simply had an appetite, Fleur was the hinge. It was like that with Him, too, Our Lord, who had obviously made the whites more shrewd, as they grew in number, all around, . . . while the Indians receded and coughed to death. It was clear that Indians were not protected by the thing in the lake or by the other Manitous who lived in trees, the bush, or spirits of animals that were hunted so scarce they became discouraged and did not mate. There would have to come a turning, a gathering, another door. And it would be Pauline who opened it, same as she closed the Argus lockers. Not Fleur Pillager. (P. 139)

Until this point Pauline has worked hard to deny her culpability for the death of the men at Argus by blacking out to avoid memory, telling Margaret that Fleur killed them, or believing that a voice in the wind told her to drop the beam. In those instances in which she has admitted her culpability, she has expressed horror at her sin and terror of the punishment she will endure "at Judgment" (p. 66). Never before has Pauline viewed her act as one of power and self-assertion; now, however, she sees that past act as proof that, guided by Christ, she has the power to wrench from Fleur the privilege of opening and closing doors. Over time her sin has become her glory. In Christ's service, she will turn the Chippewa from Fleur, Misshepeshu, and the other Manitous, who have obviously lost their power; she will gather the Chippewa souls, leading them to and through the doors of the Christian heaven. In the battle for the souls of the Chippewa, which Pauline sees as being waged between Christ and Pauline on one hand and Misshepeshu and Fleur on the other, Pauline and Christ will be victorious.

Eventually, Pauline comes to believe that by destroying Misshepeshu, she will be made whole again. "I was cleft down the middle by my sin of those days in Argus," she says, "scored like a lightning-struck tree. Deep inside, that crooked black vein, charcoal sweet, was ready to dissolve. If I did not forsake Jesus in his extremity, then He would have no other choice but to make me whole. I would be His champion, His savior too" (p. 195). At the same time, by destroying Misshepeshu, she will destroy once and for all his continuous pull on her—a pull that combines the pull of her Chippewa blood, the pull of connection, both familial and sexual, and the pull of eternal release offered through death by drowning. By killing Napoleon, in whose form Misshepeshu has chosen to appear, then, Pauline rids herself of all her personal demons and, at the same time, rids the tribe of the devil, Misshepeshu. "I believe that the monster was tamed that night," says Pauline, "sent to the bottom of the lake and chained there by my deed. For it is said that a surveyor's crew arrived at the turnoff to Matchimanito in a rattling truck, and set to measuring. Surely that was the work of Christ's hand" (p. 204). Having tamed Misshepeshu, Pauline then predicts the decline of Fleur's power, the failure of the spirits to make themselves seen or heard ever again, the death of the old conjurers, and, finally, the inability of the next generation of Indians to see or hear apparitions or voices once common on the reservation. Just as the arrival of the surveyors confirms her belief in herself as victor over Fleur and Misshepeshu, her acceptance by the Church as a bride of Christ confirms her belief that her sins have been washed away. "Now sanctified" and "recovered," Pauline sheds her past—her sins, her identity, her name—like dead skin: "I asked for the grace . . . to leave Pauline behind, to remember that my name, any name, was no more than crumbling skin" (p. 205).

No one can doubt that Pauline, despite her belief that she has "recovered," is mad. Nevertheless, within the world created by that madness, Pauline perceives—and thus experiences—herself as powerful and victorious. She has defeated and outlasted her enemies, both internal and external, and she has succeeded in extinguishing all consciousness of her past—or, that is, all conscious guilt for past sins and all conscious recognition of herself as a Chippewa. She has truly transformed herself; no reality exists for her other than the present reality of herself as "sanctified," as a bride of Christ, and as a member of the great family of the Church. Pauline now belongs; she has a place in the world, a proven identity, a worthy mission. Although Pauline's denial of one half of her identity in order to achieve this position may disturb the reader, it does not disturb Pauline. She herself recognizes that in accepting Christ's mission "to gather souls," she must renounce herself: "I must give myself away in return, I must dissolve. I did so eagerly" (p. 140). By selecting a white, Catholic identity—even though, as Rainwater suggests, that identity is an aberrant form of Catholicism—as her true identity, Pauline resolves the conflict that has disturbed her throughout the novel.

One problem with Pauline's new identity, however, is that she is required to work with the living rather than the dead. She is assigned the task of teaching arithmetic at St. Catherine's, and as she explains, "I do not like children very well" (p. 205). Readers of *Love Medicine* know that about nine years later Pauline begins to see in children the devil she once saw in herself; whereas she once abused her own body, she now begins to abuse the bodies of the children under her care. The devil that Pauline/Sister Leopolda sees hovering in the vicinity of children is particularly fearsome in that it is a monster of her own creation. As Rainwater explains, "when Pauline becomes a nun, she still believes in the lake monster, but she calls him Satan. Pauline's distorted version of the Satanic lake monster is more horrible than either the Christian Satan, who is not appeasable but who cannot victimize the truly innocent, or the Chippewa monster, who can capture the innocent but who is appeasable."[23] As a result of her transformation into a nun, Pauline sees herself as beyond the grasp of this Chippewa-Christian monster she calls Satan. Young girls, however, particularly young Chippewa girls like Marie, her own daughter, are always easy prey, and Pauline/Sister Leopolda believes that her mission as a nun is to stalk and kill Satan in all his hiding places. From a scavenger of Indian souls, then, Pauline/Sister Leopolda becomes a predator, hunting and destroying the devil as he manifests himself in young girls. Pauline/Sister Leopolda's actions in *Love Medicine*—using boiling water and a poker to drive out the devil in Marie—demonstrate the extent of her eventual madness. One power possessed by the mad, however, is that they believe that they are empowered—in Pauline's case by Christ—to commit such acts. Thus, despite one's conviction of Pauline's madness at the close of *Tracks,* one must acknowledge that she, like Fleur, emerges from this period of her life with a keen sense of her own power. She is victorious, she is transformed, and she is a survivor.

Nanapush as Trickster-Transformer

After one of Pauline's visions about the decline of the Chippewa and the rise of the Christians, she repeats a story that Nanapush had once told about an experience leading some whites on a buffalo hunt: "He said that when the smoke cleared and hulks lay scattered everywhere, . . . the beasts that survived grew strange and unusual. They lost their minds. They bucked, screamed and stamped, tossed the carcasses and grazed on flesh. They tried their best to cripple one another, to fall or die. They tried suicide. They tried to do away with their young. They knew they were going, saw their end" (p. 140). Survivors of genocide, Nanapush suggests through this story, tend to go mad. Like sufferers of windigo, they may turn cannibalistic, feeding on the flesh of fallen brothers, or they may cripple or kill the survivors, including their own offspring and themselves—all because they can see their own end in the end of those around them. The onus of survival is shared by all surviving Chippewa, but particularly by Fleur, Pauline, and Nanapush, each the small end of the "funnel" of a family's history. Fleur, the predator, directs her murderous instincts outward, attacking whites and those mixed-bloods who steal Chippewa land. Pauline, the scavenger, sustains herself by feeding on the "scraps" of her dead and dying neighbors. Nanapush, the trickster-transformer, outwits his opponents. As a hunter, Nanapush says, he prefers working with snares, allowing his game to catch itself. He uses his brain—his imagination and his ability to think like his prey—as his weapon. He uses this same technique when dealing with humans, attaining a desired end through trickery.

Nanapush is named for Nanabozho,[24] the trickster-transformer figure of the Chippewa creation myth. Although many variations of the myth exist, the basic cycle of stories includes eight episodes: Nanabozho is born, along with two nonhuman brothers, after his previously virgin mother is impregnated by the wind; he steals fire from a neighboring tribe through trickery; he kills his brothers for their part in the death of his mother; he joins a pack of wolves to gain their assistance in hunting, is expelled after several misunderstandings, but is allowed to take the youngest wolf with him as hunting companion and "brother" or "nephew"; his dream that his "brother" will be killed crossing a body of water comes true; after transforming himself into a stump at the water's edge to prevent his detection, he shoots the water lion in revenge, but the wounded lion survives; he then kills an old woman who has been curing the water lion and, wearing her skin, succeeds in killing the lion; when the other water lions flood the world in an attempt to drown Nanabozho, he re-creates the world from a few particles of soil retrieved through the aid of four animals—beaver, loon, otter, and muskrat— that die in the attempt but are later revived by Nanabozho.[25] In analyzing the relationship of this myth to the Chippewa world view, Vecsey notes several lessons provided by the stories of Nanabozho's exploits. Because animals and humans perceive the world differently, humans often need the assistance of animals, birds, and trees to defeat their adversaries. A person's success derives, then, not from "individual prowess" but from the assistance he or she receives from friendly helpers. Metamorphosis, "the fluidity between animal and human forms," is essential to success in hunting and thus to survival. Success in hunting may also require that one disarm one's opponents by addressing them as friends or relatives before killing them. Revenge is often necessary and, in fact, may be "the only means of enforcing intracommunity and intercommunity order."[26]

Vecsey's summary and analysis of the creation myth emphasize Nanabozho's role as a heroic figure whose aggression is aimed at establishing social harmony. Thus, his description of Nanabozho fits the first two of three types of trickster-transformers common to Native American literature, as identified and characterized by Paula Gunn Allen: "(1) Heroic Transformer: frequently portrayed as a monster-slayer, aggressive hero, or creator of order, who achieves power through action. (2) Cunning Transformer: frequently portrayed as a figure (human or animal) who tries to gain power by outwitting his opponents in gambling or games or through marriage or sexual encounters. The figure often changes form to take on another identity or sex or to become an animal or an inanimate object. (3) Overreacher: usually portrayed as a figure who attempts more than he can achieve and therefore suffers humiliation or injury."[27] Although Vecsey's summary and analysis minimize Nanabozho's character as an "overreacher," the cycle of Nanabozho stories collected by Paul Radin and A. B. Reagan from Sarnia, Ontario, between 1911 and 1914 include several stories presenting Nanabozho as a sort of buffoon, attempting unsuccessfully to imitate the magical feats of empowered figures or taking elaborately cunning steps to trick, ensnare, kill, and prepare game, only to be outwitted in return, losing his carefully prepared feast to other humans or animals.[28]

Of the three types of trickster-transformers described by Allen, Erdrich's Nanapush seems to be primarily a "cunning transformer," one who outwits his opponents, sometimes by assuming a different character—that is, by thinking like his prey. One senses that in his youth, Nanapush might have been more of a "heroic transformer" than he is now at the age of fifty, as he begins to experience a loss of his former powers. Concerned in 1919 about the growing feud among the reservation families over the sale of Chippewa land, Nanapush says, "I could do nothing. It is embarrassing for a man to admit his arms have thinned, his capacities diminished, and maybe worse than that, his influence over the young of the tribe is gone for good" (p. 109). Perhaps in compensation for the loss of his youthful strength, Nanapush also frequently plays the part of the "overreacher," particularly in his sexual parries with Margaret, setting himself up as the performer of tremendous sexual feats only to be knocked down by her belittling retorts. In most cases, however, particularly with Pauline, Nanapush is a "cunning transformer," presenting himself as a weak, guileless friend until, when she lowers her defenses, he makes her the butt of his jokes. Nanapush, then, gathers strength by following the example of his namesake and helper, the mythical Nanabozho, as he compensates for the weakness of age with cunning, trickery, and self-transformation.

In addition to providing the Chippewa with a role model for defeating one's adversary through trickery and transformation, Nanabozho also is credited with having created the *midéwiwin*, the Chippewa curing society and its rituals.[29] The midé shaman, Ruth Landes reports, relied on four types of vision-inspired cures: subjecting the patient to the Sun Dance torture; divining the identity of the evil shaman who has caused the illness and then admonishing or killing him or her; "sucking" the cause of the disease from the patient's body; or ritually assigning a new name bearing the power of a new mystical identity.[30] As a shaman, Nanapush develops a personal technique for curing—which is a variation of the latter two techniques described by Landes—from information revealed in a dream. "The person who visited my dream," Nanapush says, "told me what plants to spread so that I could plunge my arms into a boiling stew kettle, pull meat from the bottom, or reach into the body itself and remove, as I did so long ago with Moses, the name that burned, the sickness" (p. 188). To cure Moses, Nanapush had removed the name of the child who was ill, given him "a new name to fool death," and told his parents to pretend that their own son had died and that the child living with them "was someone else" (pp. 35–36). Historically, Chippewa were given several names, two of which—one received at the feast celebrating birth and the other received through the puberty vision—were kept secret because they identify the "essential" person.[31] The white name that Nanapush assigns to Moses is one he can use as a cover or protective device, concealing his true identity.

Nanapush says that he never revealed his own name to government officials, repeating *No Name* whenever he was asked, except for the time that he gave his name to Father Damien, who at Lulu's birth, insisted on having the name of the child's father for his records. Through this impulsive gesture, Nanapush succeeds in extending his name, even though none of his own wives and children have survived, and he also creates the "loophole" that he is later able to "reach through" to draw Lulu home from the government school (p. 225), just as he once reached into a kettle of boiling water and into the body of Moses to withdraw "the name that burned, the sickness."

In drawing Lulu home from school, Nanapush is attempting to save her from vanishing, as Pauline vanishes, within an alien world. Lulu has never forgiven her mother for having sent her away. Nanapush, in attempting to reconcile mother and daughter, explains to Lulu that Fleur sent her away because she recognized that she no longer had the weapons with which to defend her daughter against those who do not fear or respect the Pillagers. Years later, when Lulu is threatening to marry a Morrissey, Nanapush tries once again to save her, using the technique that was successful in saving her the night her feet froze. Recognizing the power of communication and words, he saved Lulu that night by creating a "string" of words to hold her fast to him and to life. Through this sustaining "string" of words, spun out through the night and into the next morning, Nanapush maintained Lulu's connection to this world, as he had once done for himself. "During the year of sickness," he says, "when I was the last one left, I saved myself by starting a story. . . . I got well by talking. Death could not get a word in edgewise, grew discouraged, and traveled on" (p. 46). Having proven the success of this curing technique on himself and on the frozen Lulu, he applies it once again in his attempt to save the adult Lulu from the dangers of marrying a Morrissey, a mixed-blood who has been afflicted by white ways.

Nanapush recognizes that the continuing encroachment of the whites on the Chippewa way of life threatens them all. As an old man weakened by age and by the hunger that strikes each winter, he dreams again a dream he had during the weakness that followed the death of his family: "I stood in a birch forest of tall straight trees. I was one among many in a shelter of strength and beauty. Suddenly, a loud report, thunder, and they toppled down like matchsticks, all flattened around me in an instant. I was the only one left standing. And now, as I weakened, I swayed and bent nearer to earth" (p. 127). Like the story of the buffalo, Nanapush's dream emphasizes the difficulty of living after the death of all one's companions; without one's family, relatives, and friends, one weakens, swaying and bending nearer to earth, longing to follow them on their journey to the west. Nanapush and Fleur were bonded as father and daughter when they together resisted the urging of the Pillager spirits to accompany them on death's journey. Fleur and Nanapush both gained the strength to endure from their knowledge that the spirits of friends and relatives lingered in the woods around Lake Matchimanito, chattering, gambling, occasionally appearing among the living. The tragedy of the destruction of those woods, foreseen in Nanapush's twice-dreamt dream, is that now the survivors are separated from the spiritual as well as the physical presence of their loved ones. During Nanapush's last journey through the square mile of oaks encircling Fleur's cabin, he takes his final farewell. "I stopped," he says, "stood among these trees whose flesh was so much older than ours, and it was then that my relatives and friends took final leave, abandoned me to the living" (p. 220). In this last journey through the woods, Nanapush sees his wives, his daughter and son, his friends, his father, his mother and sister. Lying Down Grass, the first woman with whom he slept, grasps his arm to show him "how simple it was to follow, how comforting to take the step" (p. 220). Nanapush would have done so, he says, "had only the living called from that shade. But Fleur had resisted these ghosts, at least she was not among them. So I would remain with the living too" (pp. 220–21).

As often as Nanapush has been tempted, as seriously as he has been weakened over time by the loss of loved ones, he continues to survive, choosing to stay among the living. His love for, and perhaps responsibility to, the living becomes a source of strength in times of weakness. His love has focused on a few intimates—Fleur, Eli, Margaret, and Lulu in addition to his own family—but also extends outward to include all the surviving Chippewa. Motivated by his desire "to reach through the loophole" to draw Lulu home from the government school, Nanapush transforms himself, becoming a tribal chairman. He has always fought the idea of becoming a government bureaucrat because he understands "what [is] attached" to a government job (p. 185). Later, however, when Fleur's land is lost because of a ruling on late payment fines, Nanapush recognizes his error in not having heeded Father Damien's advice: "He was right in that I should have tried to grasp this new way of wielding influence, this method of leading others with a pen and piece of paper" (p. 209). Acting ostensibly to save a specific person, Lulu, from the white world, Nanapush undergoes a transformation that will ultimately benefit the entire reservation. Replacing Pukwan Junior as tribal chairman, he will bring to governmental negotiation and policy-making a perspective that represents the old-time Chippewa. As a shaman, Nanapush often relied on his visionary powers and his helpers to cure the sick and feed the starving. Confronted with the withdrawal of Misshepeshu, the Manitous, and the spirits of the dead, Nanapush recognizes that the visionary powers of the past must be replaced with new powers, powers arising from his love to talk, his trickery, and his ability to think like his prey.

Before the coming of the whites, Nanapush, Fleur, and Pauline—like all Chippewa—lived in a universe defined and controlled by the actions of a host of supernatural beings. Although powerful and sometimes evil beings such as Misshepeshu and Windigo periodically disrupted their lives, bringing loss and grief, the Chippewa understood that it is the nature of these beings to behave in this way; they also knew that they could appease the spirits and thus, to a certain extent, control their actions, particularly when a Pillager was present. Indeed, the tribe's acceptance of the Pillagers was based on the same principle as their acceptance of the evil beings; they knew that each plays a critical role in maintaining the balance and continuity of both the community and the universe. Furthermore, the Chippewa recognized that each individual is empowered by his or her relationship with a guardian spirit, who could be called on in times of need.

The coming of the whites, however, with their greed for land, their ravaging of natural resources, their deadly diseases, and their imposition of an alien world view, overwhelms the power of the Chippewa world view not only to explain the nature of this massive destruction but also to protect and save the Chippewa from the onslaught. Surely, the Chippewa reason, the gods of the whites are more powerful than our own. Confronted with the loss of their gods—whether they have been subdued, driven out, or totally destroyed—the Chippewa are also confronted with the loss of both tribal and individual identity. Without such identity, dependent as it is on a continuing relationship with the spirit world, they are rendered powerless. In response to the intrusion of the whites into their geographical, spiritual, and cultural space, then, the Chippewa must forge a new identity if they are to survive. Fleur, Pauline, and Nanapush, as depicted in *Tracks*, demonstrate three alternative responses to the destruction of the boundaries separating the Chippewa and white worlds and the intrusion of the whites into Chippewa space.

4 Calling Tayo Back, Unraveling Coyote's Skin: Individuation in Leslie Marmon Silko's *Ceremony*

It was the story of the white shell beads all over again, the white shell beads, stolen from a grave and found by a man as he walked along a trail one day. He carried the beautiful white shell beads on the end of a stick because he suspected where they came from; he left them hanging in the branches of a piñon tree. And although he had never touched them, they haunted him; all he could think of, all he dreamed of, were these white shell beads hanging in that tree. He could not eat, and he could not work. He lost touch with the life he had lived before the day he found those beads; and the man he had been before that day was lost somewhere on that trail where he first saw the beads. —Leslie Marmon Silko[1]

Leslie Marmon Silko's *Ceremony* is similar to Erdrich's *Tracks* in that both novels describe the damage incurred when Native American world views come into conflict with the European-American world view. For Erdrich this conflict occurs when the whites intrude on Native American space, violating and eroding the boundary separating the two cultures. As a result of this intrusion, she suggests, the Chippewa are confronted with a reality that forces them to sacrifice or radically change their own beliefs. Silko, on the other hand, seems to view the Pueblo as existing within an enclosing and sheltering—although not inviolable—space. Although the Pueblo are affected by the cultural changes imposed by whites who move onto the reservation, the true danger to the individual arises, Silko suggests, when he or she crosses geocultural boundaries, wandering too far from the protective core of the home, family, and tribe. Movement across this boundary into the larger society often transforms a Pueblo into an alien creature. Both Erdrich and Silko describe characters—Pauline and Tayo, respectively—who are permanently or temporarily crazed by their inability to reconcile or mediate between two conflicting world views. Whereas Erdrich suggests that a healthy reconciliation of both world views is necessary for survival in the modern world, Silko argues that an individual can be cured of such psychological illness only within the framework of his or her own world view. She argues, furthermore, that an individual does not necessarily have to sacrifice his traditional beliefs but can choose to be guided and empowered by a return to or revitalization of those beliefs.

Silko's *Ceremony* dramatically portrays the tension of being caught between two world views, a struggle manifested not only in Tayo but also in his mother, his aunt, and the other war veterans. The story of Tayo's resolution of this tension makes a powerful statement about the personal power and well-being that accrue from successfully defining oneself in relation to the differing belief systems espoused by one's family members, one's friends, and the external society. The novel as a whole makes an equally powerful statement about the spiritual beauty of the Pueblo world view, one in which all elements of the universe, both natural and supernatural, are connected, as are the nodes of a web, with threads that are as fragile as they are strong.

Connections, Boundaries, and Divisions

"The structure of Pueblo expression," Silko explained at a 1979 meeting of the English Institute, "resembles something like a spider's web—with many little threads radiating from a center, criss-crossing each other. As with the web, the structure will emerge as it is made and you must simply listen and trust, as the Pueblo people do, that meaning will be made." Silko also warned that the Pueblo perspective on language and storytelling, as on all subjects, is one of totality and wholeness: "We do not differentiate or fragment stories and experiences. In the beginning, Tséitsínako, Thought Woman, thought of all these things, and all of these things are held together as one holds many things together in a single thought." Just as one story cannot be separated from all the others, one word cannot be separated from all other words. "We don't think of words as being alone," Silko says; "words are always with other words, and the other words are almost always in a story of some sort."[2] Each word, each story, each thematic strand of the novel *Ceremony* is part of the whole, linked by threads and filaments to every other word, story, and strand of the web. Isolating a single element of Silko's *Ceremony*, then, not only violates its weblike structure and intricately woven view of totality; it also distorts and diminishes the meaning of both the whole and the fragment. Recognizing the dangers of such an action, I nevertheless focus here on one thematic strand of *Ceremony*'s web: the process by which Tayo, as a direct result of his confrontation with, temporary transformation by, and recovery from witchery, proves himself to be a "special breed," capable of surviving drought and hardship by maintaining his connection with the land (p. 75).

Located at the physical and thematic center of *Ceremony*'s web is the story of the "witches' conference" at which an unidentified Indian witch invents the white race as a tool to be manipulated by witchery. Radiating out from this central position of power, witchery infiltrates the entire novel from beginning to end. As powerful as witchery is, however, the first story of the novel demonstrates that witchery is the invention of a more powerful creator; all things in the universe—and thus witchery—were created by Ts'its'tsi'nako, Thought-Woman, and her sisters. Similarly, the last story of the novel demonstrates that witchery can be manipulated and turned back on itself; manipulated by Tayo, witchery has "returned into its belly" and "is dead for now" (p. 261). Like all things, however, witchery will return. Its return is guaranteed not only by the law of the universal cycle—birth, death, rebirth—but also by the law of universal balance: witchery was created and continues to exist as the "counter force" to "vitality and birth." As Silko explains it, "I try . . . to see witchery as a sort of metaphor for the destroyers or the counter force, that force which counters vitality and birth. The counter force is destruction and death. . . . in recent years we've gotten into the habit of talking about black and white and good and bad. But back when, it was force or counter force. It . . . is the idea of balance, an idea that the world was created that way. In the novel it's the struggle between the force and the counter force."[3] Because witchery is cyclically bound to creativity, the struggle between the two forces—vitality and birth versus destruction and death—will continue indefinitely. The novel itself suggests that this struggle continues not only on a global scale but also within each community, each family, each individual. One step in the individuation of each person is the determination of his or her position in relation to these two forces. According to Silko, neither force is good or bad in itself. Not to know one's position, however, is likely to cause trouble when one comes up against one force or the other.

Ceremony is the story of Tayo's struggle between the force of creativity and the counter force of witchery. Silko, both in the novel and in a 1976 interview,[4] insists that witchery and white people are not synonymous; white people are merely an invention of and tool manipulated by Indian witchery. Nevertheless, Tayo's struggle between the two forces manifests itself primarily as a struggle between Native American and European-American beliefs and values. The son of a Laguna Pueblo mother, who dies while Tayo is a child, and an unknown white father, Tayo is raised in a household that exacerbates his sense of cultural division: his grandmother and uncle raise him as a Laguna, but his aunt confuses that identity by sending the message, on the one hand, that his white blood excludes him from the family and, on the other, that her own son Rocky is superior because of his ability to be "white." Despite this internal division, Tayo chooses and adheres to a Laguna identity and belief system until, seduced by the power of the word "brother," he follows Rocky into the white man's war—which proves to be a world manipulated by witchery's destroyers. Permanently transformed by his experience in the Philippines, Tayo will never be the same person he was before he left Laguna.

Framing *Ceremony*'s central story of Indian witchery are two stories that warn of the dangers inherent in wandering away from home and of the difficulty, after crossing certain boundaries, of finding one's way home again. The first story is about a boy who wanders away from his family in the mountains, ending up in bear country, where he loses his consciousness of himself as a human and assumes the consciousness of a bear. The boy's family calls on a medicine man who, by imitating the sounds and movements of the mother bear, succeeds in enticing the boy from the bear's cave. Simply finding the boy is not enough, however, for

> They couldn't just grab the child
> They couldn't simply take him back
> because he would be in between forever
> and probably he would die.

They had to call him
step by step the medicine man
brought the child back.
(P. 130)

The similarity between Tayo's experience and that of the boy who wandered into bear country is obvious. Both have wandered away from home, slipping without realizing it over a line that, once crossed, cannot be easily regained. Tayo, like the young boy, must be called back slowly, "step by step"; otherwise, he will be caught forever between two worlds, and "probably he would die," just as so many Indians who crossed into the white world—Tayo's mother, Rocky, and the Indians in Gallup—died.

Betonie, a Navajo medicine man, suggests that despite these similarities, Tayo is not really one of the bear people, not in the way that Betonie's assistant, Shush, is. Betonie explains that Shush's mental state, unlike Tayo's, is not a result of witchery but simply an accident and that Shush's existence, unlike Tayo's, is a peaceful one. Shush's condition is incurable, but Tayo's can be cured. The true distinction between the two young men is clarified by the "Note on Bear People and Witches," which follows Betonie's discussion of Shush: "Human beings who live with the bears do not wear bear skins. They are naked and not conscious of being different from their bear relatives. Witches crawl into skins of dead animals, but they can do nothing but play around with objects and bodies" (p. 131). Tayo, since his return from the war, has been cloaked in an alien skin, one that gives him the appearance and identity of a witch. Whereas Shush presumably wandered into bear country and assumed bear consciousness, Tayo wandered into witchery and crawled into the skin of a dead animal.

The second story warning about the dangers inherent in crossing certain boundaries, that of the hunter who was transformed into a coyote, begins immediately after the story of Indian witchery and continues at intervals throughout the remainder of the novel. One day while a man was out hunting, Coyote, who wanted to sleep with the man's wife, stole the man's skin and donned it himself, cloaking the man in his own coyote skin.[5] Transformed into a creature that is now more coyote than human, the man crawls from a hard oak tree to a scrub oak to a piñon to a juniper and finally to a wild rose bush, sleeping for a while under each one. To bring the man back, restoring his mind and identity, the people lead him back through hoops made of hard oak, scrub oak, piñon, juniper, and wild rose twigs, after which he walks home following the footprints of a bear. When he gets home, however, he discovers that "it wasn't over. / All kinds of evil were still on him" because "the dry skin / was still stuck / to his body" (pp. 144, 153). Although "the effects / of the witchery / of the evil thing / began to leave / his body" as soon as he arrived home, the hunter is not completely restored until "the dead skin / Coyote threw / on him" is completely unraveled along with "every evil / which entangled him" (pp. 153, 258). Because Betonie recognizes that Tayo's illness is the result of having been cloaked in Coyote's skin and thus tainted with witchery, he performs a version of the traditional Navajo coyote transformation ceremony to help restore Tayo to his true identity.[6]

As a man caught between two identities—Laguna and white—Tayo is a witch in the sense that he is a human disguised in and manipulated by the powers of a false skin. According to Paula Gunn Allen, "the Hopi refer to a witch—a person who uses the power of the universe in a perverse or inharmonious way—as a two-hearts, one who is not whole but is split in two at the center of being."[7] Tayo's physical illness after he returns from the war is a manifestation of his psychic division; he suffers from a split of his being—a split between those beliefs and actions that contribute to vitality and birth and those that facilitate destruction and death. He suffers not from a loss of belief but from a confusion of belief systems. Tayo never loses the belief, inculcated by old Grandma's "time immemorial stories" (p. 95) and his uncle Josiah's practical application of those stories to daily occurrences, that a single person or a single action has the power to destroy or heal the universe. However, influenced by his white teachers' and white doctors' dismissal of such beliefs as nonsense and superstition, Tayo begins to believe that he is crazy to hold such beliefs. One could say that Tayo's clinging to Laguna beliefs in the face of steady opposition from the white world is a cause of his illness not only because his beliefs make him feel crazy but because they make him feel shame for his errors in judgment. His belief that Josiah appeared in the jungle, where he was killed with the Japanese soldiers, and his belief that he himself caused the drought at Laguna by cursing the rain in the jungle are literally killing him. At the same time, however, the associated belief, instilled by the same "time immemorial stories," that he can make amends for his errors and bring himself back into harmony with the universe is responsible for saving him.

Tayo's doubts about the validity of the old stories are symptomatic of the change in identity incurred when Coyote's skin was thrown on him. Another sign of the false skin's power is that Tayo's sense of his relationship with the external world—the relationship among self, community, and universe—has been distorted. One process crucial to his cure is the gradual realization that his personal illness is part of a larger illness, that is, the tribal loss and shame shared by all Indians. This tribal illness is, in turn, part of a still larger illness, the witchery infiltrating the entire world. His cure is not complete, and the coyote skin is not completely removed from his body, until he understands how his personal experience—his story or ceremony—is part of the larger experience.

Tayo's return is a long, painful struggle between two forces, one tending toward self-rejuvenation, the other toward self-destruction. Half Laguna and half white, half human and half coyote, Tayo wavers between believing in and doubting the traditional stories, ceremonies, and spiritual helpers. He experiences periods of hope and piercing insight followed by periods of despair and distorted thinking. This shifting back and forth is part of the process of becoming, of growing, of unraveling the false skin. "There were transitions," Betonie tells Tayo, "that had to be made in order to become whole again, in order to be the people our Mother would remember; transitions, like the boy walking in bear country being called back safely" (p. 170). Although Betonie successfully calls Tayo back, "step by step," and although he performs the coyote transformation ceremony that helps Tayo to unravel and throw off the coyote skin, Tayo will never again be the same person he was before the war simply because his experience and understanding of the world have changed. In this case, however, the change in Tayo is empowering because he recovers a self that is stronger for having been tested, having adapted and survived, and having established its place in the larger ceremony.

My discussion of Tayo's individuation is presented in three sections. The first section focuses on his early years, a period during which the attitudes of his white teachers, Rocky, and Auntie threaten to subvert the Laguna beliefs instilled by Josiah and old Grandma. Despite this threat, however, Tayo emerges from this period with a belief that is strong enough to encourage him to pray for rain and with an incipient recognition, instilled by the Mexican woman Night Swan, of himself as a "special breed." In essence, the beliefs instilled during the first eighteen years of Tayo's life prepare him for the events that follow—both those leading to his illness and those contributing to his cure. The second section focuses on the man cloaked in Coyote's skin—a man whose cursing of the rain is symptomatic of the witchery that is manipulating not only him but the other war veterans of Laguna. The third section focuses on the way in which the ceremony to unravel Coyote's skin strengthens Tayo by helping him to see patterns and relationships among things that he would not have been able to see without the help of Ku'oosh, Betonie, and the woman Ts'eh, who serves as a spiritual guide, and, more important, without his near-disastrous journey into and "safe return" (pp. 115, 116) from the white world. One of the few survivors of such a journey, Tayo is ultimately strengthened by the experience.

The Early Years: Poised between Worlds

One morning during the drought-plagued summer before Tayo leaves for the war, he rises before dawn to pray for rain in a canyon where a spring drips continuously into a pool, even during periods of drought. Although Tayo does not know what the holy men do to call the rain clouds during drought, he enacts a ritual of his own imagining, gathering yellow flowers, sprinkling their pollen on the water, and watching a procession of animals—spider, frogs, dragonflies, hummingbird—approach the water in response to the rising sun. As each animal appears, Tayo remembers the stories that associate that animal with rain: "Everywhere he looked, he saw a world made of stories, the long ago, time immemorial stories, as old Grandma called them. It was a world alive, always changing and moving" (p. 95). Through these stories, each creature within the universe has a relation to each other, to the earth, to the sky, to the rain clouds, and to the deities who govern the fifth world. Knowing the stories helps one remember one's place in that universe, which is an endlessly changing, endlessly unfolding ceremony. Thus, in response to Tayo's prayer, Spider Woman, the frogs, the blue dragonflies, and Hummingbird join forces to bring the rain clouds back to Laguna. Tayo's later belief that his cursing of the rain has caused the drought at Laguna follows naturally from his success in praying for rain.

Tayo's visit to the dripping spring south of Laguna to pray for rain indicates the depth of his belief in the "time immemorial stories" told by old Grandma. Although Tayo has heard the stories from old Grandma, Josiah is responsible for having shown Tayo how those stories apply to day-to-day life. Once when Josiah and Tayo went to the dripping spring to fill the water barrels, Josiah told Tayo that people are responsible for drought; people bring the droughts on by misbehaving, by angering the mother of the people. Cursing the wind and the dust is wrong, Josiah told him, because they are just as much a part of life, of the cycle, as the sun and the sky. Furthermore, one must learn to expect drought periodically because people continue to make mistakes. Tayo himself makes a careless mistake, he learns from Josiah, when he kills a pile of flies for sport. When Tayo attempts to exonerate himself by explaining that his teacher said that flies "are bad and carry sickness," Josiah explains that "long time ago, way back in the time immemorial, the mother of the people got angry at them for the way they were behaving. . . . The animals disappeared, the plants disappeared, and no rain came for a long time. It was the greenbottle fly who went to her, asking forgiveness for the people. Since that time the people have been grateful for what the fly did for us" (p. 101). As soon as Josiah reminds Tayo of the story, Tayo knows that he is at fault and, furthermore, that he alone is responsible for whatever catastrophe falls on the people as a result of his act. It only takes one mistake by one person to anger the mother of the people, and he knows from the story that working out all the details of forgiveness is not an easy task. Seeing that Tayo understands the severity and the consequences of his act, Josiah comforts him, telling him that the flies understand that people make mistakes. "Next time," he says, "just remember the story" (p. 102).

Josiah has lived long enough to know that people will always make mistakes and, consequently, that drought will always plague the people of Laguna. Rather than curse the wind and the dust, he determines to accept and accommodate these conditions by raising a breed of cattle that could survive and even flourish despite frequent drought. Following the advice of Night Swan, a Mexican woman living in Cubero,

Josiah buys a herd of Mexican cattle that, descended from the desert cattle, can survive conditions that kill Herefords. The spotted Mexican cattle, Josiah explains to Tayo, are a "special breed" descended from generations of ancestors that, combining the survival techniques of several species, have learned to live with the land as it is. Those breeds that have lost their connection with the land, such as the Herefords, Josiah says, are lost, scared, and vulnerable to death and extinction.

Years later the medicine man Ku'oosh suggests that Josiah had not known enough about religious matters—about the fragility of the world and about the healing ceremonies—to educate Tayo sufficiently before he went to the war (p. 35). Although Josiah may not have educated Tayo formally in Laguna beliefs and ritual, he provided Tayo with a world view that would fully prepare him to understand and believe the later words and actions of not only Ku'oosh but also of Betonie and Ts'eh. Without the grounding in Laguna belief provided by Josiah, supplementing the "time immemorial stories" told by old Grandma, Betonie's ceremony would have had no meaning and thus no power to heal him. The problems that later arise for Tayo are caused not by a lack of education in Laguna beliefs but by the confusion arising from education in conflicting beliefs. Directly opposing and conflicting with the stories told by Josiah and old Grandma are the stories told by Tayo's science teachers, Rocky, and Auntie.

When Tayo goes to the dripping spring in the canyon to pray for rain, he is acting on his continued belief in the stories told by old Grandma, a belief nurtured and sustained despite the years he has spent at the Indian school. In spite of the science teacher's insistence that every event has a scientific explanation and his yearly demonstration that killing frogs does not result in floods, Tayo continues to believe at some level in the old stories. He clings to his belief even though that belief widens the distance between himself and Rocky, the cousin he loves as a brother. When Rocky and Tayo go hunting together, Rocky refuses to participate in the "ritual of the deer"—sprinkling cornmeal on the deer's nose to feed its spirit, thus ensuring that it will return to give itself to them another year (p. 57). During his first year at boarding school in Albuquerque, Rocky had chosen the white world over the world of the Laguna, turning to his textbooks to prove the fallacy of his family's superstition and "old-time ways" (p. 51). Rocky's only desire is to get away from the reservation, to separate himself from the family, the clan, and their beliefs and rituals. Enlisting in the Army provides him with a quick exit.

Unlike Rocky, Tayo had never wanted or planned to leave the reservation. He ends up in the war only because Rocky tells the recruiter that they are brothers: "It was the first time in all the years that Tayo had lived with him that Rocky ever called him 'brother'" (p. 65). Overwhelmed by the thought of the two of them exploring the world together, Tayo forgets that he has promised Josiah that he will help him raise the Mexican cattle. When Tayo does remember the promise and tells Rocky that he cannot go, "Rocky walked on without him: Tayo stood there watching the darkness descend. He was familiar with that hollow feeling. He remembered it from the nights after they had buried his mother, when he stuffed the bed covers around his stomach and close to his heart, hugging the blankets into the empty space of loss, regret for things which could not be changed" (p. 73). Tayo, then, goes to the war with Rocky because he cannot accept the loss of both a mother and a brother. Eventually, however, he loses both to the white world.[8]

Auntie feels so disgraced by her sister's sleeping with white men and sending home a half-breed son to be raised that she makes certain that no one will mistake her son and her nephew for brothers. Auntie never allows Tayo to forget that he is different, a half-breed, a disgrace, and a burden. Her position in relation to the boundary separating Indians from whites seems very confused; she seems to want both to maintain and to destroy that boundary. For example, despite her very strong feelings that the family was disgraced by her sister's relations with white men, Auntie supports Rocky's efforts to move into the white world: "She wanted him to be a success. She could see what white people wanted in an Indian, and she believed this way was his only chance. She saw it as her only chance too, after all the village gossip about their family" (p. 51). Auntie is willing to sacrifice Pueblo ways and beliefs, then, to gain her son's success and the respect of her neighbors.

Too often Auntie's actions are motivated by her fear of the power of village gossip. When her sister sleeps with whites and when Josiah goes to visit Night Swan, Auntie is more concerned about the stories that will be told about the family than about any effect those actions may have on the family. When she claims that the storytelling "hurts old Grandma so much," however, Tayo knows that she is wrong (p. 88). Unlike Auntie, who allows herself to be defined by the villagers' stories, old Grandma recognizes that storytelling is a continuous, interactive process. No one storyteller can tell the whole story. A master storyteller can always defuse the power of a neighbor's story by telling one of her own: "The story was all that counted. If she had a better one about them, then it didn't matter what they said" (p. 89).

Although Tayo knows that Auntie's stories about her disgrace, her burdens, and her sacrifices are only part of a larger story, he cannot help believing their underlying message. Indeed, his sense of identity necessarily derives, to a large extent, from the stories told about him and his mother. According to Silko, the stories, both positive and negative, about a person define his or her identity and place in the community: "that's how you know you belong, if the stories incorporate you into them. . . . It's stories that make this a community. People tell those stories about you and your family or about others and they begin to create your identity. In a sense, you are told who you are, or you know who you are by the stories that are told about you."[9] This process of external identification is normally beneficial. The danger, Silko warns, lies in the possibility that an enemy may change the story, telling a version that gives a distorted and damaging view of one's identity. However, "if you have already heard the story, you know your family's version of what *really* happened . . . , so when somebody else is mentioning it, you will have a version of the story to counterbalance it."[10] In Tayo's case, the stories told by his aunt confirm rather than counterbalance the stories he hears from the community. As a result, he believes that his "birth had betrayed his mother and brought shame to the family and to the people" (p. 128).

When Tayo meets Night Swan, however, she provides him with another version of his story, one to defuse the power of that told by his aunt. Night Swan explains to Tayo that the people who reject him for being a half-breed are motivated by fear: "Indians or Mexicans or whites—most people are afraid of change. They think that if their children have the same color of skin, the same color of eyes, that nothing is changing. . . . They are fools. They blame us, the ones who look different. That way they don't have to think about what has happened inside themselves" (p. 100). Tayo always remembers his meeting with Night Swan, partly because she takes him to bed, initiating him into manhood, their lovemaking accompanied by the sounds of rain falling on Laguna in response to his prayer at the dripping spring. He also remembers the day, however, because of her suggestion that being different—a "special breed"—in a world that fears change and difference will prove to be a strength rather than a weakness.

The first eighteen years of Tayo's life subject him to conflicting world views as well as conflicting attitudes about the status of a half-breed in the Indian, white, and Mexican worlds. Despite the pressure of his teachers to give up his belief in the "time immemorial stories," he clings to them, finding in them a relationship between past and present, natural and supernatural, human and animal worlds that is more satisfying than the cause-and-effect explanations provided by the science textbooks. He learns from old Grandma, Josiah, and Night Swan to choose the stories he wishes to live by, to create his own story, and to counterbalance the stories told by others with the stories of his own choice and creation. Belief in the "time immemorial stories" gives Tayo the power to call the rain clouds, to heal the drought-stricken land of his people. His agreement, however, to accompany Rocky off the reservation into the white world, into a world of war and destruction, strains his belief in the old stories. Even though the validity of his beliefs has been demonstrated by his success in praying for rain, he allows Rocky and the white doctors who treat him for what they refer to as battle fatigue to convince him that he is sick, crazy, his perceptions distorted by hallucination. The war is a devastating experience for Tayo, but as a result of that experience he begins to perceive the relationship among his personal loss and shame, the loss and shame of all Indians, and the witchery and destruction that have overtaken the world.

The War and Its Aftermath: Cloaked in Coyote's Skin

When Tayo agrees to enlist with Rocky, forgetting and breaking his promise to help Josiah raise the new breed of spotted Mexican cattle, he enters the white world, a world in which humans are manipulated by destroyers and witchery. By choosing Rocky over Josiah, Tayo is choosing the whites, the destroyers, the Ck'o'yo magic over the "special breed," the healers, the mother of the people.[11] Tayo's choice is motivated by his desire to be called brother and his need to fill the hollow permanently carved in his stomach by the loss of his mother. Perhaps he believed that Josiah, the uncle who had assumed the role of father and teacher, would always be there.

Josiah dies, however, while Tayo is at war; presumably, his death is the result of his having been worn down by efforts first to keep up with the cattle, which had continued to run south toward Mexico, and then to recover them after they had disappeared for good. Although Tayo understands the facts of Josiah's death in Laguna, he experiences his death in a different way. In Tayo's story of Josiah's death, Josiah appears to Tayo in the Philippine jungle, where Tayo has been ordered to execute a group of Japanese soldiers. Recognizing Josiah among the prisoners, Tayo is unable to shoot, but the other American soldiers fulfill the order, killing Josiah along with the Japanese. Rocky, the corporal, and later the white doctors all try to convince Tayo that the slain soldier is not Josiah, that his vision of Josiah among the Japanese is symptomatic of battle fatigue or the type of hallucination caused by malarial fever. Tayo, however, is certain that Josiah had appeared in the jungle, despite the distance separating them. Ever since Tayo was a child, believing that he could stand on "the high sandstone cliff" of Bone Mesa and reach the moon, he had known that "if a person wanted to get to the moon, there was a way; it all depended on whether you knew the directions—exactly which way to go and what to do to get there; it depended on whether you knew the story of how others before you had gone" (p. 19). Tayo knows, then, that if Josiah had wanted to come to the jungle to visit him, to deliver a message, perhaps, at the moment of his death, he could have—simply by following the directions provided in stories of "how others before [him] had gone."[12]

The message that Josiah delivers, or that Tayo hears, is that Tayo is responsible for his death, that Josiah had died because Tayo had not been there to help him find the spotted cattle after they disappeared. Later, when Tayo tells Betonie that, despite logic, he still believes that Josiah died in the jungle, Betonie assures him that seeing Josiah among the Japanese is both sane and natural: "It isn't surprising you saw him with them. You saw who they were. Thirty thousand years ago they were not strangers" (p. 124). Betonie, then, suggests that the true message conveyed by Josiah's appearance is that the Japanese are not the enemy; to kill a Japanese soldier, Josiah may have been trying to tell Tayo, is to kill a friend, a relative, a beloved uncle. Although Tayo does not consciously hear this message, Josiah's appearance among the Japanese soldiers does prevent Tayo from killing them as he had once thoughtlessly killed a pile of flies.

Although Tayo speaks to Betonie about his responsibility for Josiah's death, he does not tell either him or the medicine man Ku'oosh that he cursed the rain while he was in the jungle. Listening to Ku'oosh explain about the fragility of the world, Tayo knows that he is unable to tell him that "he had done things far worse" than killing the enemy, that in his desire to save Rocky, he had abused the power of words. To give strength to himself and the corporal helping to carry Rocky's stretcher through the jungle rains, Tayo had created a story, telling the corporal that "it wasn't much farther now, and all down hill from there" (p. 12). When, however, he had finally recognized that the flooding rain was more powerful than the story he had created, he had changed his story, using the power of words to damn the rain rather than to bolster the corporal.

Although Tayo occasionally doubts that he actually saw Josiah in the jungle and berates himself for the craziness of such a belief, he never doubts that his cursing of the rain brought drought to the people of Laguna: "He had prayed the rain away, and for the sixth year it was dry; the grass turned yellow and it did not grow. Wherever he looked, Tayo could see the consequences of his praying" (p. 14). All the "time immemorial stories" warn that one's actions, whether committed in haste, in anger, or in ignorance, have catastrophic consequences not only for the person who committed the act but for all the people. The controlling deities are easily angered and easily offended, and their usual response when angered or offended is to abandon the fifth world entirely. Tayo knows, then, that his cursing of the rain in the jungle was a terrible mistake. Floods, like dust and wind, are as much a part of life as sun and sky. Disruptions in the balance of drought and flood do not just occur randomly; they are caused by people's mistakes. Furthermore, Tayo compounds his original mistake by also cursing and killing the flies crawling on Rocky's body (p. 102). With no emissary to travel to the fourth world to ask the mother of the people for forgiveness, Tayo is left on his own to right the wrongs—the acts of destruction and death—he has committed.

Both of Tayo's mistakes—forgetting his promise to Josiah and cursing the rain—originate from his desire to hold on to Rocky in an attempt to heal the loss left by his mother. By the time he returns to Laguna, however, Tayo's loss has been quadrupled; in addition to his mother, he has now also lost Rocky, Josiah, and his connection to the land and to the mother of the people. Neither Tayo's loss, however, nor his shame for incurring those losses can be separated from a larger loss and shame shared by all Indians.

Even as a young boy, Tayo recognized that his personal loss of a mother to white men, who slept with and then beat her, was only part of a much greater loss. The people of Laguna experienced the loss of Tayo's mother, Little Sister, as the loss of a part of themselves because "what happened to the girl did not happen to her alone, it happened to all of them" (p. 69). When the Catholic priest considers Tayo's mother, he regrets the loss of another "individual soul." When the people of Laguna consider her, however, they feel within themselves "an old sensitivity," the shared consciousness that bound them generation after generation as a single clan, a single entity sharing a single name (p. 68). To lose Little Sister to the white men—or alternatively, to lose a Helen Jean to Gallup or to lose Tayo and the other war veterans to drunkenness and witchery—is to lose themselves. Thus, when a child wanders from home, the family must bring the child back, calling it home "step by step," to save not only the child but also the family and the clan.

Auntie might have succeeded in bringing Tayo's mother back if Little Sister had not already been "ashamed of herself." First "shamed by what they taught her in school about the deplorable ways of the Indian people" and then encouraged by the white missionaries to leave her home, Little Sister gradually succumbs to self-hatred (p. 69). The internalized shame that separates Little Sister from her home and that holds Helen Jean in Gallup is the same shame that drives the war veterans to try to re-create the feelings experienced during the war by drinking beer and reciting war stories. After Little Sister was first shamed by her teachers and urged to leave home, she was surprised and flattered to receive the attention of white men (p. 68). In the same way,

Emo, Leroy, and Harley were gratified to be accepted by whites, both male and female, as soon as they stepped into their Army uniforms. Putting on the uniform was like putting on a new white skin; they believed their own skin was completely covered. When the war ended, however, the uniforms were put away, and Indians, veterans or not, were treated as Indians again. Rather than attack whites for their hypocritical treatment of the Indians, for taking away the feeling they had temporarily bestowed on the Indians, the veterans "blamed themselves for losing the new feeling; they never talked about it, but they blamed themselves just like they blamed themselves for losing the land the white people took. . . . They never saw that it was the white people who took it away again when the war was over" (p. 43). For Emo and the other war veterans, life after the war becomes a continuous attempt to regain the feeling of acceptance experienced during the war and to bury the shame of having allowed the new feeling to be stolen from them just as they had allowed the land to be stolen.

Few Indians who venture into the white world, Silko suggests, receive what Rocky wished for the night before he and Tayo shipped out and what Tayo later wishes for the night he visits Betonie in Gallup—"a safe return." Some die in foreign countries; some are buried alive in white hospitals; some are stranded in Gallup, Albuquerque, or Los Angeles. Others return home but are never the same again. Although the Scalp Ceremony conducted by Ku'oosh and other medicine men sometimes succeeds in curing the war veterans of the aftereffects of warfare, it is powerless to remove the most devastating consequence of having left home: the war veterans never recover from having seen "what the white people had made from the stolen land" (p. 169). Like the man who was forever haunted by the experience of having found a strand of white shell beads that had been stolen from a grave and dropped along the trail, the war veterans never recover from having experienced the excesses of modern white cities. For the man who found the beads, the idea that anyone would violate the graves of the dead is too horrific to assimilate; but each day the war veterans experience a similar horror: "they had to look at the land, from horizon to horizon, and every day the loss was with them; it was the dead unburied, and the mourning of the lost going on forever" (p. 169). Although Tayo suffers from a personal loss and a personal shame, he also shares the loss and shame of the other war veterans—the loss of the feeling that they were finally accepted and even liked by whites and the shame of losing that feeling, acceptance, and friendship. In the same way, however, the collective loss of the war veterans is only a small part of the larger loss and shame experienced by all Indians—the loss of their land and the shame of their having allowed it to be not only stolen from them but destroyed.

When Tayo tells Betonie of his anger that the whites "took almost everything," Betonie delivers two messages. The first is that the Indians can never recover the land by fighting the whites. In a physical confrontation with the destroyers, the Indians would be easily overcome and annihilated. Also, to become a destroyer and thief in response to the destruction and thievery of others is to succumb to witchery, thus destroying in oneself those very beliefs and values that differentiate one from the destroyers. Betonie's second message is that the real battle is not between Indians and whites; the battle, rather, is against destroyers, humans of all ethnic origins who allow themselves to be manipulated by witchery to kill life because they fear it.

Emo, of course, is a prime example of an Indian, suffering from the loss and shame of being Indian, who has been transformed into a destroyer, a tool manipulated by witchery. "We were the best," Emo brags. "U.S. Army. We butchered every Jap we found. No Jap bastard was fit to take prisoner. We had all kinds of ways to get information out of them before they died. Cut off this, cut off these" (p. 61). Tayo, enraged by Emo's words of destruction and death, lunges at him, thrusting a broken beer bottle into his belly. The witchery that manipulates Emo triggers Tayo's own, a core of violence that exists deep inside him despite his conscious disdain for Emo's dependence on killing for self-definition. Half human and half coyote, Tayo finds himself behaving like a witch, contributing to the counter force of destruction and death, when what he really wants is to renew his connection with the forces of vitality and birth.

To be successful, Tayo's cure must address all three levels of his illness—personal, tribal, and global. He must be called back slowly, through a series of transitions, dealing first with the loss and shame resulting from having forgotten his promise to Josiah and having cursed the rain. Then he must deal with the loss and shame shared by all

Indians for having allowed the land to be stolen and destroyed. Finally, he must remove the false skin that has been thrown over him, threatening to transform him into a destroyer, a witch in animal skins playing around with "objects and bodies." Ku'oosh, Betonie, and Ts'eh work together to call Tayo back, providing him with the stories that tell him "exactly which way to go and what to do to get there." Tayo's belief in the "time immemorial stories," which teach that the actions of a single person can either destroy the universe or heal it, helps him to recognize that nothing is ever lost and to see his personal ceremony as part of a greater, all-inclusive one.

Tayo's Cure: Unraveling Coyote's Skin

When old Grandma decides that Tayo needs the help of a medicine man, Auntie offers two complaints so different in content that they clearly reveal her own conflict in allegiance to both the Indian and white worlds. Her first complaint is that people will believe that a medicine man should not help a half-breed. Old Grandma responds to Auntie's complaint with a clear, simple statement: "He's my grandson" (p. 33). Tayo's lineage is clear to old Grandma: in Laguna society, lineage is passed through the female, and Tayo is her daughter's son. Auntie's second response, delivered only half-heartedly because she already knows she has lost this battle, is that Tayo's white doctors will object. Tayo, however, despite being raised in the home of an aunt whose loyalties are so confused, understands that the white doctors will never be able to cure him. When he was in the hospital, they insisted that "he had to think only of himself, and not about the others, that he would never get well as long as he used words like 'we' and 'us.'" Tayo knows that "medicine [doesn't] work that way, because the world [doesn't] work that way. His sickness [is] only part of something larger, and his cure [will] be found only in something great and inclusive of everything" (pp. 125–26). Tayo's illness is not an isolated event; it is both a consequence and a cause of the continuation and spread of a greater illness that is affecting the family, the tribe, the world. Thus, his cure must be "something great and inclusive of everything," attacking the total illness, not just an individual fragment.

Ku'oosh, when called on by old Grandma, is unable to cure Tayo. Nevertheless, his visit is curative in that it forces Tayo to recognize the validity of his beliefs and to accept responsibility for his own illness, which is reflected in the illness of the land: "The old man only made him certain of something he had feared all along, something in the old stories. It took only one person to tear away the delicate strands of the web, spilling the rays of the sun into the sand, and the fragile world would be injured" (p. 38). Although Tayo refrains from confessing to Ku'oosh what he believes to be the true cause of his illness—his cursing of the rain—Ku'oosh's words are such that they force Tayo to accept responsibility not only for his past actions but also for his future cure. If Tayo does not do whatever is necessary to cure himself, he will end up destroying both the people and the fragile world.

By confirming Tayo's beliefs and establishing his responsibility, Ku'oosh helps prepare Tayo for his visit to Betonie, which constitutes the next step, or transition, of his cure. Betonie differs from Ku'oosh and is more powerful than him because of his transcultural knowledge and experience. Betonie is the grandson of Descheeny, a Navajo medicine man, and a Mexican woman who convinced Descheeny that they must use all the powers available to them—Indian, Mexican, and white—to plot a ceremony that will eventually stop the witchery originally set in motion by Indian witches. Betonie's Mexican grandmother recognized that the knowledge and power of no single culture was great enough to combat witchery. Understanding the pervasive power of witchery, she forced Betonie out into the world, sending him to Sherman Institute in California because, as she said, "It is carried on in all languages now, so you have to know English too" (p. 122). After school Betonie continued to travel, riding the train to cities throughout the country—Chicago, St. Louis, Seattle, New York, Oakland. Betonie's experience in the white world gives him knowledge that Ku'oosh does not share: he has seen and experienced what the war veterans have experienced—"the cities, the tall buildings, the noise and the lights, the power of their weapons and machines" (p. 167). Because Betonie has ventured into, seen, and experienced the white world, he understands that seclusion and separation of Indians from whites is no longer possible. Only by adapting and changing in response to the changing environment, as both Betonie and the spotted cattle have, can the Indians survive.[13]

Betonie's power derives from his understanding of, and his alignment of self in respect to, the two worlds of which he is a part. The novel suggests that half-breeds, persons of mixed blood, are more effective at surviving in the modern universe of multiple worlds and divisive boundaries. In *Ceremony* those people marked with hazel, green, or yellow eyes—Night Swan, Betonie, Betonie's grandmother, Ts'eh, and Tayo—are representative of a "special breed," capable of surviving harsh conditions. To remain separate and isolated from the white world, fixed to and bound by a single location, racial heritage, or ceremony, is, as Ku'oosh discovers, to limit one's powers during an age when more and more Indians must daily traverse previously uncrossed boundaries. Ku'oosh, however, must be credited for his wisdom in recognizing that because the Pueblo Scalp Ceremony is powerless to cure the war veterans, Tayo must seek help from a Navajo medicine man who has adapted the ceremonies accordingly. The willingness on the part of Ku'oosh to suggest an alternative—and alien—cure marks a significant crossing of previously uncrossed boundaries.

Tayo spends two nights with Betonie. The first is a talking session in which Betonie, like any psychotherapist, encourages Tayo to talk about himself and attempts to gain his trust. The second night is the night of the ceremony, and the ceremony Betonie chooses for Tayo, on the basis of Tayo's revelations, is the coyote transformation ceremony for restoring the mind of a man who has lost his identity. At the end of the ceremony, Tayo falls asleep, dreaming of Josiah's spotted cattle, and when he wakes, he wants to leave immediately to search for the cattle because he now understands that finding the cattle is necessary for his cure. Despite his enthusiasm, however, Betonie warns him that "the ceremony isn't finished yet" (p. 152). It will not be finished, and Tayo's identity not fully restored, until the dead skin that has been thrown on him has been completely unraveled and cut into pieces. Betonie's ceremony, then, is not a cure in itself but merely one of several steps in the gradual process of calling Tayo back from witchery.

The next step of Tayo's cure occurs on Mount Taylor, where he goes to search for the missing cattle. At one point during his time on the mountain, Tayo suddenly realizes that the act of searching for the cattle is curative in itself because, for the first time since returning from the war, he has forgotten its terrors. His subsequent recovery of the cattle also contributes to his cure by giving him a sense of accomplishment.

One goal of psychotherapeutic treatment in all cultures is to instill in the patient the belief that he or she is gaining control over the problems presented by the surrounding physical and social environment. Having found the cattle, Tayo can feel himself getting well, being loosened from Coyote's skin: "He had proved something to himself; it wasn't as strong as it had once been. It was changing, unraveling like the yarn of a dark heavy blanket wrapped around a corpse, the dusty rotted strands of darkness unwinding, giving way to the air; its smothering pressure was lifting from the bones of his skull" (p. 198). Finding and recovering the cattle, taking them home so that he can fulfill Josiah's dream of raising a new, resistant breed, helps him to make amends for his broken promise and Josiah's death. Furthermore, in finding the cattle on Floyd Lee's land, Tayo is forced to acknowledge that they were stolen by a wealthy white man who had no economic reason for stealing: "The spotted cattle wouldn't be lost any more, scattered through his dreams, driven by his hesitation to admit they had been stolen, that the land—all of it—had been stolen from them" (p. 192). In acknowledging once and for all that white people had stolen the land, just as they had stolen Josiah's cattle, Tayo can begin to unravel the cloak of inherited tribal shame involved in the loss of the land.

Although Tayo cannot physically recover the stolen land in the way that he has recovered the cattle, he *can* recover and nurture his connection to that land. The days and nights on Mount Taylor help to restore the connection that was broken when Tayo cursed the rain in the Philippines. His reunion with the land and the mother reaches its most complete moment when, trying to escape Floyd Lee's men, he falls from his horse, hits his head against the lava rock, and lies prone upon the ground: "He was aware of the center beneath him. . . . It was pulling him back, close to the earth, where the core was cool and silent as mountain stone, and even with the noise and pain in his head he knew how it would be: a returning rather than a separation. . . . He knew if he left his skull unguarded, if he let himself sleep, it would happen: the resistance would leak out and take with it all barriers, all boundaries; he would seep into the earth and rest with the center. . . . He could secure the thresholds with molten pain and remain; or he could let go and flow back. It was up to him" (pp. 201–2). This is a critical moment for Tayo. On the one hand, this experience of returning to the earth and to the mother's embrace is the ultimate goal: such a return, signaling the absolute forgiveness and love of the mother he offended, would end his personal illness. Reunion with the mother of the people promises to fill the hollow in his stomach left by the loss of his birth mother and compounded by all his subsequent losses.

Tayo's desire to overcome resistance, to become part of the earth, recalls another of Josiah's early stories, one in which Josiah distinguishes between human and animal relationships with the earth. "Only humans had to endure anything," Josiah had said, "because only humans resisted what they saw outside themselves. Animals did not resist. But they persisted, because they became part of the wind. 'Inside, Tayo, inside the belly of the wind.' So they moved with the snow, became part of the snowstorm which drifted up against the trees and fences. And when they died, frozen solid against a fence, with the snow drifted over their heads? 'Ah, Tayo,' Josiah said, 'the wind convinced them they were the ice'" (p. 27). In Josiah's telling, the animals that persist, becoming one with the wind and the ice and the universe around them, seem wiser than the resisting, enduring humans. The image is one of purity and an absolute peacefulness that recalls the peacefulness experienced by the bear people, those who have lost consciousness of themselves as humans. Tayo, lying prone against the earth on Mount Taylor, experiences that same peacefulness, the consciousness of himself as one with the universe, and his desire to let all resistance go is intense. Alternatively, he can accept himself as human, destined for the pain inherent in enduring; he can remain. The choice is Tayo's: "It was up to him." Josiah's story about the persistence of animals and Betonie's story about bear consciousness represent one option available to Tayo. To merge with and return to the earth—to die—would end Tayo's pain, his separation from the earth. Taking that option, however, would not save the people or the world.

Tayo's eventual safe return from Mount Taylor, after choosing to resist, is made possible, in part, by the falling of the snow, which by covering his tracks and the trail left by the cattle, signals the mother's forgiveness for Tayo's mistake in cursing the rain. The rain that continues to fall on Laguna throughout the winter and spring suggests that after seven years of drought, the mother of the people has returned. Tayo spends the months between the end of September and the end of

May at his aunt's house in Laguna. The months are marked primarily by a continuing nurturance of Tayo's renewed connection with the land and the mother of the people. Each night he dreams of Ts'eh, the mysterious woman he has come to love, and each morning he rises to greet the sun; in this way Tayo feels that he is living with Ts'eh (p. 216).[14]

Tayo's ability to feel throughout the months at Laguna that Ts'eh is living with him when she is not there at all is another step toward his cure. For the first time in his life Tayo has learned how to live with the loss of a loved one, feeling his or her continuing spiritual presence despite physical absence. One morning late in May, after Tayo has moved back to the ranch, he awakens to rain. He remembers the previous summer at the ranch, marked by the desiccation of the land and by his own illness, days torn by tears and nausea and nights shattered by a cacophony of voices and relentless dreams and memories. "The dreams," he now knows, "had been terror at loss, at something lost forever." As a result of his continuing spiritual connection with Ts'eh, despite her physical absence, Tayo understands that "nothing was lost; all was retained between the sky and the earth, within himself. . . . The mountain could not be lost to them, because it was in their bones; Josiah and Rocky were not far away. They were close; they had always been close" (p. 219). Thus, after a winter and spring of dreaming about the absent Ts'eh, rising to greet the dawn, and feeling Ts'eh's presence despite absence, Tayo has learned that "he had lost nothing" (p. 219). The mountain, the land, the mother, Josiah, and Rocky have always been there, and in that recognition, Tayo has recovered all that had ever been lost to him—all, that is, except the original loss, the loss of the mother who abandoned him.

Only a few hours after his discovery of Josiah's and Rocky's abiding presence and love, Tayo is reunited with Ts'eh; he finds her waiting for him near the dripping spring where long ago he had prayed for rain. The summer spent with Ts'eh near Pa'to'ch, Enchanted Mesa, is a period of rejuvenation, a necessary interlude for strengthening his connection with the land and for preparing for the final steps of the ceremony. Shortly before her departure in the fall, Ts'eh warns Tayo about the tactics of the destroyers: "Their highest ambition is to get human beings while they are still breathing, to hold the heart, still beating so the

victim will never feel anything again." Immediately, Tayo recognizes himself in Ts'eh's description of the destroyers' victim, remembering the deadened feeling that had enveloped him for years after the war. He remembers "the thick white skin that had enclosed him, silencing the sensations of living, the love as well as the grief" (p. 229). In the hospital, Tayo had felt as if he were invisible, cloaked in white smoke and inhabiting "a gray winter fog on a distant elk mountain where hunters are lost indefinitely." Perceiving himself as one of the dead, an "invisible one," he was both deaf and mute, cut off from the living, from the force of vitality and birth (p. 15). He had wanted to remain in that state of invisibility because it was peaceful, undemanding, devoid of memories and voices. The loss of human consciousness experienced by Tayo, however, was not the same as that experienced by the bear people; Tayo's deadened consciousness was assumed along with an alien skin, a skin thrown on him by witchery and the destroyers.

Tayo's final step in throwing off Coyote's skin is to understand how the two forces of creativity and witchery coexist in the world and to know where he exists in relation to them. During the sunrise at Pa'to'ch, Tayo gains strength from witnessing a totality of existence that perfectly contains and balances the force and the counter force: "All things seemed to converge there: roads and wagon trails, canyons with springs, cliff paintings and shrines, the memory of Josiah with his cattle; but the other was distinct and strong like the violet-flowered weed that killed the mule, and the black markings on the cliffs, deep caves along the valley the Spaniards followed to their attack on Acoma" (p. 237). For an instant Tayo glimpses the totality of the story, of the web woven by the ultimate storyteller, the Creator, who recognized from the beginning that every impulse must be balanced by an opposing impulse. As Silko explained at the meeting of the English Institute, "In the beginning, Tséitsínako, Thought Woman, thought of all these things, and all of these things are held together as one holds many things together in a single thought."[15] Tayo recognizes that the valley before him, illuminated by the rising sun, contains a multitude of stories from different points of time that together cohere in a single story existing in a single timeless moment and that this single story perfectly balances all opposing forces into a single, all-encompassing force that continuously shifts and changes in the process of becoming. This experience empowers

Tayo, providing him with the strength necessary to complete the ceremony: "The strength came from here, from this feeling. It had always been there. He stood there with the sun on his face, and he thought maybe he might make it after all" (p. 237). He recognizes that he has always had the power of the storyteller, the power to see the total pattern and to cup its totality in his mind.

The pattern that, when finally seen, releases Tayo from Coyote's skin is the pattern that emerges in the hills north of Cañoncito. For Tayo, the pattern revealed at Cañoncito clarifies what Betonie had tried to tell him about Josiah's appearance in the jungle. The Laguna and the Japanese are part of a single clan, linked by the production and detonation of the atomic bomb and "united by the fate the destroyers planned for all of them" (p. 246). For the first time Tayo sees how all the disparate voices of his dreams and all the previously entangled memories are delicately linked and interwoven into a single web. As Silko told her audience at the English Institute, "the structure will emerge as it is made and you must simply listen and trust . . . that meaning will be made."

After seeing the pattern and understanding it, Tayo need only determine his position in relation to it. Again the choice is Tayo's: whatever action he chooses will determine the ending of the story. The power to end his own illness as well as that affecting all Native Americans and the entire world lies within him. When Tayo does choose the force of vitality and birth over the counter force of destruction and death and— a more difficult task—understands how to act appropriately to fulfill that choice, he completes the story that had encircled and sometimes entangled him since his birth. Throwing off Coyote's skin, Tayo completes his journey home: "He dreamed with his eyes open. . . . Josiah was driving the wagon, old Grandma was holding him, and Rocky whispered 'my brother.' They were taking him home" (p. 254). Guided home by his family, where he crosses the river at sunrise, Tayo finally recognizes that his mother "had always loved him, she had never left him; she had always been there" (p. 255). Tayo's recovery of his connection to his birth mother[16] is the clearest indication that he has finally located a coherent identity and his place in the universe. Paula Gunn Allen says that for Keres societies such as the Laguna Pueblo, "failure to know your mother, that is, your position and its attendant traditions, history, and place in the scheme of things, is failure to remember your significance, your reality, your right relationship to earth and society. It is the same as being lost—isolated, abandoned, self-estranged, and alienated from your own life."[17] Tayo's recovery of his mother has been a process of transitions, in which he learned first to recognize Ts'eh's spiritual presence despite physical absence and then to recognize the continuing presence and abiding love of Rocky and Josiah. In Tayo's belly now, filling up the hollow carved by loss, grows the story that he will tell Ku'oosh and the other old men. A "special breed," combining white and Laguna culture, he tells a personal story—the story of how he succeeded in unraveling Coyote's skin—which in the ears of his listeners becomes one more fragment added to the ever-unfolding mystery of Ts'its'tsi'nako's web.

By the end of *Ceremony*, then, Tayo, whose passage into an alien world left him hovering between two worlds, two identities, and two systems of belief, emerges with not only a coherent sense of self but also a coherent view of the universe and his place in that universe—a universe that today includes more than one world. Tayo's illness, after he returns from the war, reflects an internal division; he is unable to reconcile the reality of Laguna, which is founded on a belief in a universe invested with and ordered by the spiritual, with the reality of the world outside Laguna, which is founded on a belief in a universe devoid of or separated from spirit and ordered by science. Although Tayo wavers between these two world views, he ultimately chooses the Pueblo-Navajo view of reality, primarily because it yields, for him, a coherent universe in which he recognizes his own place. By making a choice, privileging one belief system over the other, whether that choice is the "correct" one or not, Tayo eliminates confusion and division, achieving a whole, integrated, coherent identity. By selecting a reality that works for him, linking him with his mother, Josiah, and Rocky, he succeeds in locating his "right relationship to earth and society." Through choice and will, then, Tayo locates and assumes an identity capable of sustaining and empowering him.

5 Modern Rationality and the Supernatural: Bridging Two Worlds in Gloria Naylor's *Mama Day*

She needs his hand in hers—his very hand—so she can connect it up with all the believing that had gone before. A single moment was all she asked, even a fingertip to touch hers here at the other place. So together they could be the bridge for Baby Girl to walk over.—Gloria Naylor[1]

Like Silko's *Ceremony*, Gloria Naylor's *Mama Day* describes the collision of two worlds, two systems of belief, and two approaches to survival and growth in today's universe. New York, characterized by an emphasis on culture, alienation, and scientific reality, is a world controlled and explained by modern rationality. In contrast, the island of Willow Springs, characterized by an emphasis on nature, community, and the imagination, is a world controlled and explained by supernatural forces. Whereas the inhabitants of New York tend to believe in themselves and their own power to make things happen, the inhabitants of Willow Springs tend to draw on supernatural forces and on those humans who can communicate with and channel those forces to help or harm others. Like Tayo in *Ceremony*, Cocoa discovers the hazards of crossing the boundary that separates the world of home from the world of the dominant culture. Like Tayo, she is transformed by her experience in the external world and relies on home—and the belief instilled there that spiritual connection continues despite physical separation—as a source of healing. Unlike Tayo, however, Cocoa ultimately chooses not to return home permanently but to create for herself a new world that mediates between the two worlds known to her—New York and Willow Springs—by selectively retaining elements of belief, values, and life-style from both.

Alternative Realities: Willow Springs and New York

Patricia Olson, in her review of Naylor's *Mama Day*, suggests that the novel fails to live up to the mythic potential promised by its depiction of an "unreal" island world dominated and controlled by Miranda Day, the daughter of the seventh son of a seventh son.[2] Like Shakespeare's *The Tempest*, however, which is the precursor text that provides a framework for *Mama Day*, Naylor's novel suggests that the time for such myth—for Willow Springs—has passed: Willow Springs can no longer maintain its protected isolation from the surrounding world, and its children must leave its magical shores to confront the realities of life "beyond the bridge" (p. 7). By the year 2000, Miranda Day will have died, and with her will have died that strong voice that has led the community in saying no to the real estate developers who keep coming around to offer "community uplift" in exchange for land (p. 6). The passing of Miranda, then, threatens to bring an end to Willow Springs, which, located off the east coast of the South Carolina-Georgia state line, is connected to the world beyond by only a wood bridge that is washed away by each big storm.

Mama Day explores the necessity, as the year 2000 approaches, of bridging two worlds of belief. What happens when the children of Willow Springs move into the world "beyond the bridge"? What happens when Cocoa—directly descended from Sapphira Wade, "a true conjure woman" (p. 3), and tutored daily in the power of belief and the imagination by her great-aunt Miranda—ties her flesh and mind to George, an engineer born and raised in New York who, with no family, no past, and no future, has survived totally on a belief in himself and in the present? The most that one can hope for, Naylor suggests, is that the children learn how to hear, listen to, and interpret the voices of the air, of the sea, of the spirits of those who have gone before.

In the prologue to the novel, the collective voice of Willow Springs—"we"—faults Reema's boy for his inability to ask, his inability to listen, and thus his inability to understand. The young man, who has returned home from college to document the "ethnography" and "unique speech patterns" of Willow Springs, is frustrated in his efforts to find out what the phrase "18 & 23" means (p. 8). All that boy would have had to do to obtain the answers and understanding he needed, the voice continues, was to visit Miss Abigail Day, who would have shared her family history and sent him on over to talk to her sister, Miranda. Miranda, in turn, would have taken him to the family graveyard where, after placing a bit of moss in his shoes, he could have heard the voices of Cocoa and George as they retell their story again and again, revising and reshaping it to get it right. If Reema's boy had known how to ask and how to listen, the voice of Willow Springs tells the reader, "he coulda listened to them the way you been listening to us right now. Think about it: ain't nobody really talking to you. We're here sitting in Willow Springs, and you're God-knows-where" (p. 10). The ability to hear and to listen to the story of a place is not magical, nor is it limited to Miranda Day or the inhabitants of Willow Springs. Every person, even Reema's boy, possesses the ability to hear unspoken words just as every reader has the ability to read and give life to the words printed on a page. The reader hears the voice speaking those words even though the speaker is not present, not visible, not heard, not "living."

The reader of *Mama Day* hears three voices: those of George, Cocoa, and the collective narrator of Willow Springs. George and Cocoa speak directly to each other rather than to the reader. Their voices are so similar in their direct, rational, controlled, grammatically "correct" diction that the reader may confuse the speakers until the content of a section and the speaker's opinions are revealed. Only when Cocoa gets angry or excited does her speech reflect its origins in the African-American South and its similarity to that of the collective voice of Willow Springs. Despite their similarity of diction, George and Cocoa rarely share similar opinions. Together, they demonstrate that every difference that threatens their relationship has "four sides: his side, her side, an outside, and an inside. All of it is the truth" (p. 230). Cocoa and George are both strong-willed, stubborn individuals who believe in themselves, the "rightness" of their views, and their rights as individuals. At the same time, they love and respect each other, and they desire to build a relationship that allows the other person freedom without compromising his or her own. They both seem to want to build a relationship based on the principle that "without a slave, there could be no master" (p. 225). The result is an uneasy alliance, frequently interrupted by battles—new and old—through which they seek, paradoxically, both to maintain and to resolve their differences.

As the sections spoken by George and Cocoa focus on their own contest of wills, the novel as a whole focuses on a struggle between two worlds and the beliefs that sustain the inhabitants of those worlds. The inhabitants of Willow Springs recognize and revere the forces of God, nature, conjuration, and the spirits of the deceased, whereas the inhabitants of the world "beyond the bridge"—epitomized by New York—recognize and revere the powers of the self, the present, science, and the knowledge found in books. Caught between the two worlds is Cocoa, a child of Willow Springs who has been dehumanized by her dislocation in New York. Cocoa's childhood friend Bernice, still living in Willow Springs, and Cocoa's husband, George, represent opposite poles of belief systems available to her: whereas Bernice relies on a belief in external powers, George denies the existence of any powers other than the power of the self. Mediating between the two extremes and thus more powerful than either is Miranda, who believes in reliance on the self up to the point that one must accept one's limitations and look outward to external forces for assistance. This chapter examines the sources of Miranda Day's power, Bernice's reliance on external powers, George's reliance on the self, and Cocoa's attempt to build a new world that mediates between the worlds of New York and Willow Springs.

Mama Day: Listening, Observing, and Believing as Ways to Power
Miranda's power derives in part from her recognition that the disembodied voices that speak just beneath the wind and in the stirring of leaves possess the power to save. For ninety years Miranda has sharpened and honed her ability to hear, listen to, and interpret the voices around her. So strong is her belief in the ability of those voices to aid her in healing others that she acts without hesitation to follow the messages they deliver. The voices she hears are those of ancestral spirits—speaking out of memory or dream—and of nonhuman presences. She often remembers, for example, words spoken by her father: "*Little*

Mama, these woods been here before you and me, so why should they get out of your way—learn to move around 'em" (p. 79). She dreams the words spoken by Sapphira: *"Look past the pain"* (p. 284). She also hears unidentified voices that seem to speak from the air (p. 91), from a ticking clock (p. 138), or from some inner center of knowing (p. 262).

Miranda differs from most people by actively listening for such voices. She recognizes that they offer a source of knowing that, although it circumvents the usual process of rational thought and inference, is not only valid but empowering. Most people deny such voices, either dismissing them as unimportant or changing their meanings to make them more acceptable. George admits that when he first saw Cocoa's bent neck in the coffee shop, he "quickly exchanged" his initial feeling—*"I will see that neck again"*—with a more acceptable one—*"I've seen this woman before"* (p. 27). Cocoa does not allow herself to believe the whispers at the family plot that warn her that she will break George's heart (p. 223). Both George and Cocoa ignore the messages in their dreams, messages that would have helped them in the crisis of Cocoa's illness. Worst of all are those people who, like Reema's boy, are so closed to the possible validity of voices other than their own that they never hear any voices at all—either those of the living or those of the dead.

In addition to hearing voices that help her use the past to understand the present, Miranda also sees the future; and although she uses her foresight to prepare for the future, she never tries to change it. Much of what Miranda reads about the future is based on an acute observation of nature: "Now, sea life, birds, and wood creatures, they got ways just like people. 'Cepting they live in the sky, the earth, the tides. So who better to ask about their home? You just gotta watch 'em long enough to find out what's going on" (p. 207). Because animals are so acutely attuned to change in their habitat and environment, they "know" and prepare for change long before humans, even when aided with modern technology, become aware of it. By observing the behavior of the natural world around her, Miranda is able to predict change and, where she has sufficient experience, to identify the form that change will take.[3] Related to Miranda's ability to predict change through her observation of the natural world is her ability to read human nature. She can identify the cause of a person's illness by paying close attention to the "laughter before or after a mouth opens to speak, the number of times a throat swallows, the curve of the lips, the thrust of the neck, the slump of the shoulders. And always, always the eyes" (p. 38). Thus, she knows immediately that a woman glimpsed on the Phil Donahue show cannot sleep because she fears being awakened once again by a husband who beats her just as surely as she knows that Bernice cannot conceive because of an excess of nervous energy and the self-directed negativity resulting from her mother-in-law's criticism.

Not all of Miranda's foresight can be explained by her ability to observe the behavior of animals and humans, however. Much of her interpretation of signs seems to be purely intuitive. As a five-year-old child, she knew that "there is more to be known behind what the eyes can see" (p. 36). As an old woman, she suddenly "knows," as she stands watching a drop of moisture bead up and drip from an apricot leaf on a kitchen cabinet carved by her father, that Cocoa is arriving a day earlier than expected, that she will arrive by plane rather than by train as planned, and that the plane will land at the Charleston airport at three o'clock that afternoon. Several years later she is surprised to see her hands seemingly merge with the ridged trunk of a tree at "the other place"; in that moment she can "see" Bernice driving north with her dead son in the seat beside her. In other instances, Miranda divines the future by observing an object that represents the object or event of concern. To ascertain when Bernice will get pregnant, she studies the yolks of three eggs she adds to her cake batter and learns that Bernice will not conceive within the next three months.

Miranda's power derives to a great extent, then, from her sharpened sense of sight and hearing, her belief in what she sees and hears, and her ability to use her interpretations of natural and supernatural signs and sounds to guide and heal others. Perhaps her greatest power lies in her ability to understand and manipulate a person's belief to advance her own goals—which are usually but not always shared by the other person. Miranda understands and respects the sources, extent, and limitations of her own powers. That is, she believes in her ability to see, to hear, and to accomplish with her hands what most people cannot. At the same time, however, she believes in and reveres forces outside, above, beyond her own. She believes, for example, that a perfect sunset is a demonstration of God's inimitable art and that some external force—"whatever Your name is"—can help George in his attempt to save Cocoa (p. 299). She sees nature as an external force that she can "get under, around, and beside . . . to give it a slight push" but one that she would never try to "get *over*" (p. 262). Most empowering, perhaps, is Miranda's belief in ancestral spirits and their power to guide and aid her.

Despite her own belief in external forces, however, Miranda often scoffs at the beliefs of her neighbors. She cannot understand their notions about "the other place," which she knows is just an old, abandoned house with a large, overgrown garden. She is particularly dismayed by their belief in Dr. Buzzard's mojo hands and hoodoo bags. Miranda, who mixes roots with wisdom and love to heal and to make things grow, sees Buzzard's use of hoodoo, mixing roots with moonshine and chicanery to make money, as a desecration of her own healing arts. Despite the differences in style and motivation, however, Miranda and Buzzard are more similar than she would ever admit.

Like Buzzard, Miranda recognizes the power of belief and of the human mind. Like Buzzard, she uses the beliefs of the people of Willow Springs to achieve certain objectives even though she knows those beliefs are erroneous. For example, she often uses her neighbors' belief in her own powers to keep them in line. After Miranda suggests to Buzzard that his life might be shortened if he sells Bernice some of his hoodoo medicine to help her conceive, he refrains from "helping" Bernice. Ruby, too, backs down when Miranda confronts her with the hoodoo bag that Miranda's chicken scratched out from under her trailer.[4] When Sue Henry, "the runt of Reema's litter" who now works "beyond the bridge" as Dr. Smithfield's receptionist, acts uppity when Ambush calls for help for Bernice, Miranda gets on the phone to remind her of what will happen to her if the doctor does not show up that night: "You been knowing me a long time, ain't you, sugar? So if you don't do that, you know I ain't phoning back to find out why. You know I'm coming over the bridge tomorrow to stand in front of your face to ask you. Why, of course, there won't be no call for that. . . . You take care now. And my best to your mama" (p. 77). By lacing a specific demand with pleasantries and only a hint of a threat, Miranda assures that her demand will be met.

Paradoxically, Miranda's reputation for punishing offenders derives almost entirely from her reputation for healing. Having witnessed her power to heal for so many years, the people of Willow Springs suspect the presence of an equal power to do harm, whether or not that power is ever directly exhibited. Knowing, in addition, that Miranda is directly descended from Sapphira Wade, that she is the daughter of the seventh son of a seventh son,[5] and that a long history of grief and death has been played out at "the other place," the people of Willow Springs have developed a healthy respect for what Miranda *could* do if she set her mind to it. In this way, she helps maintain a social order, controlling the actions of the island inhabitants and limiting the powers of those, like Buzzard and Ruby, whose actions are motivated by greed or jealousy rather than a love for life. Willow Springs requires no external policing: "The folks here take care of their own, if there is a rare crime, there's a speedy judgment" (p. 79).

Miranda recognizes, as does Buzzard, that belief is critical to the success of any cure. Roots, leaves, and bark can heal physical ailments, but many physical ailments are tied to mental or emotional strain. Miranda operates on the belief that the mental or emotional obstacles blocking physical healing can be removed only through a mutual exertion of belief by both the patient and the healer. Furthermore, she recognizes the importance of ritual in heightening both participants' hope and expectation of success. Miranda's ability to arouse and sustain Bernice's belief, as well as her own, results in the conception of Bernice's child. Later, when working with George to save Cocoa, Miranda succeeds in arousing in George a belief born of desperation. However, because he is unable to sustain that belief, falling back instead on his belief in his own powers, he loses the supplementary powers offered by Miranda's ancestors. Although George does succeed in his objective, which is to save Cocoa, he must sacrifice his own life to do so; adhering to Miranda's plan for attaining his objective would, Miranda believes, have saved them both. Miranda's strength derives from her ability to believe in and use both her own powers and those of external forces. In contrast, both Bernice and George are flawed, the former by her excessive reliance on external forces rather than herself and the latter by his refusal to recognize and believe in powers outside himself.

"The Other Place": Bernice's Belief in External Forces

Bernice possesses a tremendous capacity to believe in external forces. When after several years of marriage she has still not conceived, she turns first to Miranda because, like the other inhabitants of Willow Springs, she places great faith in Miranda's healing arts. Bernice also believes, however, in supernatural powers, and when Miranda's teas do not work quickly enough for her, she asks Miranda to take her to "the other place." Miranda refuses, insisting on the use of natural measures—the passage of time and the ingestion of womb-strengthening teas of stargrass and ground raspberry. Impatient, Bernice asks Dr. Buzzard for some of his hoodoo potions and charms but, as a result of Miranda's intervention, never receives them. Although Miranda is able to protect Bernice from Buzzard's hoodoo cures by threatening him with her own superior powers, she underestimates the extent of Bernice's desperation. All she can do, after that desperation drives Bernice to take a fertility drug stolen from the pharmacy where she works "beyond the bridge," is to try to save the young woman's reproductive system from the ensuing infection. While nursing Bernice, Miranda discovers the well-stocked nursery Bernice has prepared and realizes that she had not listened carefully enough to Bernice: "If I had really listened to that child, I woulda known this day was coming" (p. 84). With this new understanding, Miranda agrees to what she had earlier refused—to go to "the other place" to help Bernice conceive.

A requirement for going to "the other place" is that Bernice keep the visit "a secret forever" (p. 87). One reason for requiring secrecy is that Miranda recognizes that the community's suspicions about her ability to call on external powers can backfire. Up to this point, she has allowed their suspicion to go unchecked because that suspicion has helped her to maintain a gentle control over them—a control that is intended to help and protect them. *Knowing* that Miranda works with external powers, however, is far different from *suspecting* it. Knowledge about her activities with Bernice at "the other place" would change the community's perception of Miranda, replacing their trust and respect for a "healer" with dread and fear of a "conjurer." A second reason for requiring secrecy is that secrecy enhances belief. The secrecy surrounding Bernice and Miranda's intended visit to "the other place" will encourage Bernice's belief that something special will indeed occur, thus increasing the level of her hope, her faith, and her expectation of success. Such expectation will go a long way toward promoting Bernice's belief in herself—the ability of her body to conceive, carry, and bear a child—the lack of which has been a crucial factor in her continuing infertility. The secrecy is also important because it will protect both Bernice and Miranda's belief from the doubt that might be cast by others. Miranda does not even tell her sister, Abigail, about her plan for Bernice because not only Bernice but Miranda, too, must believe in both Miranda's powers and the powers to be called on at "the other place."

Miranda spends the months between autumn and spring preparing Bernice for the visit to "the other place." The preparation is both physical and psychological. The first objective is to redirect Bernice's nervous energy, showing her how to expend that energy each day through work and exercise so that by nighttime she is tired enough to get a good night's sleep and to stop worrying about whether and when she will conceive. Miranda's plan includes teaching Bernice how to make foods, as she and Abigail did in the old days, rather than opening up ready-made, store-bought products. In addition to filling Bernice's days with work and exercise, Miranda also develops a magical ritual, which involves planting black seeds to drive off negative thoughts and gold seeds to encourage hope. Abigail believes that Bernice is too smart for Miranda's "hocus-pocus" and will know that the black and gold seeds are just pumpkin seeds (p. 97). Miranda, however, who recognizes the power of the mind in witnessing and experiencing miracles, tells her sister: "The mind is a funny thing, Abigail—and a powerful thing at that. Bernice is gonna believe they are what I tell her they are—magic seeds. And the only magic is that what she believes they are, they're gonna become" (p. 96).

Miranda knows that Bernice's belief is secure when, on the night of Candle Walk, Bernice tells Miranda about the success of the seeds she has planted. Looking at Bernice's "eager and hopeful eyes" on Candle Walk night, Miranda thinks, "I'm not so sure about myself, but I ain't gotta worry about you. You're gonna make it over that line. And maybe, you'll just have to drag this tired old lady with you" (p. 116). As artist and magician, Miranda is fully aware of her own limitations: a human, she possesses no supernatural forces or magic seeds or potions for performing miracles. Her sole power lies in her ability to prepare Bernice so that the young woman is both physically and psychologically ready to conceive. She recognizes that, like any artist, she has limited control over her creation, the being she has helped form. At some point Bernice must take control, as an artist's creation does, leading her creator where *she* must go rather than waiting to be led.[6]

When the time comes to go to "the other place," Miranda does not tell Bernice what to expect, just to come. Bernice must bring fear and enough hope to overcome that fear; she must find within herself a knowing that overcomes confusion. As Bernice approaches "the other place," Miranda, sitting on the porch with a hen in her lap, "can taste the fear that hesitates on the edge of the garden walk. . . . Fear trembling at the bottom of the porch steps, watching the gleaming of two pair of eyes, hearing the creak of wood against wood under the soft rumbling from feathers, the humming begun in eternity. But it's hope that finds a voice: Mama—Mama Day?" (p. 139). As soon as Miranda hears the hope in Bernice's voice, she proceeds with the ritual she has devised. Based on sympathetic magic, the ritual requires the ingestion into Bernice's body of two freshly laid hen's eggs—the first by mouth and the second by womb. Confused about what is expected of her, Bernice waits too long to take the first egg offered. Together, Miranda and Bernice wait, and when the second egg, "still pulsing and wet," is offered, Bernice knows intuitively to take it and eat (p. 139). After Bernice eats the hen's egg, both women move inside the old house. Bernice lies on the dining room table, which has been covered with a sheet, and closes her eyes as Miranda's hands begin to stroke her body. As the stroking continues, Bernice becomes increasingly aware of that body's openings—not only its nine obvious openings but all the pores of her skin—until, experiencing her entire body as one opening, a receptacle, she is ready to receive the second hen's egg: "She ain't flesh, she's a center between the thighs spreading wide. . . . Pulsing and alive— wet—the egg moves from one space to the other. A rhythm older than woman draws it in and holds it tight" (p. 140). Nine months later, Bernice bears a son, and no mention is ever made about the night spent at "the other place."

Not until four years after her son's birth, at the party Abigail gives for

George and Cocoa, does Bernice acknowledge Miranda's assistance in the boy's conception. "I never thanked you for my son," Bernice says, but Miranda is quick to tell her that she was right not to have thanked her: "I ain't in the business of miracles, so I wasn't the one to thank" (p. 239). Despite this warning, however, Bernice still believes that Miranda can work miracles. When her son dies, she again meets Miranda at "the other place." Bernice carries her dead child to Miranda because she believes that if the old woman has the power of conception, she must also have the power of resurrection. Miranda, however, recognizes the limitations of her powers and of her belief. Bernice's belief alone is not enough, and Miranda's own belief can never extend that far. Miranda is overwhelmed by grief, both for Bernice's loss and for her belief: "More crushing, just a bit more crushing than that baby's death, is the belief that his mama came to her with" (p. 261).

Bernice never apologizes for her belief in Miranda's powers, but she does recognize that taking her son's body to Miranda was wrong for other reasons. At the "standing forth" for Little Caesar, the neighbors who knew him stand up one at a time to commemorate the first time each saw him and to express their belief that when they see him again, he will be engaged in a similar, although more advanced, activity. When it is Bernice's turn to stand forth, she apologizes for her temporary belief that her son was lost to her: "when I see you again, you'll be forgiving of your old mama, who didn't remember for a moment that you were still here" (p. 269). Bernice recognizes that resurrection of her son by Miranda is unnecessary because he is not really gone; he is "still here," continuing to exist and grow, changing and aging at the same rate as she and the neighbors are.

Cocoa's Illness: George's Belief in Self

Whereas Bernice's belief in external powers occasionally extends beyond what even the greatest belief can achieve, George's belief in himself to the exclusion of external forces can be equally excessive. When George sees Bernice carry her dead child into the woods, heading for Miranda and "the other place," his whole concept of reality is threatened: "It was one of those moments when your mind simply freezes to protect itself from the devastation of a thousand contradictions. . . . If this was reality, it meant I was insane, and I couldn't be—

and she couldn't be, because I had met that woman" (pp. 257–58). A belief such as Bernice's is inconceivable to George, a modern, rational man who does not believe in God; does not believe in luck, superstition, or fate; and does not believe in Ruby's hoodoo or in Miranda's power to counteract that hoodoo. George believes only in himself: "I've always made my own luck," he says. "Always" (p. 204).

Miranda believes that George's belief in himself can be used to save Cocoa. She knows that, without George's help, she cannot save Cocoa from the hoodoo triggered by Ruby's misplaced jealousy. "He's a part of *her*, Abigail," she tells her sister. "And that's the part that Ruby done fixed to take it out of our hands" (p. 267). All the trappings of hoodoo— ground glass and pepper, pins and needles, graveyard dust, hair and pee, Van-Van oil—are powerless, Miranda knows, unless the body or the mind is already poisoned. Thus, more powerful than the physical poisoning of the nightshade rubbed into Cocoa's scalp is Ruby's exploitation of the division between Cocoa and George that she witnessed at their party. Cleansing Cocoa's body of the physical poison—the nightshade—presents little difficulty, but cleansing her mind of the mental poison requires understanding that mind and all of the past events that have contributed to its makeup.

The form that Cocoa's hallucination takes is directly influenced by the quarrel she and George had on the night of their party. The quarrel arose, in part, from Cocoa's anxiety about her appearance, which in turn reflects years of feeling shame because of the light color of her skin, which she believes indicates the presence of white blood. Miranda remembers a time when Cocoa came home from school and sliced her finger to see whether her blood was really white. She laughs, remembering the incident, particularly in light of her certainty that Cocoa is "pure black" (p. 48). George makes a similar statement, knowing that no matter what mix of white and black blood Cocoa may have, her temperament, action, and behavior are those of a *black* woman: "We only had to get into an argument for me to be reminded . . . you were, in spirit at least, as black as they come" (p. 219). Despite the perceptions of others, however, Cocoa has never believed in her blackness. All she can see is the difference between her skin color and that of other blacks; all she can remember is the years of being ostracized, teased, called a leper by her classmates. On the night of the party, George is angered by Cocoa's continuing insecurity, which seems irrational to him, and at one point in their fight he calls her a "living nightmare" (p. 235). During her illness, brought on initially by the nightshade, Cocoa actually perceives herself as a living nightmare, seeing in her mirror "the flesh from both cheeks . . . hanging in strings under [her] ears" so that moving her head "caused them to wiggle like hooked worms" (p. 276). As the illness progresses, the red welts caused by the nightshade take on a life of their own, becoming worms burrowing beneath her skin. Cocoa is thus literally being devoured from within by her own self-doubt. Although much of what Cocoa sees and experiences—such as worms cascading from the shower nozzle—continues to be hallucination, there comes a point when she stops recognizing that her perceptions are false (i.e., hallucinations) and begins to believe that worms have invaded her body. As soon as Cocoa begins to believe that the worms are real, they become real; and as George soon discovers, her body is truly infested by worms.[7]

In an attempt to understand Cocoa's mind and to free it of Ruby's hoodoo poison, Miranda retreats to "the other place" to communicate with her ancestral spirits. Although she believes that the individual histories that constitute Cocoa's past can be helpful in understanding her mind, Miranda recognizes that anything she discovers will prove insufficient without George's assistance. This assistance, however, as both Miranda and Abigail know, will be difficult to attain. The sisters have no doubt that George will do anything in his power to save Cocoa. The problem, they fear, is that he will never believe in their way of saving her—that, indeed, such belief may not lie within his power. Thus, when Buzzard, at Miranda's request, explains to George that Cocoa's illness is the result of Ruby's hoodoo, George's response is exactly what Miranda, Abigail, and Buzzard all expect it to be: "What do you do when someone starts telling you something that you just cannot believe? You can walk away. You can stand there and challenge him. Or in my case, you can fight the urge to laugh if it wasn't so pathetic" (p. 286). George's ideas about hoodoo do not differ significantly from those often expressed by Miranda: he refers to the belief in "snakeroot," "powdered ashes," "loose hair," and "chicken blood" as "madness," whereas Miranda has always called it foolishness (pp. 286–87). Miranda does, however, recognize and respect the power of hate and the power of the mind—two powers associated with hoodoo that George, born and raised in New York, does not know enough to allow for. He does not believe that any force originating outside the self can wield such power.

The belief in a power outside himself is the "missing piece" (p. 285) that Miranda needs and that George, ultimately, cannot give. What Miranda learns from the message she receives from "the great, grand Mother" (p. 48), whose name she never learns, is that what links Cocoa to Ophelia and to Sapphira is that all three are tied up with the same kind of men: men who believe that they possess in their hands the power to hold on to the women they love despite the desire of one of those women to go—to leave—with peace and the other to go with her dead baby, Peace. George is another in this line of men who believe in themselves, and his belief, if handed over to Miranda so that she can connect it with the belief of John-Paul and Bascombe Wade, can save Cocoa. Miranda "needs that belief buried in George. Of his own accord he has to *hand* it over to her." All Miranda needs from him is "his hand in hers" because to give her his hand is to give her his belief (p. 285).

In an attempt to obtain George's hand joined with hers in belief, Miranda creates a ritual as she did for Bernice. George must walk to "the other place," accept from her John-Paul's cane and Bascombe Wade's black ledger, carry them back to the chicken coop at her trailer, look in a red hen's nest in the northwest corner of the coop, and bring back to her what he finds there. Although the hen is not, of course, a life-threatening opponent, Miranda knows that George, a city boy, feels wary and anxious in the presence of her chickens and that he would never initiate a confrontation with one unless he believed that its outcome would help save Cocoa. The confrontation with the old red hen, then, becomes a test of George's belief. Like Bernice at "the other place," George does find sufficient belief and hope to overcome fear, and he struggles with the hen to find what is hidden in its nest. Unlike Bernice's belief, however, George's is insufficient to provide him with the knowing necessary to overcome confusion. When he realizes that the only thing in the hen's nest is his own hand and that his hand is what Miranda wants, George's belief in her evaporates while that in himself reasserts itself. As he later tells Cocoa, "There was nothing that old woman could do with a pair of empty hands. . . . I brought both palms up, the bruised fingers clenched inward. All of this wasted effort when these were *my* hands, and there was no way I was going to let you go" (p. 301).

Ultimately, then, George cannot find within himself the belief that would allow him to work with Miranda to save Cocoa. Earlier, Buzzard had accused George of being a "boy," telling him that "a man would have grown enough to know that really believing in himself means that he ain't gotta be afraid to admit there's some things he just can't do alone" (p. 292). For George, however, to believe in some power greater than himself threatens his own sense of control: "When things were under control—and I lived my life so that was usually the case—there was no need to think about having to deal with some presence that might be governing what was beyond my own abilities" (p. 251). He has always controlled events in his own life; thus, when given a choice between acting on his own or giving himself up to the power of another being, he will always rely on himself. Nevertheless, for a moment in the chicken coop, George almost yields to belief in a greater power. A week earlier, he experienced a similar desire to yield when during the hurricane, he recognized the power of the winds as a manifestation of God: "Every thought, ambition, or worry diminished as it became my being against the being on the other side of two inches of wood. Fear never entered the picture: at first an exhilaration of the possibility of having the barrier broken and, for one brief moment, to be taken over by raw power. Pure power. What a magnificent ending to an insignificant existence" (p. 252). Overwhelmed by the force of the hurricane, George momentarily experienced the desire to destroy divisive barriers, of giving himself over to "pure power." The recognition of and desire to submit to a greater power, both during the hurricane and later in the chicken coop, are fleeting, however, and belief in the other is quickly replaced by belief in the self.

In Miranda's view, a belief in the self such as George possesses is a rare and extremely valuable commodity. When such a belief in self is insufficient, however, or when it is lacking, as in the case of Bernice, a belief in external powers provides an alternative source of strength. Although Bernice's belief in Miranda's ability to resurrect her son is so radically misplaced as to be ineffective, her belief in the continued existence of her son's spirit is empowering. To combine both sources of strength—

George's belief in the self and Bernice's belief in external powers—is to become nearly invincible. Miranda is such a person, and her grand-niece, Cocoa, has the potential to become one.

Cocoa as the Future: Bridging Two Worlds

Although Naylor's depiction of Willow Springs and of Miranda Day may make one long to return to such an existence, the novel ultimately suggests that the twenty-first century, which looms at the novel's end, belongs to some world other than that of either Willow Springs or New York. George's death seems to suggest that the inability of modern rationality to accommodate a belief in the supernatural signals the defeat of both world views. The power of Miranda's magic depends on the power of belief; the mind, and only the mind, can transform a handful of black and gold pumpkin seeds into magic seeds. When belief is lacking, as in George's case, Miranda is rendered powerless. For-tunately, belief, like Candle Walk, will never completely die; but the form and practice of belief, as well as the power derived from it, must necessarily change with time and with the increasing contact between alternative world views.

The increasing contact with the culture, alienation, and science "beyond the bridge," for example, inevitably transforms the children of Willow Springs. Their beliefs waver, falter, and become ever more distorted until, like Reema's boy, they become strangers to home, no longer able to hear its voices or understand its ways. Even the strongest believers, who like Bernice have always relied on the external powers alive in Willow Springs, are swayed by contact with life "beyond the bridge," placing their faith in science—in degreed doctors, modern hospitals, and miracle drugs—rather than in magic. To counteract the sense of impending loss suggested by the passing of Miranda Day and the passing of the century and the world in which her powers reign, Naylor offers Cocoa. Cocoa discovers, after her loss of the world she shared with George, the power to construct a new world—one that is fixed in neither Willow Springs nor New York but that is founded on beliefs drawn from both worlds, supplementing a belief in self with a belief in external powers. The hope for the future lies, Naylor suggests, in the new world and new world view developed by Cocoa, who—through struggle, illness, and loss—learns "the meaning of peace" (p. 312).

Although Cocoa's mother died soon after she was born, Cocoa was fortunate enough to be lavishly loved and nurtured by her grandmother Abigail and tutored daily in the powers of belief and the imagination by her great-aunt Miranda. Years later, while visiting "the other place" with George, Cocoa remembers her delight as a child walking with Miranda in the garden because "her trees sang and her flowers took flight" (p. 224). As a child, Cocoa believed without doubt the wonders that her eyes perceived; only as an adult does she perceive that the singing trees are actually rustling leaves and the flying petals startled butterflies. Also as an adult, Cocoa discovers that she must leave Willow Springs and enter that other world "beyond the bridge." When she does, she finds that her training in belief and the imagination are not strong enough to sustain her in New York.

In fact, life in New York transforms Cocoa. Dehumanized by her fear of "change and difference" and by the daily competition for work, housing, and love, she becomes harsh, abrasive, manipulative, and bigoted (p. 63). When the children of Willow Springs move to the northern cities, as Cocoa does, they lose a part of themselves. When Cocoa talks about going to college "to 'find herself,' " Miranda admits that "Baby Girl did have something lost to her, but she wasn't gonna find it in school" (p. 150). Only when Cocoa returns home to Willow Springs on her annual vacation does she recover a sense of who she is. "Home," she says, is "being new and old all rolled into one. Measuring yourself against old friends, old ways, old places. Knowing that as long as the old survives, you can keep changing as much as you want without the nightmare of waking up to a total stranger" (p. 49). Despite the sustenance Cocoa derives from her connection to home, however, that connection becomes increasingly strained by her years in New York and by her experience of the city as a world distinctly different from Willow Springs, one in which her belief in Miranda's power and wisdom dissolves. With time, Cocoa's visits home become more disruptive than healing as she struggles to prevent Miranda and Abigail from dominating and manipulating her life. As comforting as it is to return home and reexperience herself as a child, protected and coddled by great-aunt and grandmother, Cocoa must continually assert herself as an adult against an overprotectiveness that threatens to reduce her to the powerlessness of a "Baby Girl."

Had George lived, Cocoa would have been faced with the possibility of either continuing to live in New York or, as he had suggested a few days before his death, returning to Willow Springs. Both worlds are dangerous for Cocoa—one because it threatens her with "the nightmare of waking up to a total stranger" and the other because it has the power to keep her a child forever, to show her "she's still carrying scarred knees, a runny nose, and socks that get walked down into the heels of her shoes" (p. 48). In both worlds, Cocoa would have had to struggle to find and to maintain a sustaining self-identity. George's death, then, despite the loss it brings, releases Cocoa to create a new world in which to live.

Unlike her forefathers—Bascombe Wade and John-Paul—who allowed their lives to be destroyed by the women who left them, Cocoa learns that after one world collapses, you use what you learned from it to build a new one. Later, settled in her new world, she remembers her feelings at the time of George's death: "Being so young," she says, "I didn't understand that every hour we keep living is building material for a new world, of some sort" (p. 302). For Cocoa a requirement for building a new world is to avoid both the pull of New York, exemplified by George's excessive belief in self, and the pull of Willow Springs, exemplified by Bernice's excessive belief in external forces. Her new world must reflect a relationship with Miranda in which she neither denies Miranda's powers nor falls under her control. Like Miranda, she must seek to find some balance of internal and external powers, but rather than patterning herself after Miranda, she must develop a system of belief that works for her in the time and place in which she lives. Each century since Sapphira's short reign over the world of Willow Springs has exhibited a change in power: the exhibition and expression of power that was appropriate for Sapphira in Willow Springs in 1823 would not have been appropriate or viable for Miranda in 1985; by the same token, what was appropriate for Miranda in Willow Springs in 1985 would not have been appropriate in New York in 1985, nor will it be appropriate for Cocoa in any city "beyond the bridge" after the year 2000.

As a first step toward building a new world after George's death, Cocoa chooses to live in Charleston, a location that combines the rationality of New York with a closeness, both geographical and emotional, to Willow Springs. As she explains, "It was easier in Charleston: . . . I drew strength from moving in the midst of familiar ground. Enough strength to build around—and on—that vacant center in me" (p. 309). Living in Charleston allows Cocoa to reclaim her belief in herself—she finds a new job, marries another good man, and raises two sons—while simultaneously allowing her to supplement that belief with beliefs in external powers retained from her childhood and still shared by the people of Willow Springs. Living in Charleston makes it easy for her to visit the family graveyard at Willow Springs overlooking The Sound where George's ashes were scattered and to talk with him about the events that led them to this point in time. Although they go over and over those events, reshaping and refining them in each telling, Cocoa knows that she and George will never agree on exactly what happened. "When I see you again," she tells him, "our versions will be different still" (pp. 310–11). Cocoa's new world becomes possible, then, because she learns that physical separation does not preclude spiritual connection; she learns, that is, as her ancestors never did, how to let a loved one "go with peace." By understanding that George is "still here," Cocoa discovers, as Bernice did, the "meaning of peace."

Mama Day is, first and foremost, an examination of the nature and limits of belief. Belief in supernatural forces and belief in the self are both powerful; both types of belief, however, are necessarily limited in their ability to perform miracles. Belief in supernatural forces can help one conceive a child, just as it can convince one that the spirit of a dead child lives on, but it cannot restore the spirit of life to a dead body. Similarly, belief in one's own powers can enable a person to free himself or herself from the definitions—and thus shackles—imposed by others, but it cannot free a loved one from a destructive self-definition or identity. The ideal, Naylor suggests, is to recognize the powers and limitations of both types of belief, striving to reconcile and mediate between them, allowing one to take over where the other fails. To insist on only one type of belief, on only one type of reality, is not only limiting but potentially destructive.

6 The Ghost as Demon and Savior: Confrontation with the Past in Toni Morrison's *Beloved*

As long as the ghost showed out from its ghostly place—shaking stuff, crying, smashing and such—Ella respected it. But if it took flesh and came in her world, well, the shoe was on the other foot. She didn't mind a little communication between the two worlds, but this was an invasion. —Toni Morrison[1]

All the novels discussed to this point suggest the double-edged nature of belief in the supernatural: although such belief often sustains, it can also weaken or kill. In Smith's *Oral History,* for example, Granny Younger's belief in the supernatural allows her to define herself in self-empowering ways, but it also leads her to mistakenly—and destructively—define an innocent woman as a witch. In Erdrich's *Tracks,* Pauline, constructing a personal world inhabited by demanding gods and vindictive devils, locates a place, identity, and mission that empower her while simultaneously driving her to physically and emotionally abuse herself and others. In Silko's *Ceremony,* Tayo's belief in the ability of an individual either to destroy or to save the universe triggers his illness but also enables his consequent healing. Finally, Naylor's *Mama Day* demonstrates that the same belief that can help Bernice, a seemingly barren woman, conceive a child can also drive Cocoa, after she falls under the power of Ruby's hoodo, mad.

Toni Morrison's *Beloved* delivers a similar message about the positive and negative consequences of belief in the supernatural. Belief in the life of the human spirit after death sustains and consoles the ex-slaves living in and around 124 Bluestone by providing them with a sense of connectedness with those loved ones who have passed on. Such belief, however, when distorted by guilt, jealousy, or excessive love or need, can transform the spirit of a loved one from a benign presence into a vindictive, possessive, threatening, consuming monster—a projection, that is, of one's own internal conflicts. Such is the case with Beloved; with no identity of her own, she tends to reflect the conflicted identity of the person who perceives her. Thus, Sethe, Denver, and Paul D all defined Beloved in relation to their own needs and fears to the point that they endow her with the power to destroy, erase, or move them against their will. The community also defines Beloved, seeing in her a vindictive devil who has returned to torment Sethe. When the women of the community intervene to save Sethe, they destroy the boundary that has excluded Sethe and her family from their midst, thus saving themselves as well as Sethe. Beloved, then, like the previously discussed novels, not only reveals the double-edged nature of belief but also emphasizes the need for self-definition and warns of the danger imposed by a divisive boundary—not, in this case, a boundary separating two cultures but one separating an individual from the community.

Separation and Connection

Beloved, Morrison's fifth novel, continues to explore the central question introduced and expanded upon in her previous works: how does the self assert and claim autonomy while maintaining essential ties to the other—that is, to parent, child, lover, friend, or community? Both separation and connection are essential to healthy growth and development, but for many people one response tends to preclude the other. In its exploration of the consequences of separation and connection, Beloved focuses on many of the same issues examined in Morrison's earlier novels: the killing power of mother love, the struggle to form mutually liberating relationships between male and female, the acts and beliefs that isolate an individual from a community, the importance of rootedness in the past through ties to an ancestral figure, and the strength imparted through female friendships and membership in communities of women. Furthermore, Beloved exhibits once again Morrison's proven mastery in blending an "acceptance of the supernatural" with "a profound rootedness in the real world" in such a way that neither dominates the other.[2] Despite such similarities, however, *Beloved* is distinguished from Morrison's previous novels by its emphasis on slavery.

The idea for *Beloved* grew out of a slave story Morrison discovered while helping prepare *The Black Book*, a collection of articles, photographs, advertisements, and other memorabilia documenting the African-American experience. An article published in *American Baptist* in 1856 tells of a young woman who attempted to kill her children, killing one and injuring two, rather than allow them to be returned to slavery. When asked if she had taken this action in a moment of "madness," the woman replied: "I was as cool as I now am; and would much rather kill them at once, and thus end their sufferings, than have them taken back to slavery, and be murdered by piece-meal."[3] Writing *Beloved* provided Morrison with the opportunity not only to examine the life of this woman but also to relate the stories that the writers of the slave narratives were unable to tell. These writers, Morrison explains, suppressed details about the horrors of slavery because the purpose of the narratives—"to persuade the [white] reader of the evil of slavery"—prohibited the use of language or detail that might anger or offend the intended audience: "Over and over, the writers pull the narrative up short with a phrase such as, 'But let us drop a veil over these proceedings too difficult to relate.' In shaping the experience to make it palatable to those who were in a position to alleviate it, they were silent about many things, and they 'forgot' many other things."[4] The narrator of *Beloved* suggests another reason why the stories were suppressed. For Sethe, the narrator says, "every mention of her past life hurt. Everything in it was painful or lost. She and Baby Suggs had agreed without saying so that it was unspeakable" (p. 58). For Sethe and Baby Suggs, then, as for all slaves and former slaves, the past was "unspeakable"; their stories were not stories "to pass on" (p. 275). In *Beloved* Morrison seeks to rectify that error. The past may indeed be "unspeakable," she argues, but the stories must be passed on; they are part of a collective past that must be acknowledged, confronted, and only then laid down.

Beloved tells the story of Sethe, a slave who takes flight, safely transporting her four children to the home of her mother-in-law, who had been bought out of slavery by her son, Halle. After twenty-eight days of freedom, Sethe is found by Schoolteacher, who, accompanied by his nephew, a slave tracker, and the local sheriff, enters the yard of 124 Bluestone to reclaim his property. Sethe, however, claims herself and her children as her own possessions to care for as she deems fit. She attempts to kill them all, believing that in this way she can escort them all to safety on "the other side," thus preventing them from ever experiencing the degradation of slavery. She succeeds in killing only one child, her two-year-old daughter. This daughter returns first as a ghost, taking possession of 124 Bluestone for eighteen years, before returning in the flesh as a twenty-year-old woman named Beloved.

Beloved's own feelings of abandonment and her desire to rejoin her mother, compounded by Sethe and Denver's refusal to let her go, to let her rest on "the other side," are sufficiently powerful to give life to first the baby ghost and then the fully fleshed embodiment of the dead baby's spirit. As a result of her death at the age of two and her experience of death, an experience not shared by her mother and sister, Beloved is not exactly what Sethe and Denver believe her to be. Beloved is the embodiment of Sethe's dead daughter's spirit and of Denver's dead sister's spirit, but neither Sethe nor Denver recognizes who or what that spirit—Beloved—really is. Sethe believes that, as her resurrected daughter returned to her at the age of twenty, Beloved shares with her a history, a past, and a connection (mother-daughter) that enable Beloved to understand her in a way no one else can. Similarly, Denver believes that Beloved, as her resurrected sister, shares with her a history, a past, and a connection (sister-sister) that yield desires, needs, and objectives that are identical to her own. Both Sethe and Denver see Beloved, then, only in a direct relation to themselves—as daughter and as sister—that does not allow for Beloved's consciousness of herself.

Having been cut off from her mother at the age of two, before she developed an ego, and having experienced death, the spirit of Beloved is no longer just the spirit of Sethe's daughter and of Denver's sister. According to Baby Suggs, "death [is] anything but forgetfulness" (p. 4), and Beloved's own thoughts (pp. 210–14) suggest that with death she was plunged into the collective memory of the African-American experience. Egoless at the time of her death, her identity as Sethe's daughter has apparently merged with that of other dispossessed spirits of the

African-American past: "Beloved is not only Sethe's dead daughter returned," writes Karla F. C. Holloway, "but the return of all the faces, all the drowned, but remembered, faces of mothers and their children who have lost their being because of the force of EuroAmerican slave-history."[5] Possessing an amorphous, all-encompassing identity rather than a discretely defined self, Beloved is easily transformed in the minds of others into a reflection of their own desires, fears, and needs. Not only Sethe and Denver but also Paul D and the community define Beloved in terms of their own experience and their own past rather than on her own terms. As a reflection of the other, Beloved is paradoxically both powerless and empowered: although powerless to be herself and to make herself known to others, she is tremendously empowered to affect the lives of those who believe, mistakenly, that they know who and what she is. As the ghost of herself—a two-year-old girl—Beloved is benign; but when endowed with the powers attributed to her, both consciously and unconsciously by others, she can become a formidable adversary, or alternatively, she can become a supernatural agent of liberation and rebirth. This chapter examines Beloved; her relationships with and impact on the lives of Sethe, Denver, Paul D, and the community; and the way in which, through Beloved's return, the inhabitants of 124 and their neighbors save themselves through resolution of their past.

Beloved as Mirror of the Other

Baby Suggs finds nothing unusual about a two-year-old baby ghost taking up residence at 124 Bluestone: "Not a house in the country ain't packed to its rafters with some dead Negro's grief" (p. 5). The emotions of the dead, she suggests, outlive corporeality.[6] The neighbors, too, show no surprise when they hear about the ghost's existence, but they avoid 124, reluctant to tangle with the ghost of one who has "die[d] bad" (p. 188). The neighbors' ready acceptance of the presence of Beloved, both as a ghost and in her corporeal form, accords with their world view, one that blends Christian belief in the resurrection of the dead with African religious belief in the behavior of the living-dead.[7] According to African belief, the living-dead—the spirits of the recently deceased, those who are still remembered by surviving family members and friends—are still part of their families, continue to live close to their homes, and frequently visit their surviving relatives. A living-dead, explains John Mbiti, author of *African Religions and Philosophy*, retains his or her personal name as well as identifiable physical features.[8]

Despite the community's acceptance and even expectation of a close interaction between the living and the deceased, however, Sethe's neighbors do not tolerate excess in any form; certain limits must not be breached. Thus, when Ella learns that Beloved is plaguing Sethe, she decides to act, believing that ghosts should remain ghosts, not take on flesh and move into the real world. Driven away from 124 Bluestone by Ella and the other women of the community, Beloved disappears, first from the daily consciousness and then from the memory of those whose lives she has touched. Although no longer remembered, her spirit continues to exist, hovering around 124, leaving footprints that, if noticed, would be found to accommodate anyone, child or adult, who attempted to step in them. In this unremembered, undefined, sub-stanceless existence, Beloved can be anyone and everyone. Eventually, the last traces of Beloved disappear, and those breaths, whispers, and accidents that continue to stir the visible world of 124 Bluestone are dismissed as oddities of the weather. Without memory, the narrator says, "the rest is weather. Not the breath of the disremembered and unaccounted for, but wind in the eaves, or spring ice thawing too quickly. Just weather. Certainly no clamor for a kiss" (p. 275). According to African religious belief, a living-dead, when no longer remembered, "enters the state of collective immortality. It has 'lost' its personal name, . . . and with it goes also the human personality. It is now an 'it' and no longer a 'he' or 'she'; it is now one of myriads of spirits who have lost their humanness."[9] The spirits of the unremembered dead continue to live near their original homes, residing in the surrounding forests, rivers, and mountains, but they are no longer distinguished as indi-vidual spirits of humans as the living-dead are. The existence of the living-dead, then, is a continuous struggle between two phases of ex-istence—Sasa (human) and Zamani (spirit). "Everyone wants to 'be remembered,' even if the body and spirit have been separated," writes Mbiti. Thus, "it is the sacred duty of the family . . . to keep the living-dead within temporal sight of the Sasa period."[10]

The strength of Beloved's ties with the living, then, reflects the extent to which she is remembered. The stronger the memories of those who loved her and the stronger their need to keep her alive, the stronger she herself is. Those who remember Beloved—primarily Sethe and Denver—not only keep her alive but also invest her with power. Because Beloved will never truly die until she is entirely forgotten, she embodies and keeps alive the past of those who remember her. Beloved, Morrison suggests, is the past incarnate, a past that continues to haunt, that refuses to disappear, until it is experienced and confronted. Speaking of Beloved, Morrison says, "I wanted it to be our past which is haunting, and her past, which is haunting—the way memory never really leaves you unless you have gone through it and confronted it head on. But I wanted that haunting not to be really a suggestion of being bedeviled by the past, but to have it be incarnate, to have it actually happen that a person enters your world who is in fact—you believe it, at any rate—the dead returned."[1] The past embodied by Beloved, Morrison suggests, is not just "her past," an individual past, but "our past," the collective past of all African Americans.

With death, which is "anything but forgetfulness," Beloved sinks into the collective memory of all the beloved African-American daughters abandoned by their mothers as a result of slavery. In death, Beloved "remembers" a female who collected flowers, placing them in a round basket, in the place where the tall grass parts, where they lived before they were separated by the clouds. As critic Deborah Horvitz explains, Beloved is remembering a daughter's separation from her mother during a slave raid in Africa, when clouds of gunsmoke prevent her from rejoining her mother. In death, Beloved also remembers crouching in the dark with other bodies, some dead already and others trembling in their attempt to release spirit from body. She remembers watching the white men, who appear to her to have no skin, push a pile of bodies into the sea and then being separated from a beloved female who, with others, jumps voluntarily into the sea.[12] Submerged in death, Beloved compounds the personal experience of her own separation from and abandonment by Sethe with the collective experience of all the abandoned daughters of the "Sixty Million and more"—those who did not survive captivity in Africa or the Middle Passage—to whom Morrison dedicates the novel. In fact, Beloved appears to have no recollection at all of her own death at Sethe's hands. She has repressed that specific experience, remembering only Sethe's name and face and the experience of fear, loss, and anger at being abandoned, an experience vastly magnified by her absorption of the similar experiences of others. When Beloved later reproaches Sethe, she accuses her not for having sliced her throat with a handsaw but for having severed the connection between mother and child, for having left her.

In returning to 124 Bluestone, Beloved is not interested in explanations of how and why she died; her only objective is to renew the bond between self and mother. Beloved is not, as Paul D and the neighbors believe, evil. Poised between life and death, she clings to life, and life as she remembers it depends on reconnection with Sethe, the mother. Cut off from her mother at the age of two, Beloved developed no ego, no sense of self separate from the other and in relation to the external world. As critics Wilfred D. Samuels and Clenora Hudson-Weems explain, "With the murder, Beloved never has the opportunity to come into her own, to find a central self by moving beyond the stage of infantile ego. . . . Still mired in the world of primary identification— her mother—Beloved does not differentiate herself from Sethe when she reemerges eighteen years after her death. . . . For Beloved, to see Sethe's face is, in fact, to see her own face."[13] Thus, Beloved's only desire—in fact, the driving force of her continued existence—is reconnection with the mother; life for her depends on "the join" (p. 213), on reclaiming Sethe's face, body, and life as her own. When Sethe is not available or sufficiently responsive, Beloved satisfies her appetite with mother substitutes, connecting with Denver as sister and with Paul D as lover. As her body fattens on the sweets Denver feeds her and grows pregnant with Paul D's child, Beloved's spirit feeds off the stories told by and about Sethe because these stories define her own individual rather than collective identity.[14] Sethe's stories are Beloved's stories. Sethe's past is Beloved's past. Without the past and the identity provided by Sethe, Beloved is any motherless child, any African-American female—she is nobody and everybody, nothing and all.

Because Beloved is not self-defined, she takes on a chameleon-like identity, becoming what others believe her to be. Egoless and undefined, she is a blank slate, a mirror reflecting the feelings, fears, or unresolved conflicts of others. After the community drives Beloved away, "those who had spoken to her, lived with her, fallen in love with her . . . realized they couldn't remember or repeat a single thing she said, and began to believe that, other than what they themselves were thinking, she hadn't said anything at all" (p. 274). Although Beloved exists, she has no true self, no voice of her own; she simply reflects what others are thinking. She is unable to cross to "the other side," then, not only because she "die[d] bad" but also because others will not let her go. Their needs demand that she continue to exist on this side until they are able to confront and then release the past she embodies. The power that Beloved appears to hold over others is a power bestowed by them as a consequence of their own needs, desires, fears. Thus, to understand Beloved's relationship with Sethe, Denver, Paul D, and the community, one must understand exactly what she represents for each.

Sethe: Protective Mother and Abandoned Daughter

Sethe's flaw is that she loves her children too much. Although such excessive mother love can be empowering, it can also be destructive. Empowered by her love for her children, Sethe accomplishes the near-impossible: unlike her own mother, who abandoned Sethe and lost her own life when she tried to run, Sethe escapes slavery with all her children intact. She is tremendously proud of her act, of her courage to attempt an escape and her ability to accomplish it without the assistance of her husband, Halle, and the other Sweet Home men. "I did it," she tells Paul D. "I got us all out. Without Halle too. Up till then it was the only thing I ever did on my own. . . . It felt good. Good and right. I was big, Paul D, and deep and wide and when I stretched out my arms all my children could get between them. I was *that* wide" (p. 162). Sethe's pride is justified because the accomplishment of this feat enables her to know and define herself—a self that combines the masculine tendency to fly, to leap, to dare with the feminine instinct to feed, nurture, and protect.[15] Freed from her definition of self as slave by her discovery of self as mother and savior, Sethe invests all her energies into developing this self to the point of excluding all other potentialities of self.

Eventually, Sethe sacrifices everything—both self and children—in the name of mother love. After she makes her second attempt to save her children, this time to keep them from being returned to slavery, Sethe again believes and takes pride in her success in accomplishing her goal: "I stopped him [Schoolteacher]," she tells Paul D. "I took and put my babies where they'd be safe" (p. 164). She believes that her attempt to save her children was successful because in her view nothing can be worse for her children than slavery, and her impulsive but determined action did prevent their enslavement. As she herself recognizes, however, the cost of running from slavery is too high: she loses her husband, who was left behind on her first flight; she loses her two-year-old daughter, who dies in her arms during the second flight; she loses her sons, who leave home to escape the spite of the baby ghost; she loses Baby Suggs, who gives up her faith in the human heart after Sethe's act; and she loses the community, who while understanding her rage, cannot accept her claim to the right to kill her children. Sethe's initial flight liberates her; her second flight grounds her, imprisoning her in 124 where her energies are consumed in "keeping the past at bay" and in protecting Denver from "the past that [is] still waiting for her" (p. 42) and where the spite of the baby ghost is welcomed as the solitary manifestation of life.

When Paul D arrives at 124, the "spite of the house" had grown so strong that Sethe "was oblivious to the loss of anything at all. . . . There was no room for any other thing or body until Paul D arrived and broke up the place, making room, shifting it, moving it over to someplace else, then standing in the place he had made" (p. 39). Driving out the baby ghost, Paul D restructures life at 124, not only reviving Sethe's sexuality but also introducing the possibility of making plans for a future. In addition to awakening the future, however, Paul D also awakens Sethe's past. Together they begin to explore, to piece together, their shared history at Sweet Home and what they know of the attempted escape of the Sweet Home slaves. Hopes for the future dissolve, however, when Paul D asks Sethe about the newspaper article Stamp Paid has given him. Sethe has never felt the need to explain her action to others, to seek understanding or approval from the external world, but when Paul D asks, she tries to tell the story behind the article. For Sethe her action and her reasons for taking that action are simple: no one will ever list her children's animal characteristics on the right side of a page. "It's my job," she explains to Paul D, "to keep them [my children] away from what I know is terrible. I did that" (p. 165). Paul D is so shocked to learn what Sethe already knows—that "unless carefree, motherlove [is] a killer" (p. 132)—that he does not stay to hear all of Sethe's reasons for trying to kill her children. Four days after his leaving, Sethe realizes with a "click" that Beloved is her resurrected daughter (p. 175). With that knowledge she dismisses, once and for all, any need for Paul D, a future, or the external world: "Whatever is going on outside my door ain't for me. The world is in this room. This here's all there is and all there needs to be" (p. 183).

Locked inside 124 with Beloved and Denver, Sethe begins to voice her thoughts, reliving aloud all the events that led up to Beloved's death. Beloved, however, is not even listening. She is too busy reliving and voicing her own past pain, her separation from her mother. Neither woman can hear or understand the other: "Sethe began to talk, explain, describe how much she had suffered, been through, for her children. . . . Beloved accused her of leaving her behind. . . . And Sethe cried, saying she never did, or meant to—that she had to get them out, away. . . . Beloved wasn't interested. She said when she cried there was no one. That dead men lay on top of her. . . . Ghosts without skin stuck their fingers in her and called her beloved in the dark and bitch in the light. Sethe pleaded for forgiveness, counting, listing again and again her reasons" (pp. 241–42). Communication between the two is impossible. Sethe is unable to understand that Beloved truly has no interest in any events leading up to her death or in any reasons justifying that death. All Beloved wants is "the join," to be assured that she will never again be separated from Sethe. Nor can Sethe understand that Beloved's memory encompasses far more pain and experience than that caused by Sethe alone; as a result of Beloved's absorption of a collective African-American memory in death, most of what Beloved says is incomprehensible to Sethe. She cannot understand Beloved's need—reconnection and merger—any more than Beloved can understand Sethe's—understanding and forgiveness. Confronted with the daughter whom she believes is refusing understanding and forgiveness, Sethe begins to see Beloved as her accuser and judge.

Sethe sees Beloved as her accuser because although she does not understand Beloved on a conscious level, she does understand her on a subconscious one. Beloved's accusations reflect Sethe's unspoken, unconscious accusations against her own mother. In an unspoken monologue directed at Beloved, Sethe says, "You came right back like a good girl, like a daughter which is what I wanted to be and would have been if my ma'am had been able to get out of the rice long enough before they hanged her and let me be one. . . . I wonder what they was doing when they was caught. Running, you think? No. Not that. Because she was my ma'am and nobody's ma'am would run off and leave her daughter, would she? Would she, now?" (p. 203). The accusatory, unforgiving, forever unsatisfied Beloved is a reflection of Sethe, the daughter, whose mother abandoned her when she tried to escape. The possibility that her mother might have "run off and [left] her daughter" is so unacceptable to Sethe that she has always denied it. Sethe's memories of her mother are vague, Horvitz writes, not only because their contact was severely limited, but also because those memories "are inextricably linked with feelings of painful abandonment." Those pictures and words that do occasionally creep into Sethe's conscious memory, Horvitz continues, "come from that place inside her that stores, but can never lose, forgotten memories."[16] Sethe's struggle with Beloved is, then, an external enactment of a struggle within: Sethe the mother knows that she made the right, the only, choice; Sethe the daughter knows that no explanation justifies the severance of the tie between mother and child. As mother, she knows she would make the same choice again; as daughter, she will never forgive her own mother for having abandoned her.

Caught in this endless struggle, Sethe loses her spirit and begins to waste away, a process that is exacerbated by physical starvation as she gives her portion of whatever food remains in the house to her daughters. Denver believes that Beloved is killing Sethe—eating up Sethe's life, swelling and growing taller on it—and intervenes to save Sethe by reaching out to the community (p. 250). By the time the community gathers outside 124 to rescue Sethe from Beloved, Sethe is completely broken and diminished by the trauma of remembering, reliving, and explaining her past to an unforgiving accuser—the child in her that can never forgive her mother, and thus herself, for abandoning a daughter. She is so immersed in the past that she misunderstands the community's reason for being there and does not spurn them. Thus, Sethe is saved in spite of herself, for she would never have acknowledged the need for help herself. Because the community does intervene to help her, however, Sethe loses Beloved again and regains a chance, under Denver and Paul D's care, for a resurrected life of her own.

Denver: Separation and Responsibility for Self

Beloved is not the only child to suffer from Sethe's excessive mother love. Although a "charmed" survivor who never experienced separation from her mother, as Beloved did, Denver also suffers (p. 209). As a consequence of Sethe's desire to save her children from slavery, Denver grows up in a state of unbearable loneliness, of paralyzing fear of both her mother and the world outside the yard of 124, and of endless stasis as she waits to be rescued by her father. Because Sethe's act has alienated her from the community, Denver's only companions for the first six years of her life are her brothers. At the age of seven, Denver does venture out on her own, discovering and being invited into Miss Lady Jones's school for black children. After a year, however, another student, Nelson Lord, asks her, out of curiosity rather than meanness, whether she had been with her mother when Sethe was in jail for murder. As soon as the question is asked, some "thing that had been lying there all along" leaps up in Denver, preventing her from asking Sethe if Nelson is right (p. 102). When she does ask, she withdraws into two years of silence, going "deaf rather than hear the answer" to her questions (p. 105).

Denver's two-year silence provides a hiatus in the child's growth and development during which she assimilates the information that her mother once attempted to kill her children and that some unknown thing that exists outside the yard at 124 might cause her mother to try again. Denver's feelings for her mother become terribly mixed, combining both fear and love: "I love my mother but I know she killed one of her daughters, and tender as she is with me, I'm scared of her because of it" (p. 205). Denver's solution to this dilemma is threefold: she spends "all of [her] outside self" loving Sethe so that Sethe will not kill her; she refuses to leave 124; and she waits for her father, Halle, to come rescue her (p. 207). From the age of seven until the moment twelve years later when she gathers the courage to leave 124 by herself, Denver believes that her father will eventually find her, rescuing her from her mother. Until that time, she remains imprisoned within the boundaries of the yard at 124 Bluestone, as if awaiting delivery from the womb or resurrection from the grave. Sethe contributes to Denver's paralyzed womb/tomblike existence because of her desire to protect Denver from the past that exists as "rememory" outside the yard (p. 36). As Judith Thurman explains in her review of *Beloved,* despite Denver's miraculous delivery in a rowboat, "Sethe has, in fact, never fully 'delivered' Denver. Fat, dreamy, submissive, fearful of the world, . . . Denver will be forced to complete the labor by herself."[17] Sethe's protectiveness, combined with Denver's mechanisms to defend herself from Sethe, the past, and the external world, becomes as imprisoning as slavery itself.

The answers to Nelson Lord's questions, in addition to locking Denver inside 124, change her perception of and relationship with the baby ghost: "the monstrous and unmanageable dreams about Sethe found release in the concentration Denver began to fix on the baby ghost. . . . Now it held for her all the anger, love and fear she didn't know what to do with" (p. 103). During her two-year silence Denver has transformed her perception of the baby ghost from that of a separate, irritating, and wearying presence to a reflection of herself, the emanation of Denver's feelings toward Sethe—"anger, love and fear"—which, out of fear for her life, she cannot express. Thus, as soon as Denver begins to hear again, the baby ghost has a new character. From the moment that Denver hears the baby climbing the stairs—the first sound she hears in two years—"the presence was full of spite. Instead of sighs and accidents there was pointed and deliberate abuse" (p. 104). Thus, the change in the baby ghost appears to be a change motivated by Denver herself: Denver's own feelings toward Sethe are being expressed through the baby ghost as spite. Denver's spite, reflected and expressed by the baby ghost, drives off everyone but Sethe: Howard and Buglar run off to the war, and Baby Suggs dies soon after. Thus, Sethe, Denver, and the baby ghost become locked in a passive triadic relationship in which the only life in 124 is Denver's spite, expressed through the baby ghost.

Over the next nine years, life at 124 becomes increasingly colorless and barren. Denver's only escape from this lifeless existence is a further retreat into a small boxwood grove, which, like a second, life-giving womb within the imprisoning womb/tomb of 124 and its yard, envelops and sustains her, changing what it gives in response to what she needs—play, refuge, and eventually life itself: "In that bower, closed off from the hurt of the hurt world, Denver's imagination produced its own hunger and its own food, which she badly needed because loneliness wore her out. *Wore her out.* Veiled and protected by the live green walls, she felt ripe and clear, and salvation was as easy as a wish" (pp. 28–29). Denver's boxwood grove, then, appears to be a miniature replica of Baby Suggs's Clearing, a spot in which Denver ministers to herself, imagining love, grace, and salvation. Only through imagination can Denver, in her awful isolation, experience life at all. In producing "its own hunger and its own food," Denver's imagination sustains her until Beloved appears, after which looking at Beloved becomes "food enough" for Denver, "but to be looked at in turn was beyond appetite; it was breaking through her skin to a place where hunger hadn't been discovered" (p. 118). Once Beloved arrives, Denver has no further need for her boxwood grove and never returns.

Before the arrival of either Beloved or Paul D, Denver had always relied on being the object of her mother's gaze. On the first night that Paul D appears at 124, however, Denver is rocked by the knowledge that this man has the power to draw Sethe's gaze from Denver to himself. Threatened for the first time in her life by separation from her mother, Denver longs for a sign of the baby ghost's spite and exhibits her own. By announcing the presence of the baby ghost in 124, Denver invokes her sister's spirit to help her break the intimacy growing between her mother and Paul D: "'We have a ghost in here,' she said, and it worked. They were not a twosome anymore" (p. 13). The ghost, Denver explains, is neither sad nor evil but "lonely and rebuked" (p. 13); it is, in essence, a reflection of herself. Denver, who drank her dead sister's blood along with the milk from her mother's blood-smeared breast, discerns no separation between self and sister, and thus she assumes that they share the same feelings and desires. When Beloved appears on the stump outside 124, then, Denver believes that Beloved shares her desire to keep each other company and to hold onto their mother until their father arrives. Because Denver has no concept of Beloved as separate from herself, she is unable to comprehend—despite the power of her imagination—that Beloved is driven by desires different from her own. Beloved is driven solely by the need to merge with her mother. She does not remember her father at all, and her interest in both Denver and Paul D is minimal; they exist only as they help or hinder her efforts to regain her identity, her life, through merger with Sethe.

With Beloved's arrival, Denver transfers her former desire for her mother's attentive gaze to Beloved. In fact, Beloved's gaze becomes much more powerful and satisfying than her mother's ever was. Whereas Sethe has always seen Denver as an extension of her own being, Beloved sees her as a separate entity, giving Denver for the first time (outside the boxwood grove at least) a sense of self.[18] This sense of self as separate and worthy of "the interested, uncritical" gaze of the other becomes so important to Denver that she recognizes that she must protect Beloved from her mother, who might try to kill her daughters again (p. 118). Should Sethe and Beloved become engaged in some life-threatening conflict, as they did at the Clearing, Denver knows that "the choice between Sethe and Beloved [is] without conflict" (p. 104). Although Denver still depends on her mother for physical sustenance, she now depends on Beloved for psychological sustenance, for her sense of self as separate.

Denver's dependence on Beloved's gaze for a sense of self is both destructive and constructive. Her dependence is destructive because the belief that she exists only when perceived by the other continually threatens Denver with loss of self through loss of that other. One day while they are playing in the cold house, Beloved disappears. Deprived of Beloved's gaze, Denver discovers that "she has no self. . . . She can feel her thickness thinning, dissolving into nothing. She grabs the hair at her temples to get enough to uproot it and halt the melting for a while" (p. 123). Separated from the gaze of the loved one, Denver begins to experience the dissolution into nothingness, the sense of being swallowed by the dark, that will be Beloved's eventual fate. Dropped from the sight and memory of one's loved ones, one simply fades away, no longer existing as a clearly defined individual spirit but as an amorphous spiritual presence, invisible, voiceless, and indistinguishable from the weather.

On the other hand, Denver's dependence on Beloved inspires the desire to care for and protect another—to nurse Beloved to full health by bringing her water, cleaning up after her initial incontinence, and feeding her endless sweets, and to protect her from Sethe. Thus, Denver's relationship with Beloved is constructive in that it begins to give her a sense of self, transforms her fear into a desire to protect, allays her paralyzing loneliness, introduces to her the power of creating stories, and prepares her to give rather than receive care, nurture, protection. Although Beloved has no real interest in Denver, she tolerates her company when Sethe is not available, and Denver gradually assumes the role of mother substitute. Having already assumed this role in her relationship with Beloved, Denver is prepared, then, to assume a similar role in her relationship with Sethe: when she recognizes that Sethe's efforts to meet Beloved's excessive demands for love and attention threaten to kill Sethe, Denver decides that she must intervene to save her mother.

In saving Sethe, Denver saves herself. Watching her mother struggle with the past, believing that she must now protect her mother from Beloved rather than vice versa, and recognizing that the relationship is viable only if all three are alive, Denver exerts "an effort of the will" necessary to move from the house and the yard into the world.[19] Motivated by an urge to life that is stronger than her fear of the external world, she delivers herself into that world, giving herself over to the mercy of the community. The community responds, offering food, friendship, and the opportunity to work to feed herself and her mother. In making this step, Denver delivers herself from the encircling womb created by her mother's desire to protect her from the past that is waiting for her, releases herself from the dream that her father will rescue her, and relieves herself of her reliance on her dead sister as her only source of companionship. She no longer depends solely on the gaze of her sister to make her self visible to herself. Nelson Lord, whose casual questions once locked up Denver's mind, now unlocks it by casually commenting, "Take care of yourself, Denver." The idea of "having a self to look out for and preserve" is so novel that Denver hears Nelson's words as if they "were what language was made for" (p. 252). This new recognition of self and of her ability and responsibility to care for that self enables Denver to separate from her mother—both from her fear of her mother and from her dependence on her; she can now share with Paul D the responsibility of protecting and caring for her mother.

Paul D: Freedom, Desire, and Manhood

When Paul D arrives at 124 Bluestone after eighteen years of attempting to free himself from white men, he finds Sethe, Denver, and a ghost. This triadic relationship at 124 has existed in an established, if not particularly harmonious, order for the nine years since Denver began to hear again, Sethe's sons left 124, and Baby Suggs died.[20] His arrival disturbs this order, displacing the ghost of Sethe's past with his own desires for a future; but just as he begins to build a life with Sethe and Denver, Beloved appears. Paul D is perplexed by Beloved—her sudden appearance, her new shoes, her vagueness when questioned about her past—and wants her to leave because he sees her as an obstacle to attaining what he most desires—a life, a family, a chance for a future. Despite his desire that Beloved leave 124, however, Paul D begins to notice that he rather than Beloved is the one moving out of the house. Perplexed, he moves from Sethe's bed to a rocker in the kitchen to the keeping room and finally to the cold house. Not until he ends up in the cold house does Paul D realize that his movement is involuntary, that he is "being prevented" from remaining in the house (p. 116). With this realization comes a sense of waiting; soon Beloved comes to the cold house, forcing him—against his will, he believes—to have sex with her. Unable to understand how he, a grown man, can be forced by a twenty-year-old girl to do something that he does not want to do, Paul D concludes that Beloved has bewitched him.

Although Beloved is a supernatural being, she is no witch; her true power over Paul D lies in her ability to arouse in him long-buried desires, fears, and conflicts that must be acknowledged and resolved before he can progress to a new life, liberated from the past. Although Beloved clearly resents Paul D's ability to distract Sethe's attention from her, the omniscient narrator gives no indication that Beloved is actually using supernatural powers to move Paul D out of 124. Paul D believes that Beloved is moving him because *he* wishes to move *her* out, and he projects his own desires onto her. What is moving him is not Beloved but his own unresolved past, which continues to haunt him, plaguing him with doubts about whether he is indeed a free man.

For Paul D freedom is defined as the ability to move and to love as one chooses. As a slave, he was denied these two freedoms, with the result that even though he wants to build a life with Sethe, he fears he will not be able to stay with her: "walking off when he got ready was the only way he could convince himself that he would no longer have to sleep, pee, eat or swing a sledge hammer in chains" (p. 40). Paul D equates movement with liberation, with escape from the threat of enslavement, whether by a white man or by a woman. In sharp contrast, Sethe sees moving not as liberation but as running away. When Paul D suggests that she leave 124 to escape the wearying spite of the baby ghost, she replies angrily, "No more running—from nothing. I will never run from another thing on this earth! I took one journey and I paid the ticket, but let me tell you something, Paul D Garner: it cost too much! Do you hear me? It cost too much" (p. 15). Sethe has learned the hard way that movement is, ultimately, ineffective: whatever you leave will eventually catch up with you. Beloved becomes, in essence, the past that catches up with Paul D. When he moves from Sethe's house, he is running not from Sethe but from Beloved, from a past that will continue to haunt him, driving him away from every place in which he hopes to settle until he stops long enough to turn and confront it.

When Paul D moves from 124, he is moving away from Beloved's shining; the radiation from her sexual arousal confuses him because it is not directed at him, the only man in the house. Beloved's shining is the two-year-old's desire for Sethe manifested as the sexual desire of a twenty-year-old woman. It is also, however, a reflection of Paul D's own desire. Although Paul D consciously loves and desires Sethe the woman, Beloved arouses his long-submerged and never-to-be-fulfilled desire for the young Sethe of his dreams. Beloved, Paul D tells Stamp Paid, "reminds me of something. Something, looks like, I'm supposed to remember" (p. 234). Beloved, unknown to Paul D, is Sethe's daughter and at twenty years old is about the same age Sethe was in 1856, the last time he saw her before she escaped from Sweet Home. When, in 1873, Paul D follows Sethe up the stairs on his first night at 124, he drops "twenty-five years from his recent memory. A stair step before him [is] Baby Suggs' replacement, the new girl they dreamed of at night and fucked cows for at dawn while waiting for her to choose" (p. 20). The sexual union he had anticipated for so many years is, of course, bitterly disappointing: "His dreaming of her had been too long and too long ago" (p. 20), and Sethe is no longer the young girl of his dreams but an aging, scarred woman. When Beloved later approaches Paul D in the cold house, he finds himself unable to resist her plea for connection because in having sex with her, he relives the act he imagined and dreamed of but never consummated. Subconsciously perceiving Beloved as the young Sethe, Paul D releases twenty-five years of unconsummated desire as he finally has sex with the person he had wanted but had been prevented from having.

Having sex with Beloved releases far more than pent-up desire. It also releases long-buried memories of life at Sweet Home and serious questions about how his experiences there affected his sense of himself as a man. Each time Beloved "turned her behind up, the calves of his youth . . . cracked his resolve" (p. 126). Sex with Beloved reminds him of the manly restraint he and the other four slaves were forced to practice at Sweet Home. When Sethe first arrived at the plantation, Paul D and the other slaves, despite being "so sick with the absence of women they had taken to calves," allowed her the time and freedom to choose one of them as a husband. Determined to treat her as a human rather than as an animal or a slave, they denied themselves the "luxury" of rape, thereby confirming to themselves that they were, indeed, "Sweet Home men—the ones Mr. Garner bragged about" (p. 10).

Paul D has always believed that his restraint in allowing Sethe the freedom of choice was the ultimate proof of his manliness. Twenty-five years later, however, living in the cellar of the Church of the Holy Redeemer, he begins to realize that the restraint itself was unnatural, that it was necessitated by his enslavement to the very person who had labeled him a man.[21] He begins to recognize that his own self-definition as a man has depended too heavily on Mr. Garner's labeling him and the other slaves as men: "Garner called and announced them men—but only on Sweet Home, and by his leave. Was he naming what he saw or creating what he did not? . . . Suppose Garner woke up one morning and changed his mind. Took the word away" (p. 220). Paul D realizes that during those years at Sweet Home, he had been called a man but never allowed the freedom to test and discover the truth about himself on his own terms.

Later, when Schoolteacher replaced Mr. Garner, the new master deprived the Sweet Home slaves of their status as men, redefining them as boys, which was such a drastic change that it forced them to try to escape. When Paul D was caught, his ankles were chained, a three-spoke collar was placed around his neck, and an iron bit was inserted in his mouth. Too late Paul D recognizes the danger of believing in an assessment, a definition of self, that is imposed from without: "they were only Sweet Home men at Sweet Home. One step off that ground and they were trespassers among the human race. Watchdogs without teeth; steer bulls without horns; gelded workhorses whose neigh and whinny could not be translated into a language responsible humans spoke" (p. 126). Deprived of the word bestowed by Mr. Garner and cast out of Mr. Garner's Eden, the Sweet Home men were magically transformed, through redefinition by a different authority, into animals—domesticated, impotent, and unintelligible.

Paul D makes his final, most distancing move from Sethe when, in response to her attempt to explain that she killed her children out of love, he says, "You got two feet, Sethe, not four" (p. 165). In suggesting that Sethe's act was that of a beast rather than that of a human, Paul D is projecting his own shame, his own fear that he is more beast than man. Sethe has not told him that by attempting to kill her children, she was guaranteeing that no white man would do to her children what Schoolteacher had done to Paul D—"dirty" them, convincing them that they were not fully human but creatures embodying both human and animal characteristics (p. 251). Eventually, Paul D recognizes that Sethe's life has been dedicated to preventing those she loves from perceiving themselves as less than human. He remembers "her tenderness about his neck jewelry. . . . How she never mentioned or looked at it, so he did not have to feel the shame of being collared like a beast. Only this woman Sethe could have left him his manhood like that" (p. 273). She returns to him the favor he once gave her—the perception and treatment of the other as a human rather than as a beast or a slave.

Paul D's perception of Beloved as "a low-down something" and a "bitch" (p. 235) never changes, however, because he never recognizes her as the agent of his own change.[22] Later, after Beloved has been driven from the community and Paul D is returning, step by step, to 124 and Sethe's bed, he can no longer imagine "the desire that drowned him there and forced him to struggle up, up into that girl like she was the clear air at the top of the sea. Coupling with her wasn't even fun. It was more like a brainless urge to stay alive. Each time she came, pulled up her skirts, a life hunger overwhelmed him and he had no more control over it than over his lungs. And afterward, beached and gobbling air, in the midst of repulsion and personal shame, he was thankful too for having been escorted to some ocean-deep place he once belonged to" (p. 264). While at Alfred, Georgia, Paul D had beat life to a pulp, killing it again and again each day in order to survive. When the rains came, however, threatening to bury him and the other prisoners living in boxes below ground, the desire for life had become so strong that "they just plunged, simply ducked down and pushed out, fighting up, reaching for air" (p. 100). His delivery from the mud at Alfred was a physical rebirth: he rediscovered the desire to live, to survive, to escape. What Beloved offers is a spiritual rebirth, guiding him down into, reconnecting him with, and delivering him from the womb/tomb of three hundred years of shared African-American misery, abandonment, and grief. As a result of his immersion in the past that is embodied in Beloved, Paul D discovers the strength not only to return to 124 but also to fulfill a new role, that of healer and nurturer.

Community: Accusations, Sins, and Atonement

When Janey spreads the news that Beloved has returned in the flesh to whip her mother, the community's first and immediate reaction is gratification. The story that is created by Janey and reshaped and passed on by the women—"Sethe was worn down, speckled, dying, spinning, changing shapes and generally bedeviled" (p. 225)—is readily believed because it fulfills their own expectations: no one can commit such a crime without eventually receiving the just punishment of God. The only means to avoid such punishment, within their Christian world view, is to ask pardon, beg forgiveness, seek atonement from God and from the universe (the community) that has been disturbed by the crime. Sethe, however, believing that she was both right and had the right to kill her children to prevent their return to slavery, has taken none of these steps.[23] Outraged by Sethe's claims as a mother, by the pride that keeps her from asking for help, and, perhaps worst of all, by the self-sufficiency that enables her to survive without their help, the community believes that Sethe's punishment is long overdue. Thus, Beloved's bedevilment of Sethe reflects their own desire to punish Sethe: "Just about everybody in town was longing for Sethe to come on difficult times. Her outrageous claims, her self-sufficiency seemed to demand it" (p. 171).[24]

Guided by Ella, however, community opinion changes. Soon Beloved is no longer seen as a God-sent punishment; she becomes, as defined by Ella and the community, "sin moving on in the house" and "the devil himself." In addition, she seems to signify the potential threat of "past errors taking possession of the present." Thus, Beloved can be seen as the past errors, the sin, and the evil committed by the community itself, both individually and collectively. "The past," Ella believes, "is something to leave behind. And if it didn't stay behind, well, you might have to stomp it out" (p. 256). Led by Ella, the women gather at 124 to stomp out Beloved and, in so doing, stomp out their own past and their own sin, exorcising the collective spirit of "meanness" that has encouraged them to punish Sethe not only for her crime but also for her subsequent pride and self-sufficiency.

The interdependence between asking for, giving, and receiving help forms one of the unspoken codes that bind the community. Not to ask for help when it is needed, no matter what one's motive, is seen as prideful. Immediately after Sethe kills her daughter, the community gathers outside 124 to offer consolation but then withholds it because she does not appear to need that consolation: "Was her head a bit too high? Her back a little too straight? Probably. Otherwise the singing would have begun at once. . . . Some cape of sound would have quickly been wrapped around her, like arms to hold and steady her on the way" (p. 152). When, in contrast, Denver leaves 124 and moves into the community to ask for help, the women respond, giving freely whatever they have to spare from their own limited supplies. When Denver visits to thank them, the conversations, laden with memories, begin: "All of them knew her grandmother and some had even danced with her in the Clearing. Others remembered the days when 124 was a way station. . . . One remembered the tonic mixed there that cured a relative. One showed her the border of a pillowslip, the stamens of its pale blue flowers French-knotted in Baby Suggs' kitchen" (p. 249). Remembering Baby Suggs, the Clearing, the way station at 124, and the celebration party, the women reach out to Denver, wrapping her in the embrace they had denied Sethe.

The response of the community to Denver's request for help is motivated by more, however, than a simple sense of duty. The community is atoning for its own sin, its own unpardonable "meanness," committed eighteen years earlier. When the four strange white men rode into town in 1856 on the morning after Baby Suggs's feast to celebrate the safe arrival of her daughter-in-law and four grandchildren, no one warned Baby Suggs and her new family. That warning, had it been given, might have allowed Sethe the time to come up with a solution other than the one she chose. By acting, the people of the community could possibly have saved Sethe's children or, if not, at least have had the satisfaction of knowing they had tried to help. Instead, they waited passively to see what events would unfold. Stamp Paid knows that "it wasn't the exhaustion from a long day's gorging that dulled them, but some other thing—like, well, like meanness—that let them stand aside, or not pay attention, or tell themselves somebody else was probably bearing the news already to the house on Bluestone Road" (p. 157). The people of the community did not warn Baby Suggs because when they woke up the morning after the celebration, they discovered they were angered by her "reckless generosity" (p. 137). They were unable to accept Baby Suggs's generosity, unable to receive graciously what she wished to share in her thanksgiving for the safe delivery of four grandchildren, because they believed it to be excessive. Suddenly jealous of Baby's good fortune, they created a new fiction, saying that although Baby Suggs was an ex-slave, she had never really suffered—at least not to the degree that they had. Jealous of the easy life they imagined for Baby Suggs, in comparison with their own histories of hardship and abuse, they decided to let her fend for herself against the four white men.

When the women gather outside 124 to drive off Beloved, they come up against their past. They see themselves as they were eighteen years earlier at Baby Suggs's celebration, "younger, stronger, even as little girls lying in the grass asleep" (p. 258). Banded together to save Sethe from her "past errors," the women save themselves from their own. Michael Awkward, in his discussion of the "phenomenon of scapegoating" in Morrison's *The Bluest Eye*, suggests that a community may rid itself of its own feelings of guilt by projecting the negative aspect, or "shadow," of its behavior onto an external, "alien" personality. "In combatting the shadow that has been externalized and can, thus, be perceived as Other," Awkward explains, "the group is able to rid itself ceremonially of the evil that exists within both the individual members and the community at large."[25] In perceiving Sethe as a monster for having killed her child, the community projected its own guilt for its complicity in that act. Now by perceiving Beloved as a demon whipping Sethe, the community projects its guilt for having whipped her themselves for eighteen years. Furthermore, by setting up Beloved as the ultimate scapegoat for both sources of communal guilt, the community is able to re-vision Sethe as a victim, leading to her reincorporation into the community, an action that, by removing the cause of the people's guilt, heals the community.[26] By exorcising Beloved, the community exorcises the past, opening the way for the old harmony, inspired and nurtured by Baby Suggs, before it "was buried amid a regular dance of pride, fear, condemnation and spite" (p. 171).

In fact, there is some suggestion that Baby Suggs is helping the community to recover that harmony from "the other side." Beloved says that a woman on the bridge, the bridge connecting the human and spirit phases of life, directed her to 124 Bluestone (p. 65). Sethe, too, thinks that Baby Suggs helped Beloved come back to her in the flesh (p. 200). If so, then it appears that Baby Suggs recognized that Beloved must return, touching and releasing those whose lives had been paralyzed by the past. Beloved acts as a supernatural agent—experienced as daughter, sister, witch, or demon-child—who engages others in a seemingly external but actually internal struggle resulting in rebirth, renewal, resurrection. Representing the living past, both individual and collective, with which the modern African American must engage in order to experience selfhood and build a future, Beloved is sacrificed so that others may live and grow.

For Morrison, the past, as incarnated in the ghost of the beloved or as embedded in the geography of a place, lives on in the present. One must neither ignore the past nor allow it to dominate one's life but, rather, confront it, examine it, and understand how it has shaped one's own identity. Furthermore, one's individual past cannot be separated from the collective past of the group; African Americans, Beloved suggests, share a common heritage—captivity in Africa, the Middle Passage, and three hundred years of slavery in America. By confronting that shared past and then exorcising it, African Americans can liberate themselves from enslavement to a past that, when repressed or left unspoken, possesses all the more power to destroy. To know oneself, to claim or to construct an identity, Morrison suggests, one must know the past, both individual and collective.

7   Warring with Ghosts: Power through Individuation in Maxine Hong Kingston's *The Woman Warrior*

Medical science does not seal the earth, whose nether creatures seep out, hair by hair, disguised like the smoke that dispels them. She had apparently won against the one ghost, but ghost forms are various and many. Some can occupy the same space at the same moment. They permeate the grain in wood, metal, and stone. Animalcules somersault about our faces when we breathe. We have to build horns on our roofs so that the nagging once-people can slide up them and perhaps ascend to the stars, the source of pardon and love. —Maxine Hong Kingston[1]

Maxine Hong Kingston's autobiography, *The Woman Warrior: Memoirs of a Girlhood Among Ghosts,* traces the process by which she defined herself in relation to her parents, the Chinese emigrants living in Stockton, the Chinese—both living and dead—in China, and the non-Chinese Americans. Like Morrison's *Beloved, The Woman Warrior* argues that one cannot know or define oneself until one confronts the ghosts of one's past. Kingston recognizes, as does Morrison, that to believe in ghosts is to give them the power both to destroy and to heal. Thus, although haunted by ghosts, Kingston refuses to be dominated by them; neither, however, does she exorcise them. Instead, by imagining the lives of her ghosts, she gives them substance, solidity, and permanence. By reconstructing the lives of the ghosts who haunt her, Kingston also constructs an identity for herself—one that is neither Chinese nor American but Chinese-American. Because her girlhood in Stockton, California, demanded a daily crossing and recrossing of the boundary separating the world of the emigrant villagers from the world of the English-speaking Americans, she refuses as an adult to allow that boundary either to entrap her in one world or to exclude her from the other. By locating a voice and an identity that transcend the potential barrier, a common language that speaks to the inhabitants of both worlds, Kingston overcomes the power of boundaries—or of ghosts—to circumscribe or control her development as an individual.

Living among Ghosts

As the subtitle of her autobiography suggests, Kingston experienced childhood as a continuous struggle among and against a multiplicity of supernatural beings. "When I was growing up," Kingston explains in a 1989 interview with Angeles Carabi, "people around me saw spirits and creatures. . . . It wasn't just that they brought ghost stories from China, but that they saw spirits and magic people in the world around them, and that they tried to use the magic for or against themselves." As a result of this encroachment of the supernatural into her everyday world, Kingston says, "I was terrified all the time. I was always afraid of forces I couldn't control. I thought the world was made of spirits, ghosts, vampires." To overcome her terror of the supernatural beings that peopled her childhood world, Kingston continues, she attempted to control and destroy the supernatural world by leading a "very rational life," that of a scientist or engineer.[2] Instead, however, Kingston became a teacher and writer, learning, as those around her had, how "to use the magic" of the supernatural world for herself. In *The Woman Warrior,* Kingston examines the ghosts that haunted her as a girl—as "Maxine."[3] Born in America of Chinese emigrants—that is, a man and a woman who, after more than thirty-five years living in America, still view China as "home"[4]—the young Maxine is not only surrounded by ghosts of both American and Chinese origin but is herself viewed as a "half ghost" (p. 183). To know herself, to liberate herself from a ghostly existence, Maxine is forced to confront those ghosts who threaten to mislead her by silencing her, enslaving her, or driving her crazy—thus enticing her to live the nonlife of a ghost rather than the life of a human being. Her intent is not to destroy those ghosts but to control their power *over* her, thereby gaining power *from* them.

From her earliest days Maxine experiences the world as thoroughly infiltrated by ghosts. One type of ghost that she interacts with daily is the white ghost that dominates life outside the small area inhabited by the emigrants from her parents' village in China. Taught by her parents to view all non-Chinese as ghosts,[5] Maxine experiences her immediate world—the city of Stockton, California—as "so thick with ghosts" that she can "hardly breathe" (p. 97). Her difficulty in breathing arises not only from the feeling that she is being suffocated by the vast numbers of non-Chinese in California[6] but also from fears arising from the belief that ghosts are haunting, demonic, nightmarish spirit beings.

Many children fear ghosts. Maxine, however, thanks to her powerful imagination, her confused interpretation of scattered bits of "knowledge" gained from her mother's stories, and her own experiences of bicultural life in America, is particularly adept at creating ghosts— ghosts that haunt her, challenging her to pattern her life on theirs. Thus, despite her fear of the Newsboy Ghost, Maxine is also fascinated by him, imagining herself as taking his place: "We used to pretend we were Newsboy Ghosts. We collected old Chinese newspapers . . . and trekked about the house and yard. We waved them over our heads, chanting a chant: 'Newspapers for sale. Buy a newspaper.' But those who could hear the insides of words heard that we were selling a miracle salve made from boiled children" (p. 97). Maxine's ability to "hear the insides of words" makes her particularly susceptible to the powers of ghosts, one of which is to entice her to imitate their own mode of existence. To overcome the power of external ghosts, she must discover and strengthen the ghost, or spirit, of herself.

The individual spirit possessed by each person—the spirit that bestows breath, life, and personality—is another type of ghost that haunts Maxine. She is surrounded by emigrants whose true spirit, the spirit that guided their feelings, thoughts, and actions in China, has been subdued or driven away by life in America. Some emigrants, Maxine says, gain strength from living among other emigrant villagers, who, remembering their exploits in China, know, for example, that despite appearances an "old busboy is really a swordsman" (p. 52). The busboy's knowledge of his true spirit, shared by his neighbors, helps sustain him in a country whose inhabitants insist on defining and treating him as a busboy rather than a swordsman. To lose this spirit, Maxine knows, is to experience insanity; a person goes crazy and may eventually die when his or her spirit wanders or is driven away from the body, gets lost, and cannot find its way back home. No matter what fears, what terrors, what ghosts one confronts and battles, however, one's own spirit can be called safely home to rest as long as one has family and friends. When Brave Orchid "got scared as a child," Maxine explains, "one of my mother's three mothers had held her and chanted their descent line, reeling the frighted spirit back from the farthest deserts" (p. 75). The chanting of one's descent line provides the directions necessary to lead a spirit through generations and across geographical boundaries to one's true home.

The emigration of the Chinese to a new "home" in America, however, tended to confuse the emigrants' spirits; when frightened by events in the new country, an emigrant's spirit might very well return to the village of its origin in China, which most emigrants continued to recognize as "home," rather than to the newly established village in California. The loss or displacement of self in relation to home explains Moon Orchid's insanity as well as Brave Orchid's inability to chant her spirit back to its body. Brave Orchid "had whisked her sister across the ocean by jet and made her scurry up and down the Pacific coast, back and forth across Los Angeles. Moon Orchid had misplaced herself, her spirit (her attention, Brave Orchid called it) scattered all over the world" (pp. 156–57). Brave Orchid's cure for fear and for the insanity that often follows from fear is founded on the principle that health, strength, and well-being derive from the recognition of one's connection to family, home, and village and from the feeling of love, security, and protection that this recognition instills.

To break that connection, to remove one's name, to destroy one's descent line, then, is to relegate a spirit, whether that of the living or the dead, to endless wandering. The endlessly wandering spirit of Maxine's nameless aunt, denied by her family because of her impregnation by an unknown lover, is one of the personal ghosts that haunt Maxine. After the villagers raided and destroyed the home of the aunt's family, "the family broke their silence and cursed her. 'Aiaa. . . . Look what you've done. . . . Ghost! Dead ghost! Ghost! You've never been born'" (pp. 13–14). "The real punishment" suffered by her nameless aunt, Maxine explains, "was not the raid swiftly inflicted by the villagers, but the family's deliberately forgetting her. Her betrayal so maddened them, they saw to it that she would suffer forever, even after death" (p. 16).

Maxine is haunted by the memory of her two aunts, each of whom suffered from having lost her family, her home, and thus her spirit. They haunt her, in part, because she sees them as her "forerunner[s]" (p. 8), who seem at times to entice her, as the Newsboy Ghost did, to follow in their footprints. At times Maxine fears the spiteful power of her nameless aunt, who drowned herself in the family well, because the Chinese believe that the ghost of a drowned person "waits silently by the water to pull down a substitute" (p. 16). Maxine fears the power of both aunts to pull her into a way of life that imitates their own lives, ghostly lives spent in fulfilling the traditional role of the female in China followed by a ghostly afterlife spent wandering alone, forever separated from home and family. To counteract her visions of the "Chinese-feminine" (p. 11) role personified by her aunts, Maxine has the examples of two Chinese women warriors: her mother, a doctor and exorcist of ghosts, and Fa Mu Lan, swordswoman and "female avenger" (p. 43). As Maxine discovers, however, spirits and ghosts are difficult to pin down, difficult to characterize, define, and conceptualize in such a way that they provide "ancestral help" (p. 8). Although she sees Fa Mu Lan as "the swordswoman who drives me" (p. 48), portions of her story, in its retelling over time and its transportation to another country, have not "translated well" (p. 209). The same is true of Brave Orchid's story; a heroic exorcist in China, Maxine's mother is a tyrannical and suffocating nightmare in America. Maxine must examine and reconceptualize the role of the woman warrior in twentieth-century America in such a way that she can experience both Fa Mu Lan's and Brave Orchid's lives, like the life of her nameless aunt, as "branching into mine" (p. 8).

"Memory," Kingston commented in an interview with Paula Rabinowitz, is "insignificant, except when it haunts you and it is a foundation for the rest of the personality."[7] This chapter examines the ways in which Maxine's memories and imaginative re-creations of her forerunners' lives haunt her and, through that haunting, drive her to discover and create her own spiritual essence—one that refuses the role of wife, slave, and victim and reconceptualizes the role of the female as a warrior to fit the needs of a twentieth-century Chinese-American female. The sections in this chapter focus on the ways in which the ghosts of five Chinese females—Maxine's nameless aunt, Moon Orchid, Fa Mu Lan, Brave Orchid, and Ts'ai Yen—shape, guide, and strengthen Maxine's own spirit. In writing about the ghosts who haunted her girlhood, Kingston told Rabinowitz, she was not attempting to exorcise them but rather to give them "substance" and "solidity": "I have learned that writing does not make ghosts go away. I wanted to record, to find the words for, the 'ghosts,' which are only visions. They are not concrete; they are beautiful, and powerful. But they don't have a solidity that we can pass around from one to another. I wanted to give them a substance that goes beyond me."[8] The Woman Warrior demonstrates the process by which Maxine, through a creative act of the imagination, gives life, substance, and solidity to the ghosts of her childhood and, in so doing, comes to know them and, through her knowledge of them, to discover the power to create—to give life, substance, and solidity to—herself.

"No Name Woman": Ghost of Silence

At the time of Maxine's first menstrual flow, Brave Orchid tells her the story of Maxine's father's sister, who violated "the law" of family and village by committing adultery and bearing an illegitimate child. Although the stated reason for telling the story is to warn Maxine that sexual indiscretion can lead to the loss of one's family and thus one's descent line, a second warning lies in the secrecy with which the story is imparted. The second warning Maxine hears in her mother's story, more powerful than the stated warning, is that telling her aunt's story would surely damage her father and would perhaps harm the entire family: "I have believed that sex was unspeakable and words so strong and fathers so frail that 'aunt' would do my father mysterious harm. I have thought that my family, having settled among immigrants who had also been in the ancestral land, needed to clean their name, and a wrong word would incite the kinspeople even here" (p. 15). To protect her father and her family, Maxine remains silent, participating in the denial of her aunt's existence, even though her curiosity demands that gaps in her mother's story be filled. She knows, however, that asking her mother for details or for her aunt's name would have been useless: "My mother has told me once and for all the useful parts. She will add nothing unless powered by Necessity" (p. 6).

Given only "the useful parts" of her aunt's story, Maxine is haunted by its missing details: "My aunt haunts me—her ghost drawn to me because now, after fifty years of neglect, I alone devote pages of paper to her" (p. 16). Driven by curiosity, sympathy, and guilt, Maxine restores her dead aunt, denied and neglected for fifty years, to life. As the only family member who still remembers her, she attracts her aunt's wandering spirit and attempts, as that spirit hovers and haunts, to give it substance and solidity. She feeds the spirit in hopes that it will give her, in return, "ancestral help." Attempting to understand her aunt's story and what it means to her own life, Maxine imagines the details withheld by her mother. After imagining her aunt first as a woman commanded by a man "to lie with him and be his secret evil" (p. 6) and then as a woman who gave herself freely to men, Maxine finally concludes that her aunt was an eccentric woman, tending toward western ideas of individuality: "At the mirror my aunt combed individuality into her bob" (p. 9).[9] Her aunt, Maxine decides, was the victim of an eastern way of thinking that values social order and cohesion over individuality and selfhood. Furthermore, she was the victim of a worldwide process of socialization that allows men to wander, even to err, while expecting women to maintain both the home and tradition: "She was the only daughter; her four brothers went with her father, husband, and uncles 'out on the road' and for some years became western men. . . . They expected her alone to keep the traditional ways, which her brothers, now among the barbarians, could fumble without detection. The heavy, deep-rooted women were to maintain the past against the flood, safe for returning. But the rare urge west had fixed upon our family, and so my aunt crossed boundaries not delineated in space" (p. 8). Her aunt, Maxine imagines, was part of a family that tended toward the west, toward the expression of individuality, toward the crossing of oceans and boundaries. Expected to stay at home, to preserve tradition and the past, Maxine's aunt rebelled; daring to cross "boundaries not delineated in space," she violated the social mores and codes that keep the home and the village intact, untouched by time or change.

This vision of her aunt as a rebel against the "traditional ways" that bind the women of China to husbands and husbands' families, both of whom value women only insofar as they fulfill the role of "perfect filiality" (p. 45), haunts Maxine. She knows that she, too, must at some point assert her own individuality even though such action will, she believes, set her adrift like her aunt, separating her from a family that denies her. Despite the courage displayed by Maxine's aunt in asserting her individuality, however, she later betrays that act by acquiescing to her fate in silence, never revealing the name of the man who impregnated her. Perhaps she believed that silence would ensure her protection.

At about the time that Maxine's mother tells her the story of her aunt, Maxine is struggling to overcome her own fear of talking, a fear that originated in kindergarten when she realized that she must speak English. "The other Chinese girls did not talk either," she says, "so I knew the silence had to do with being a Chinese girl" (p. 166). By the sixth grade, however, Maxine has overcome her fear of talking, and empowered by her own newly found speech, she torments another Chinese girl who can read aloud but who cannot, or will not, talk in any other situation. Beginning as adolescent nastiness, the tormenting escalates into a scene of torture that eventually drives both girls to tears:

> Why won't you talk? . . . You don't see I'm trying to help you out, do you? Do you want to be like this, dumb . . . , your whole life? Don't you ever want to be a cheerleader? Or a pompon girl? What are you going to do for a living? . . . you are a plant. . . . That's all you are if you don't talk. If you don't talk, you can't have a personality. . . . You've got to let people know you have a personality and a brain. You think somebody's going to take care of you all your stupid life? You think you'll always have your big sister? You think somebody's going to marry you, is that it? Well, you're not the type that gets dates, let alone gets married. Nobody's going to notice you. And you have to talk for interviews, speak right up in front of the boss. Don't you know that? You're so dumb. Why do I waste my time on you? (Pp. 180–81)

Maxine's attack on her classmate is not, of course, motivated by concern for the other girl's welfare; it is motivated by Maxine's own self-hatred, which she projects outward on the girl who disgusts her because she is, like Maxine herself, such a "Chinese-feminine" person rather than the "American-feminine" ideal (p. 11) to which Maxine aspires: "I hated her when she was the last chosen for her team and I, the last chosen for mine. I hated her for her China doll haircut. I hated her at music time for the wheezes that came out of her plastic flute" (p. 173). Maxine hates the girl's fragility, her timidity, her helplessness. Her verbal and physical abuse of the girl, Joanne S. Frye writes, "is clearly an effort to expunge those parts of her Chinese-female identity which she abhors and to mark out her own possibilities for strength in resisting that identity."[10] When Maxine harangues the girl about the necessities for talking, however, she clearly reveals, in addition to her self-hatred, her fears about the bad things that happen to those who cannot speak up, who cannot find "some voice, however faltering" (p. 172). For one thing, without a voice, one can never be "American-feminine." Maxine wants to be accepted by Americans as an American; she wants to be an integral member of the team or, failing that, a "cheerleader" or "pompon girl." At the same time, she fears that she, like her classmate, is not "the type that gets dates, let alone gets married," primarily because she will never succeed, she believes, in becoming "American-feminine." If she does not marry, she reasons, she will have to support herself, which will require that she "talk for interviews, speak right up in front of the boss." In confronting her classmate's silence, Maxine is confronting her own fear of a future that will continually require a facility in speaking as well as her own desire, in the face of that fear, to retreat into silence. Brave Orchid's story about Maxine's nameless aunt confirms two ideas that had already begun to form in Maxine's mind about the nature of speech and silence: words, possessing the potential to destroy, are powerful, whereas silence offers neither safety nor comfort.

Maxine's aunt's rebellion, followed by both her own silence and that of her family, haunts Maxine for twenty years before she finds the courage to resurrect her aunt, capturing, solidifying, and fixing her wandering spirit through the power of the written word. Maxine feels guilty for the years of silence, but as she herself knows, the silence before speech is a necessary and powerful interlude, a moment of infinite potentiality: "My silence was thickest—total—during the three years that I covered my school paintings with black paint. I painted layers of black over houses and flowers and suns, and when I drew on the blackboard, I put a layer of chalk on top. I was making a stage curtain, and it was the moment before the curtain parted or rose" (p. 165). Maxine's teachers, not too surprisingly, fear that her blacked-out pictures, combined with a silence so thick it is total, suggest emotional problems. The silence, however, is a result of her inability to understand and speak English while the blacked-out pictures are the expression of a personal vision, unknown by and unshared with the teachers. Maxine is entranced by that moment of potentiality before the stage curtain rises, before the word is uttered. Just as her later silence about her fear of marriage and slavery is eventually shattered in one tremendously liberating outburst, in which "she shouts [her] grievances" to her parents (p. 37), so her silence about her aunt's life and death is similarly shattered once she finally finds the voice, the courage, and the vocabulary with which to speak. In fact, as she grows older, Maxine begins to understand that "talking and not talking made the difference between sanity and insanity. Insane people were the ones who couldn't explain themselves" (p. 186). If Maxine had been unable to find "a voice, however faltering," and the words with which to explain herself, the curtains would have remained drawn, the stories entombed in silence, and the teller forever lost and wandering in a private, interior world.

Moon Orchid: Ghost of Craziness

One of Maxine's greatest fears as she moves through adolescence is that she will prove to be the "crazy one" in her family (p. 190). From her observation that "within a few blocks of our house were half a dozen crazy women and girls, all belonging to village families," Maxine deduces that "every house had to have its crazy woman or crazy girl, every village its idiot. Who would be It," she wonders, "at our house?" (pp. 186, 189). She and her brothers and sisters had, for example, witnessed the erratic behavior of a neighbor until the day she disappeared once and for all. The children had also spent a good deal of time with Crazy Mary, who sprang at them from dark corners when they visited her house before she, too, disappeared. The children also had to deal with Pee-a-nah, whom they believed to be a witch because she chased them when they went to the slough to play. The one commonality among these diverse manifestations of female craziness is that all the women eventually disappear. Having lost their wandering spirits somewhere along the journey between the old world and the new, the "crazy women and girls" are eventually separated from family and village—from "home"—and are incarcerated in the local crazyhouse. Another similarity among the "crazy women and girls" is their eccentricity in behavior and appearance; their response to the external environment, like that of Maxine's nameless aunt, is individual and thus abnormal. Furthermore, the eccentricity, individuality, and abnormality of such females disturbs the social order, inspiring fear among the villagers, which in turn drives them to separate the individual from the group.

Having heard—and imagined—what happened to her own aunt in China and having observed what happened to three villagers (the woman next door, Crazy Mary, and Pee-a-nah) in America, Maxine begins to fear that her own abnormality—an exceptionally active imagination—marks her as the "crazy one" of the family. "There were adventurous people inside my head to whom I talked. With them I was frivolous and violent, orphaned. I was white and had red hair, and I rode a white horse. Once . . . I asked my sister, just checking to see if hearing voices in motors and seeing cowboy movies on blank walls was normal, I asked, 'Uh,' trying to be casual, 'do you talk to people that aren't real inside your mind?'" (pp. 189–90). Terrified of the abnormal, eccentric, and individual imagination that dominates her life, transforming her from a black-haired Asian girl to a red-haired Caucasian, Maxine maintains her silence. Afraid to be different, to be abnormal, to be crazy, she keeps her secret life to herself and, in so doing, unwittingly submits to a potentially crazy-making silence: "Insane people were the ones who couldn't explain themselves."

Maxine's fears about the fate of crazy Chinese women and girls are exacerbated by the example of Moon Orchid, who misplaces her spirit when, late in life, she crosses geographical boundaries as well as "boundaries not delineated in space." Thirty years after her husband left China to make his fortune in America, Moon Orchid arrives, her emigration arranged and paid for by her sister Brave Orchid. Against her better judgment, Moon Orchid allows Brave Orchid to pressure her into confronting her husband. As soon as he understands who Moon Orchid is, he tells her, "It's a mistake for you to be here. You can't belong. You don't have the hardness for this country" (pp. 152–53). Brave Orchid herself has already recognized the truth of this statement but knows also that, because her sister cannot be sent back to China, she must "toughen up" and adjust to her new life (p. 127). Moon Orchid, however, is unable to "toughen up." Soon after the meeting with her husband, Moon Orchid, having "misplaced herself, her spirit . . . scattered all over the world," slips into what others view as a totally insane paranoia. When Moon Orchid insists that the drapes and blinds be drawn and begs the children not to leave the house for fear they will never return, first Maxine's father and then her mother conclude that Moon Orchid is truly and irretrievably mad.

Although Moon Orchid's behavior is abnormal and eccentric, her perception of the world is not as mad as it seems. During the years after her husband and her sister left China, Moon Orchid continued to live in a country gone mad: in this "new" China, Maxine's own "uncles were made to kneel on broken glass during their trials and had confessed to being landowners. They were all executed, and the aunt whose thumbs were twisted off drowned herself. Other aunts, mothers-in-law, and cousins disappeared" (p. 50). Although Moon Orchid seems to have fared relatively well in Communist China, the ghosts of the family and friends who died or disappeared arise to haunt her once she is spirited to an alien country populated by ghosts and barbarians. Moon Orchid transfers what was a legitimate fear in China to America, where the fear is no longer legitimate or "rational." The fear is the same, but the environment has changed. Unable to explain to the "overseas Chinese" (p. 136) why her fear is valid, Moon Orchid slips ever more deeply into insanity. Her paranoia arises from her inability to communicate with those around her; unable to understand the language spoken by the ghosts, she believes that they are talking about her, plotting to kill her.[11] At the same time she finds that even among those who do speak Chinese, she is unable to explain herself. Like the other "overseas Chinese," Maxine's parents, not having experienced the Communist takeover of China and thus unable to understand Moon Orchid's "Chinese" experience, are more "American" than they realize. Because Moon Orchid cannot make herself understood, she eventually becomes, in Maxine's view, one more in a continuous line of insane Chinese women and girls who disappear into the crazyhouse.

Moon Orchid and Maxine are similar in that neither can explain herself—her uniquely "Chinese" or "American" experience of reality, respectively—to Maxine's parents, who represent the norm of the emigrant villagers and "overseas Chinese." Similarly, neither Moon Orchid nor Maxine can understand Maxine's parents, who seem very foreign and "American" to Moon Orchid and very foreign and "Chinese" to Maxine. Thus, both Moon Orchid and Maxine suffer from the same crazy-making experience—the inability to know and to make themselves known to Maxine's parents, who offer to both of them their only tie to family, village, home. Thus, the experience of being separated both from the family and from the world at large by cultural differences and misunderstandings is a primary cause of Moon Orchid's craziness and Maxine's crazy-making confusion.

Much of Maxine's confusion arises from her inability to understand who she is in relation to, on one hand, her parents and the emigrant villagers and, on the other, the world at large. Her parents do not always share information with their children, distrusting them because, Maxine says, "we had been born among ghosts, were taught by ghosts, and were ourselves half ghosts" (p. 183). Maxine understands that her parents use the word "ghost," as they use the word "barbarian," in a derogatory way to distinguish the nonhuman and barbaric Americans from the human and civilized Chinese. At times, however, she is confused about the use of these words and the distinctions they make between racial groups. If Americans are nonhuman and barbaric while Chinese are human and civilized, as the epithets imply, how then does one explain the seemingly barbaric actions and beliefs of the Chinese, the villagers, her family, and her parents? She is terrified by the stories of torture and execution in China, related in letters that make her father scream in his sleep. She is sickened by the stories about the villagers' raid on her aunt's home, their stoning of the village idiot, and the Chinese enjoyment of a "monkey feast." She is disgusted by her second cousins' great-grandfather, who, surrounded by six girls, shouts at them, "Maggots! Where are my grandsons? I want grandsons!" as she also is by her own great-uncle, who takes only boys—"No girls!"—when he goes shopping (pp. 191, 47). She is angered when the audience at a Chinese opera laughs raucously each time the daughter-in-law sings, "Beat me, then, beat me" (p. 193). Looking at the world through "Chinese" eyes, as her parents do, Maxine knows that the American racists and tyrants are barbaric and inhuman; but when looking at the same world through "American" eyes, she cannot help seeing the Chinese as equally barbaric and inhuman.

Perhaps most disturbing to Maxine is her confusion about what exactly her parents believe about the value of females. Can she believe that when her parents say, "When fishing for treasures in the flood, be careful not to pull in girls," they are only repeating a common saying about daughters (p. 152)? When her family finally returned "home" to China, would her parents sell her as a slave or, virtually the same thing, force her to marry, to become a daughter-in-law beaten by her husband and his family? Stories Maxine hears about the treatment of girls and rebellious women in China, as well as her hatred of those physical features that mark her as "Chinese-feminine" rather than "American-feminine," contribute to a sort of craziness in which she imagines herself as "white" with "red hair." More serious than her imagined crossing of racial boundaries, however, is her imagined crossing of the boundary that separates the human from the nonhuman: "I had vampire nightmares; every night the fangs grew longer, and my angel wings turned pointed and black. . . . Tears dripped from my eyes, but blood dripped from my fangs, blood of the people I was supposed to love" (p. 190). Believing herself to be monstrous—barbaric, ghostly, nightmarish—because of the depth of her anger, fear, and resentment toward those she "was supposed to love," Maxine is convinced of her own craziness and inevitable disappearance.

Because keeping her fears inside becomes intolerable and because she recognizes that "talking and not talking made the difference between sanity and insanity," Maxine attempts to tell her mother about the bad things she has done, which she has compiled in a list of two hundred items. She is driven by the need to explain herself, to make herself known to another person: "If only I could let my mother know the list, she—and the world—would become more like me, and I would never be alone again" (p. 198). By explaining herself to and thus making herself understood by others, Maxine believes that she can eliminate the difference—the abnormality—that separates her from the rest of the world. Unfortunately, Maxine's attempt to save herself by revealing herself to her mother fails. "I wish you would stop," Brave Orchid says when Maxine begins to recite her list. "I don't feel like hearing your craziness." Years later Maxine understands that her mother's rejection of her was founded on her own need "to ride off with the people in her own mind" (p. 200). What Maxine believes is a clear indication of her own craziness—her imaginative re-creation of the world—is actually the strongest tie linking her to her mother. At the time, however, Brave Orchid's response simply confirms Maxine's belief in her own "craziness," which is exacerbated by her mother's refusal to listen to her attempts to explain herself. "Maxine is afraid," King-Kok Cheung writes, "of losing her identity, of being erased or unhinged—as her two aunts have been respectively erased and unhinged—through silence."[12]

Having been denied this rather sane attempt to explain herself to another person, Maxine eventually unleashes all her thoughts and feelings in a volcanic eruption of threats and accusations. "I am not going to be a slave or a wife," she shouts at her parents. "Even if I am stupid and talk funny and get sick, I won't let you turn me into a slave or a wife. I'm getting out of here. . . . Ha! You can't stop me from talking" (pp. 201–2). This outburst, this act of talking that was so long silenced and suppressed, saves Maxine from the fate of so many Chinese females living in America. She refuses to be one of those women and girls crazed, as Moon Orchid is, by a misplacement of their spirits or, as she herself almost is, by the experience of living in a society that, through its own comparatively liberating treatment of women, glaringly reveals the barbaric treatment of women by the Chinese.[13] At the time, however, Maxine's outburst is rewarded with the punishment she has always dreaded, the fear of which has for so long ensured her silence. Brave Orchid, "champion talker," not to be outdone by her daughter, shouts back at her, "Leave then. Get out, you Ho Chi Kuei. Get out. I knew you were going to turn out bad. Ho Chi Kuei" (p. 204). Although Maxine does not understand the words "Ho Chi," she does know that "Kuei" means "ghost." Her mother's words, as she tells her to leave their home, recall the epithet shouted at Maxine's aunt fifty years earlier in China: "Look what you've done. . . . Ghost! Dead ghost! Ghost! You've never been born." The words spoken by herself and by her mother, Maxine knows, mark a significant break in her connection with the family, the village, the Chinese—a connection that, although eventually restored, will never be the same as when, still a child, she had agreed to be a participant in and slave to silence.

Fa Mu Lan: Spirit of Rebellion

When Maxine, no longer able to maintain her silence, speaks out against her parents, she discovers the power of speech to liberate herself. Like the mythological woman warrior Fa Mu Lan, Maxine brandishes her sword to cut down the tyrants who would sentence her to a ghostly, silent existence as wife or slave. That the tyrants she opposes are her parents, however, rather than her parents' enemies confuses Maxine. Furthermore, her verbal battle with her parents, in which she refuses to submit to their wishes that she become a wife or a slave, demonstrates that she, unlike Fa Mu Lan, will never kneel before the feet of her parents-in-law to say, "Now my public duties are finished. . . . I will stay with you, doing farmwork and housework, and giving you more sons" (p. 45).

The ghost of Fa Mu Lan inspires Maxine, but it also disturbs her, primarily because she knows that she herself does not possess the temperament of a warrior; she does not like armies, nor does she care for bloodshed (p. 49). When Maxine imagines herself as performing the exploits of Fa Mu Lan, an imaginative act that personalizes and fills in the gaps of the existing Fa Mu Lan chant,[14] she alternates between experiencing warfare as glorious and experiencing it as horrendous. When Maxine, masquerading as Fa Mu Lan, reaches Peiping, she fully experiences the glory of "the People of One Hundred Surnames" united and victorious in their rebellion against tyranny (p. 42). Caught up in her imagination, Maxine experiences the joy of being one among many heroic peasants, who together put down their hoes, picked up their swords, and discovered the power of a united voice as they rebelled against and dethroned the emperors who had erred by allowing them to go hungry for so long: "The last emperors of dynasties must not have been facing in the right direction, for they would have seen us and not let us get this hungry. We would not have had to shout our grievances" (p. 37). Shouting their grievances and wielding their swords, the peasants liberate themselves from tyranny.

The sense of empowerment that Maxine receives from her imaginary identification with Fa Mu Lan cannot be denied. Nevertheless, she is all too aware of flaws in Fa Mu Lan's story as well as the discrepancies between her own character and that of Fa Mu Lan. Thus, in mentally reenacting Fa Mu Lan's exploits and reexperiencing her feelings of glory, Maxine also introjects feelings of horror and grief. When she imagines Fa Mu Lan's killing of the giant Chen Luan-feng, for example, she cannot help seeing the giant's wives "holding each other weeping," their white mourning garments fluttering in the wind (p. 38). As much as Maxine might like to isolate the glory of battle, she recognizes that warfare can never be separated from bloodshed and mourning.

The story of Fa Mu Lan confuses Maxine, then, because she does not know how to reconcile the heroism of a just revenge with the bloodshed and mourning that necessarily accompany acts of vengeance. She is also confused about other flaws she discerns in Fa Mu Lan's heroism; the flaws lie both in the original story and in Maxine's imaginative re-creation of the swordswoman and her military exploits. To fulfill her objective of avenging her family, Fa Mu Lan puts on "men's clothes and armor" and ties her hair in "a man's fashion" (p. 36). The soldiers of her army, when they tell of their victories, refer to themselves as being "on *his* side" of the battle. "I never told them the truth," Fa Mu Lan says, because "Chinese executed women who disguised themselves as soldiers or students, no matter how bravely they fought or how high they scored on the examinations" (p. 39). Ultimately, Fa Mu Lan, who disguises herself in battle as a man and who returns, after fulfilling the objective of avenging her family, to the traditional role of a daughter-in-law serving her husband and his family, does little to avenge or liberate the women of China. When she confronts the baron who sent her brother to fight, she announces herself as a "female avenger," meaning that she is a female come to avenge her family. Because she is disguised as a man, however, the baron misunderstands, believing that she is a male come to avenge the enslavement and forced prostitution of the villagers' daughters. Fa Mu Lan's actions, however courageous, glorious, and victorious they may be, ultimately focus on the preservation and con-tinuity of males: she goes to battle in her father's place, she leads an army of men, she kills the baron to avenge the conscription of her brother and the villagers' sons, and she bears one son during battle and promises her parents-in-law to bear more sons—not daughters—in the future. Compare Fa Mu Lan's motivations for fighting with those of the women whom she releases from a locked room in the baron's palace. According to Fa Mu Lan, these women, when they later formed an army of swordswomen, "did not wear men's clothes like me, but rode as women in black and red dresses. They bought up girl babies so that many poor families welcomed their visitations. When slave girls and daughters-in-law ran away, people would say they joined with these witch amazons. They killed men and boys" (pp. 44–45). For these true female avengers, openly wearing women's clothing as they fight to avenge male tyranny over females, the enemy—"men and boys"—is clearly defined.[15]

Maxine is both haunted and driven by the figure of the swordswoman Fa Mu Lan. To receive "ancestral help" from this ghost, however, Maxine must "see her life branching into [hers]"; she must be able to translate Fa Mu Lan's story in such a way that it becomes "a story to grow up on," and her translation will not necessarily coincide with Brave Orchid's. Over time Maxine sifts through the details of Fa Mu Lan's story, identifying and retaining the "useful parts." Some of the most "useful parts" come from Maxine's imaginative re-creation of Fa Mu Lan's training on the mountain.[16]

Fa Mu Lan's training on the mountain provides her with several insights, one of which is gained during a visionary experience resulting from excessive hunger. As a result of this experience, she develops the ability, frequently renewed during periods of fasting, to "stare at ordinary people and see their light and gold." "I could see their dance," she says. "When I get hungry enough, then killing and falling are dancing too" (p. 27). What at first seems to be a mystical vision of life—the ability to see the "light and gold," the "dance," the spirit that informs and unites all humans despite differences in external form and appearance—eventually becomes the means by which Fa Mu Lan distances herself from the reality of warfare. "Falling and killing" are not a "dance"; to see them as such is to separate oneself from the consequences of one's actions.[17] Maxine herself is never able to separate the bloodshed of warfare from its glory, and later in life she totally rejects this mystical endowment of the universe with a spirit of "light and gold." As an adult who determines to rid her world of ghosts and spirits, she says, "Now when I peek in the basement window where the villagers say they see a girl dancing like a bottle imp, I can no longer see a spirit in a skirt made of light, but a voiceless girl dancing when she thought no one was looking" (p. 205). Thus, Maxine rejects her childish inclination to transform the villagers' sayings and similes into ghosts as well as Fa Mu Lan's tendency to transform an ordinary person into a spirit of "gold and light." To see "a voiceless girl dancing when she thought no one was looking" as "a spirit in a skirt made of light" not only peoples the earth with ghosts that do not really exist; it also ignores the reality of "a voiceless girl." By destroying the ghost, one can see the girl, giving her substance, solidity, and a voice so that she may be known.

The first part of Fa Mu Lan's training, culminating in the survival test, is directed at developing her physical strength and endurance. The second part, the training in "dragon ways," is directed at developing mental prowess and control. During battle Fa Mu Lan will rely primarily on physical warfare. Nevertheless, more than half of her training is dedicated to developing mental control, and her mentors will not allow her to leave until she can "point at the sky and make a sword appear, a silver bolt in the sunlight, and control its slashing with [her] mind" (p. 33). Maxine imagines Fa Mu Lan drawing on this strength only once when, having wandered away from her army's camp, she is surprised by the enemy: "My fear shot forth—a quick, jabbing sword that slashed fiercely, silver flashes, quick cuts wherever my attention drove it. . . . two more swords appeared in midair. They clanged against mine, and I felt metal vibrate inside my brain. I willed my sword to hit back and to go after the head that controlled the other swords. But the man fought well, hurting my brain" (p. 41). In this ability of Fa Mu Lan, when physically overcome, to engage the enemy in mental battle, matching her brain against that of her opponent, Maxine finds a strategy for attacking and overpowering her own opponents. She knows that she can easily be physically overcome by her enemy, the bosses who tower two feet above her. She also knows that beheading or gutting the enemy is no longer an effective means of swordsmanship. Thus, to avenge herself, her family, and the women of China, Maxine develops mental prowess and control, learning to engage the enemy in verbal combat. She does well in school, wins a scholarship to college, and dares to break the code of silence universally imposed by tyrants in both North America and Asia: "The swordswoman and I are not so dissimilar," Maxine says. "What we have in common are the words at our backs. . . . The reporting is the vengeance—not the beheading, not the gutting, but the words" (p. 53). Just as Maxine realizes that "the real punishment" imposed on her aunt "was not the raid swiftly inflicted by the villagers, but the family's deliberately forgetting her," she also realizes that the true "vengeance" against silence, against tyranny, against racism and sexism—and a form of battle at which she is highly skilled—is found not in a bloody beheading or gutting but in the words that report, that reenact, the crime.

An equally important lesson gained from Fa Mu Lan's training in "dragon ways" but perhaps more difficult to incorporate into her own life is that true wisdom, true mental strength, comes from "learning to make [one's] mind large . . . so that there is room for paradoxes" (p. 29). Learning to stretch her mind to encompass paradox is the most difficult lesson for Maxine to learn, as it was for Fa Mu Lan. With time Maxine becomes adept at stretching her mind, at understanding that the Chinese people are both tyrannical and heroic, that the villagers can both sustain and stone their neighbors, and, the most difficult paradox of all, that her mother is both an exorcist of ghosts and a nightmare that threatens to suffocate her. Maxine learns that she can infer the whole woman who is Brave Orchid, as one "infer[s] the whole dragon," only by studying "the parts you can see and touch" (p. 28).

Brave Orchid: Exorcist and Nightmare

If Maxine is haunted and driven by the ghost of Fa Mu Lan, she is equally driven by the woman who first, through her chanting and singing, brought the swordswoman to life for her. Whereas Fa Mu Lan was a woman warrior fighting and overpowering tyrants, Brave Orchid was a woman doctor struggling against and overpowering ghosts. For Maxine, however, Brave Orchid's exploits as doctor, shaman, and exorcist in China seem as mythical, legendary, and ghostly as Fa Mu Lan's exploits as swordswoman. From the photographs of her mother at age thirty-seven and from her mother's ghost stories, Maxine attempts to reconstruct a portrait of Brave Orchid that captures her spirit and its paradoxes.[18]

The stories that Brave Orchid tells her children about her battles with ghosts, from which she consistently emerges victorious, suggest that she, like Fa Mu Lan, was always courageous and unafraid. Maxine believes, however, that, if her mother *had* ever experienced fear, she would have felt challenged to destroy it. Like Fa Mu Lan, Brave Orchid, when she experiences fear, forges swords out of the air. She does not deny the existence of fear-evoking entities and events, but she believes that, in their presence, one must not submit but "toughen up." One must "make herself not weak." "Plain people who were lonely and afraid," people like Maxine herself, earn Brave Orchid's contempt (p. 67).

Thus, when the other female scholars at To Keung School express their fear of a ghost that haunts one of the dormitory rooms, Brave Orchid tells them with authority that "most ghosts are only nightmares" (p. 65). A modern post-Freudian would interpret Brave Orchid's statement as meaning that ghosts are projections of one's inner conflicts while in a dream state. Long before Freud, however, some people believed that a nightmare was not just a dream but "a female spirit or monster supposed to beset people and animals by night, settling upon them when they are asleep and producing a feeling of suffocation by its weight."[19] The Sitting Ghost that Brave Orchid encounters when she tests her theory about ghosts by spending the night in the haunted room possesses all the characteristics of a classic, pre-Freudian nightmare. This ghost—no shadowy, substanceless spirit—has mass and weight and solidity, and it sits on Brave Orchid, pinning her to the bed, sapping her energy, and gaining size and strength as it feeds on her thoughts (p. 69). Recognizing that the nightmare-ghost's strength lies in its superior physical size, which increases in relation to the increasing flow of her own thoughts, Brave Orchid fights the Sitting Ghost by controlling those thoughts. Like Fa Mu Lan, Brave Orchid recognizes that this battle is a test between her brain and that of her opponent, and she releases a stream of words aimed at belittling and demeaning the enemy while asserting her own superior strength. She controls and subdues the Sitting Ghost by reassuring herself—as she talks aloud to the ghost—of her own superior strength, her certain victory, her refusal to submit no matter what pain it inflicts, and her knowledge that "there are no such things as ghosts" (p. 70).

The ghost is real, however, inasmuch as some previously unacknowledged, long-submerged fear of Brave Orchid's has materialized in the form of a nightmare, making its existence and strength known in graphically and suffocatingly clear terms. Brave Orchid is haunted by her own loneliness and fear, originating in the death of her children and the ten-year absence of her husband. She has attacked that loneliness and fear, however, by crossing geographical boundaries as well as "boundaries not delineated in space" to train as a doctor, thus ensuring that she will no longer be a slave—either to her husband's family or to her own loneliness and fear. Thus, when that loneliness and fear arise out of the dark as a nightmare-ghost threatening to suffocate her, sapping her energy, strength, and resolve, she fights and subdues it through the power of words and rationalism. Confronted with the apparent reality of the ghost, Brave Orchid paradoxically draws on her modern skepticism—her belief that "there are no such things as ghosts"—as a weapon in her struggle.

The Sitting Ghost encountered by Brave Orchid is a personal ghost; her struggle with it is a personal battle, and her success in subduing it is a personal victory. She recognizes, however, that the ghost that haunts the dormitory room is also a communal ghost. She knows that when her classmates learn that she has, indeed, encountered a ghost in that room, they will continue to fear it unless they, too, participate in its exorcism. In telling the story to her friends, then, Brave Orchid does not belittle the ghost as she did when she was speaking directly to it. Instead, she exaggerates its size, its strength, and the danger it poses, presenting it as a communal rather than a universal threat: "The danger is not over. The ghost is listening to us right now, and tonight it will walk again but stronger. We may not be able to control it if you do not help me to finish it off before sundown. . . . It is dangerous. It is real" (pp. 73–74). Whereas Brave Orchid once argued that her friends need not fear because ghosts did not exist except as nightmares, she now attempts to confirm their belief in ghosts. Their belief in both the reality and the danger of the Sitting Ghost is necessary to ensure their belief in their power to destroy it. Brave Orchid, having encountered a personal ghost, having experienced fear in her confrontation with that ghost, and having gained the power that comes from subduing it, has decided that she must teach her friends how to exorcise ghosts. This ability is important to them not only as women subject to ghostly visitations but also as future doctors "who would have to back up their science with magic spells should their patients be disappointed and not get well" (p. 74). For some of their patients, the women will have to serve as both traditional shaman and modern doctor.[20]

The image of Brave Orchid, both as a female doctor in China and as an exorcist of ghosts, inspires Maxine as much as the image of Fa Mu Lan as swordswoman. Maxine sees Brave Orchid as a woman warrior who succeeded in translating the story of Fa Mu Lan to meet her own

needs as a woman who, living in China in the 1930s, had been abandoned for years by a husband who had gone to America to make his fortune. Unfortunately, Brave Orchid, transported from China to America in 1939, has not "translated well": "In America," says Maxine,
"my mother has eyes as strong as boulders, never once skittering off a
face, but she has not learned how to place decorations or phonograph
needles" (p. 59). Brave Orchid still has the strength, courage, and
endurance of a woman warrior, but in Maxine's view these qualities
have become misdirected in America. For Maxine, Roberta Rubenstein
notes, Brave Orchid is "ambivalently both a woman of exceptional
power within the female world of her culture and a powerless female in
the larger bicultural situation."[21] Brave Orchid's inability to speak English means not only that she is unable to practice medicine in America
but also that she must bully her children to speak for her: "You can't
entrust your voice to the Chinese, either," says Maxine. "They want to
capture your voice for their own use. They want to fix up your tongue to
speak for them. 'How much less can you sell it for?' we have to say. Talk
the Sales Ghost down. Make them take a loss" (p. 169). Maxine is
repeatedly humiliated by having to speak for a mother who does not
understand that Chinese ways are inappropriate in America. Rendered
powerless by her voicelessness in an English-speaking world, Brave
Orchid depends on the voices of her children. Fearful perhaps of that
dependency, Brave Orchid becomes tyrannical, demanding silence of
her children unless they speak as she commands them to speak.

Maxine is, then, understandably confused about her mother's true
identity and spirit. Is she a hero—a warrior among ghosts—or a tyrant?
As closely as Maxine examines the photographs of her mother, as atten-
tively as she listens to the stories of her exploits, and as critically as she
attempts to understand her words and actions in America, Maxine can
never quite stretch her mind large enough to "infer the whole dragon"
that is her mother. Eventually, fearing that her mother is more loyal to
traditional than mythical ideas of womanhood, Maxine sees her as a tyrant and a nightmare. Like Fa Mu Lan, Maxine engages in mental combat, wielding a sword forged from the air, her brain and her words clang-
ing against those of her mother. Like Brave Orchid battling the Sitting
Ghost, Maxine confronts her own personal nightmare—the fear of
being forced by her parents into a life as wife or slave—with a steady

stream of words, asserting her refusal to submit, her superior mental powers, her ability to fend for herself, her freedom and power of speech.

Although Maxine succeeds in subduing the ghost-nightmare, she never truly overcomes its power to return, to haunt, and to weaken her. Years later when her mother asks her to return to Stockton to live, Maxine explains that the nightmare who continues to haunt her lives in Stockton:

> When I'm away from here, . . . I don't get sick. I don't go to the hospitals every holiday. I don't get pneumonia, no dark spots on my x-rays. My chest doesn't hurt when I breathe. I can breathe. And I don't get headaches at 3:00. I don't have to take medicines or go to doctors. Elsewhere I don't have to lock my doors and keep checking the locks. I don't stand at the windows and watch for movements and see them in the dark.
>
> . . . I don't hear ghost sounds. I don't stay awake listening to walking in the kitchen. I don't hear the doors and windows unhinging.
>
> . . . I've found some places in this country that are ghost-free. And I think I belong there. (P. 108)

For Maxine, confronting the nightmare-ghost that dominated her girl-hood—Brave Orchid—through speech is only a first step toward con-trolling its power over her. To free herself, to regain the power to breathe, she must distance herself from her mother, her family, the emigrant villagers. Brave Orchid, after listening to her daughter, agrees that Maxine must "stay away," suggesting that "the weather in Califor-nia must not agree with you." Whether or not Brave Orchid can "hear the insides of words," thus understanding that it is she as much as the California weather that does "not agree" with her daughter, Maxine is relieved by what appears to be her mother's blessing: "A weight lifted from me," she says (p. 108). She has learned to use words to confront and subdue and even to ask for the blessing of the nightmare-ghost who, weighing on her chest, sapping her energy, and feeding on her thoughts, has made breathing so difficult at home.

In making a break with her family, Maxine asserts her right to forge her own role in life rather than to submit to one dictated by Chinese tradition or tyrannical parents. In gaining autonomy, however, she also must sacrifice the protective, encircling cocoon offered by the tradi-tional Chinese family. As an adult, Maxine discovers that the silent classmate she had tormented years earlier succeeded in living her whole life in such loving, protective seclusion. "I was wrong," Maxine says, "about nobody taking care of her. Her sister became a clerk-typist and stayed unmarried. They lived with their mother and father. She did not have to leave the house except to go to the movies. She was supported. She was protected by her family" (p. 182). Such an option, however, is never viable for Maxine, who is driven by such powerfully haunting female ghosts as her nameless aunt, Moon Orchid, Fa Mu Lan, and Brave Orchid, all of whom deliver, whether explicitly or implicitly, whether through examples of success or failure, the same message: to liberate yourself, you must find "a voice, however faltering."

Ts'ai Yen: A Voice Transcending Difference

When Ts'ai Yen, the daughter of a famous scholar, is captured by the Southern Hsiung-nu, she is abruptly and forcibly transplanted from a "civilized" world to a "barbaric" one. As a captive, she becomes, against her wishes, a woman warrior as well as the wife of the captain who captured her and the mother of two children born in the sand between battles. With her captivity, Ts'ai Yen learns the meaning not only of enslavement but also of voicelessness. For Ts'ai Yen, life among the Southern Hsiung-nu, whom she believes to be "barbarians" and "primitives" (p. 208), means total alienation, separation not only from home but also from civilization. Her alienation is compounded by her inability to communicate with those around her.[22] Not even her own children speak Chinese.

Ts'ai Yen believes that the nomadic, warring Hsiung-nu have no art form—no literature, no architecture, no sculpture or etchings, no music. Their only music, she believes, is the terrifying, whistling "death sounds" of their arrows, made from reeds carved into whistles, hurtling through space during battle. One night, however, Ts'ai Yen hears "music tremble and rise like desert wind." Leaving her tent to investigate this source of music, she discovers that it is coming from the flutes of the barbarians: "They reached again and again for a high note, yearning toward a high note, which they found at last and held—an icicle in the desert." Ts'ai Yen is disturbed by the paradox that the barbarians' music forces her to grasp: these primitive and barbaric people have produced a music that, in "its sharpness and its cold," is so powerful and so penetrating that it makes her "ache" (p. 208). Ts'ai Yen must stretch her mind to understand and believe that an icicle has materialized, assuming form and clarity, in the heat and aridity of a barren desert.

The music of the barbarians' flutes, transcending barriers separating one culture from another, penetrates Ts'ai Yen's being, piercing the silence surrounding her and disturbing her to the point that she must speak up, joining her song with theirs: "Ts'ai Yen sang about China and her family there. Her words seemed to be Chinese, but the barbarians understood their sadness and anger. Sometimes they thought they could catch barbarian phrases about forever wandering" (p. 209). By adding her own voice to the music of the barbarians' flutes, Ts'ai Yen creates a song, a form of communication, that for brief moments unites the two cultures. Although she sings in Chinese, the barbarians understand the "sadness and anger" of her song. The feelings behind the words—"the insides of words"—translate well even though the words themselves are indecipherable. Furthermore, by sprinkling her song with "barbarian phrases about forever wandering," Ts'ai Yen demonstrates that some of the "barbarian phrases" have also "translated well"; she has not only been able to understand the meaning of those phrases that express the "sadness and anger" of "forever wandering" but has also chosen to incorporate those phrases into her own song because they express far better than any Chinese words the essence of her own bicultural experience among the barbarians. The nomadic Hsiung-nu know more about the loneliness and fear of "forever wandering" than do the Chinese, who have led a sedentary, village-based existence since 2500 B.C. Separated from family, home, and village, Ts'ai Yen merges her own "sadness and anger" at her captivity, enslavement, and separation from home with the "sadness and anger" she shares with the barbarians— that of "forever wandering."

Ts'ai Yen discovers that despite the barrier she herself has constructed by labeling the Hsiung-nu as "barbarians," "primitives," and aliens—a barrier that is made even more formidable by the differences in their behavior and the unintelligibility of their language—she and the barbarians can find a common voice, one that transcends the barrier. Similarly, Moon Orchid, rendered speechless by her life among the barbarians in America and separated from her family by her inability to explain her experience, also finds a voice that transcends seemingly insurmountable barriers. When Brave Orchid visits Moon Orchid in the asylum, she is surprised to find that Moon Orchid is happy. "'Oh, Sister,'" Moon Orchid says, "'We are all women here. . . . And you know, . . . we understand one another here. We speak the same language, the very same. They understand me, and I understand them.' Sure enough, the women smiled back at her and reached out to touch her as she went by" (p. 160). Moon Orchid, of course, is still unable to speak English. She cannot converse with the other "crazy women and girls" in the asylum any better than she was able to converse with the Mexican ghosts she believed were trying to kill her. Despite the inability to express themselves through words and despite the fact that each woman is submerged deep within her own private, interior, and individually constructed world, however, the women "understand one another." They "speak the same language, the very same," a language conveyed through smiles and by touch, a communication made possible perhaps because, in Moon Orchid's words, "we are all women here," and because the asylum is just that—a haven that protects the women, isolating them from the confusion and fear that separate spirit from body.

Maxine too, of course, as so many others have noted before me, finds a voice that translates well, transcending cultural boundaries, a voice that is especially powerful among women. The finding of her voice, however, has less to do with creating a common language among women than with overcoming the power of female ghosts to haunt. Maxine discovers that she can transform the ghosts that haunt her by giving them a voice. What may appear to be a ghost, "a spirit in a skirt made of light," is actually just another "voiceless girl dancing when she thought no one was looking." To rid the world of ghosts, Maxine does not exorcise them, as her mother did. Instead, she gives them a voice with which to speak, one that she then translates and captures on paper, thus giving them solidity and permanence, releasing them from a ghostly, voiceless existence as "forever wandering," "forever hungry," forever sad and angry spirits. To make her world "ghost-free," Maxine must stretch her mind wide enough to accept several paradoxes, the ultimate paradox being that to rid the world of ghosts, she must not destroy them but instead give them life and permanence. Only by giving her ghosts substance and solidity can Maxine control their power over her so that she can gain power from them.

8 Boundaries and Belief

The fifth condition for work was . . . to make connections among ourselves, while recognizing and respecting our differences, as an integral way of knowing. —Bettina Aptheker[1]

Ts'ai Yen, in the fourth of her eighteen laments describing her captivity among the Southern Hsiung-nu, cites several cultural differences—customs, thought, food, drink—that make living with them so difficult for her. Her sense of isolation from her captors is compounded, she says, by her inability to share her feelings with others.[2] Her isolation is perhaps also increased by her perception of her captors, based on her own experiences growing up under the Han dynasty, as primitive and barbaric. The Southern Hsiung-nu are a warring, nomadic tribe, and she is forced to ride on horseback behind her husband when the tribe travels; to fight, along with the other captive soldiers, against the tribe's enemies; and to give birth to her children in the sand. This mode of existence, so natural to the Southern Hsiung-nu, is not only alien to Ts'ai Yen but also, because of beliefs instilled in her as a child about the nature of civilized behavior, perceived to be uncivilized, and thus inferior, to her own. To protect herself, to survive, she would likely cling to her past life, holding it safe and intact within herself. She would, that is, hold on to her difference because only by maintaining her difference can she remain Han, remain civilized.

Ts'ai Yen's belief, then, that the Southern Hsiung-nu are uncivilized and the people of Han civilized creates a boundary, real and uncrossable, between herself and her captors. Not until she hears the music of their flutes and is forced to comprehend the paradox of such disturbing music being produced by an uncivilized tribe does the boundary that separates them begin to disintegrate. Through music the two cultures begin to communicate and to discover not only that they understand each other, comprehending the meaning of previously unrecognized words and phrases, but also that they share similar feelings. To shatter belief, then, is to destroy—or at least to weaken—the boundary.

Kingston, in *The Woman Warrior*, offers Ts'ai Yen's story as an analogy to her own experience growing up among a people her parents had labeled as ghosts and barbarians. Like Ts'ai Yen, Maxine is conditioned from a very young age to believe that Chinese thought, customs, food, and drink are civilized whereas those of the American ghosts are barbaric. Because her parents, living primarily within the confines of the community of Chinese emigrant villagers, do not learn English, they are unable to teach Maxine the language. Thus, when Maxine, reaching school age, is abruptly thrust into the white, English-speaking world, she experiences the same sort of cultural collision experienced by Ts'ai Yen. The thought, customs, food, and drink of the Americans differ from her own, and as for Ts'ai Yen, the differences are compounded by Maxine's speechlessness, her inability to speak the language of those around her.

Maxine's experiences differ from those of Ts'ai Yen, however, in that the longer she lives among the American barbarians, the more she wants to be like them. She wants to be "American-feminine," not "Chinese-feminine," and for several years she is obsessed with the physical and cultural differences that threaten to prevent her from living an "American-normal" life.[3] Maxine, then, far from isolating herself from the alien culture because she judges it to be uncivilized and barbaric, wants to be included. She wants to participate in certain types of "barbaric" behavior and customs, such as American sports, music, dating rituals, and gender relations. Whereas Ts'ai Yen believes unfailingly in the superiority, the preferability, of her own culture over that of the Southern Hsiung-nu and wants only to be reunited with her family and culture, Maxine, recognizing the flaws in both cultures, understands that only through separation from her family and community can she create an individual, eccentric, self-empowering identity.

The rigidity of Ts'ai Yen's beliefs about the superiority of Han culture, instilled over a period of twenty years before she is captured, creates a boundary, a separation of worlds, that Maxine, who mixes with American barbarians—Newsboy Ghosts, Bus Ghosts, Meter Reader Ghosts, Garbage Ghosts—from earliest childhood, never experiences. Despite her parents' self-imposed isolation primarily within the Chinese emigrant community, Maxine herself always lives in a dual world, part Chinese and part American. Thus, her demarcation of the universe into "our" civilized world and "their" primitive, barbaric, uncivilized world is never as rigid as that of Ts'ai Yen or, for that matter, of her parents. From her earliest years, Maxine is subjected to conflicting stories, conflicting views, conflicting beliefs about which thought, customs, food, and drink are barbaric and which are civilized. As a child, for example, she is often repulsed by the food her mother serves; as she grows older, she is equally repulsed by what she hears about Chinese attitudes toward and treatment of females.

Maxine, then, is subjected to a multiplicity of conflicting beliefs by the time she is twenty, the age that Ts'ai Yen was when she was captured by the Southern Hsiung-nu. Her problems arise not from a rigidity of belief but from a confusion of beliefs. Like Ts'ai Yen, however, Maxine does believe that a boundary separates her from the other Americans— a boundary based on both physical and cultural differences. She hates the black hair, weak neck, and fragile features as well as the timidity, fragility, and lack of athleticism that she believes mark her as Chinese because she believes they create an uncrossable boundary. Like Ts'ai Yen, however, she discovers that the boundary can be dissolved by overcoming her voicelessness. By locating a voice, she is able to carve, as Gloria Anzaldúa has, a space for herself, an identity that crosses boundaries, that takes beliefs from both cultures available to her to create a world and identity that is not only Chinese-American but also uniquely individual.

Beliefs, then, arising from acquiescence with—or reaction against—cultural or familial conditioning, create boundaries between cultures. Only when the beliefs change, either as a result of some isolated experience that clearly refutes the validity of previous experience or as a result of gradually reevaluating and reformulating one's beliefs over time, do the boundaries dissolve. Silko's *Ceremony* and Erdrich's *Tracks* both demonstrate, although in different ways, the power of Native American beliefs in creating boundaries that have historically separated Native Americans from European Americans. Tayo's experience, in *Ceremony*, of crossing the boundary separating the two cultures demonstrates that his psychological and physical health depends on an adherence to his Laguna Pueblo beliefs despite the pressure to accept the scientific world view of the European Americans. Because his illness derives from these Laguna Pueblo beliefs, as instilled by the stories of his grandmother and his uncle and as later confirmed by his own experience, it cannot be cured by white doctors. Healing depends on a shared belief system between patient and healer. Tayo can never be healed by a doctor who categorically dismisses as hallucination his belief that he saw his uncle Josiah die in the Philippine jungle; he can only be cured by a doctor who not only accepts that he did see Josiah in the jungle but also explains why he saw him there. The boundary separating the two cultures, Silko suggests in *Ceremony*, is based on a difference in world views that can never accommodate one another. Although the Pueblo-Navajo healing ceremonies may change to allow for the pervasive influence of the European-American world, the boundary itself remains.

Erdrich's *Tracks* also examines the relationship between Native American beliefs and the boundary that separates Native Americans from European Americans. The focus here, however, is on the damage incurred by the encroachment of whites into Chippewa space. The devastation by the whites—the decimation of whole families through disease, the destruction of game and habitat, the acquisition of land previously held by the tribe—overwhelms the Chippewa with a sense of their own powerlessness as well as that of their gods. Thus, *Tracks* suggests that because beliefs and boundaries coincide, not only can a shattering of beliefs destroy boundaries but, conversely, a destruction of the boundaries can shatter beliefs. A culture that loses its sustaining belief system consequently loses that difference—the boundary—that sets it apart from other cultures and eventually dies out through assimilation and homogenization.

The works by Erdrich, Silko, and Kingston, then, point to the advantages and disadvantages of adhering to culturally based beliefs. The two Native American authors both suggest that the psychological and physical health of Native Americans and thus the survival of Native American cultures depend on the maintenance of and adherence to the belief systems that sustain them. Kingston's autobiographical account of her coming of age in America suggests that, for her, psychological and physical health depends on claiming a geographical and cultural space that is neither Chinese nor American but Chinese-American, an identity that is individual and eccentric. *The Woman Warrior* demonstrates that the creation of such a space requires an evaluation, rejection, acquisition, and modification of beliefs. Kingston even claims the right to adapt the stories of her ancestors and the myths of her culture to create a new story and a new myth to sustain her as a Chinese American living in the modern (or postmodern) world.[4] The story of Ts'ai Yen, however, which concludes Kingston's autobiography, points to the blindness caused by rigidly held beliefs about the primitive, barbaric, uncivilized—rather than merely different—thought, custom, food, and drink of other cultures.

By demonstrating that beliefs instilled through cultural conditioning create boundaries, these three works suggest a strong relationship between belief and ethnicity. The question, however, of whether ethnicity is inherited or constructed comes down, I fear, to a question of belief—of whether one believes that beliefs are inherited or whether one believes that they are constructed.[5] What the works discussed here suggest is that one's childhood beliefs are inherited but that it is the right and the responsibility of every adult to question, to examine, ultimately to choose—and, in some cases, to construct—a self-sustaining, self-empowering belief system. (In some cases, as most clearly demonstrated by Silko's *Ceremony,* only a system that sustains the group would also sustain the individual.) Of more concern to me here, however, than the question of whether beliefs, and thus ethnicity, are inherited or constructed, is the fact that, as demonstrated by the works of Smith, Naylor, and Morrison, the same relationships between boundaries and beliefs that occur between cultures or ethnic groups also occur within them. Differences in belief also create boundaries between an individual and his or her community, and those boundaries are weakened only through a shifting of beliefs on one or both sides.

The beliefs in the supernatural held by the inhabitants of the mountains of Appalachia at the turn of the century, as described in Smith's *Oral History*, are, like those of the Native Americans in Erdrich's and Silko's novels, empowering and sustaining. Unlike Erdrich and Silko, however, Smith suggests that with the passage of time these beliefs have become confining, preventing individuals, particularly women, from identifying and attaining new roles and identities. Granny Younger's belief in witchcraft blinds her to the reality that Red Emmy, despite her years of living outside the community, is simply a woman. During her months with Almarine, Red Emmy clearly displays her capability to be just as effective and conscientious a housewife, field-worker, and companion as Pricey Jane is. Granny Younger, however, sees only those signs that confirm her existing belief that Red Emmy is a witch. As a result of community belief in the power and nature of witches, Red Emmy is denied membership in the community.

Dory Cantrell, too, is denied the opportunity to cross the boundary that separates the primitive, uncivilized, *passionate* mountain life of Appalachia from its town life. Richard Burlage, like Granny Younger, believes that a woman raised in one environment is unable to change her nature, to adapt to the codes and manners of life in a different sphere. In listing the reasons why he should forget Dory, Richard first mentions the difference in social class and then the related difference in education: "She is ignorant and largely uneducated," he writes. "Such a gap exists between us that it could never be truly bridged, not even by any attempt on my part to educate her."[6] Such beliefs, like those of the Han people about the primitive, barbaric Southern Hsiung-nu, are so deeply ingrained and rigidly held that, no, the gap can never be bridged, not even by the passion that Dory awakens in Richard, the feeling that for the first time in his life he is truly alive. Red Emmy, Granny Younger, Dory Cantrell, and Richard Burlage are all Appalachians, sharing a similar ethnic background; yet the beliefs that separate them are just as divisive as the beliefs that separate different cultures or ethnic groups.

Naylor's *Mama Day* also focuses on the beliefs that separate members of the same ethnic group. George Andrews is similar to both Richard Burlage and Ts'ai Yen in that he is an outsider who believes that the community in which he finds himself—in this case, a southern, rural African-American community—is primitive and its beliefs in hoodoo ludicrous. In his pride of superior scientific knowledge, George is unable to believe that the people of Willow Springs may understand some things as fully as he does. When lightning strikes Ruby's trailer twice, for example, George knows that the electric field necessary to cause such a phenomenon can be manufactured artificially. That someone in Willow Springs could have manufactured such an electric field, however, is inconceivable to him. Proud of his own knowledge and abilities as an engineer, George consistently underestimates the knowledge and abilities of what he perceives to be a backward community. Because he cannot believe in the existence of powers different from—perhaps even greater than—his own, whether those powers are held by Miranda Day or by Ruby or by some supernatural force, George is rendered powerless in the world of Willow Springs. Differences in beliefs held by the people of New York and those of Willow Springs create, for George, an un-bridgeable gap.

The multiple beliefs that separate Sethe and her daughter Denver from the rest of the African-American community in Morrison's *Beloved*, although not as clearly dichotomous as those that separate the worlds of New York and Willow Springs, are just as rigidly held and just as destructive. The division is caused by differences in belief surrounding Sethe's attempt to kill her children to protect them from slavery. Sethe believes that it is her duty as a mother to protect her children from harm, which means to her the harm caused by being defined and treated as animals by white slavemasters. She also believes in life after death on "the other side." Thus, when Schoolteacher enters the yard of 124 Bluestone to reclaim his property—Sethe and her four children—she believes that killing her children and then herself, delivering them all safely to "the other side," is the most effective way under the circumstances to protect them from harm. When this attempt fails, she continues to try to protect Denver from harm by "keeping her from the past that was still waiting for her" outside the yard of 124 Bluestone.[7] Denver participates in and supports her mother's self-imposed isolation from the external world because of her own beliefs: she believes that although Sethe loves her, something may cause her mother to kill her too; she believes that the thing she fears will originate outside the yard of 124 Bluestone, which is the only place where she is safe; and she believes that her father, Halle, will eventually come to rescue her from her dangerous mother.

The community, on the other hand, believes that Sethe had no right to kill her daughter. Despite this belief, the women of the community would have wrapped her within their cloaking embrace had she shown some remorse, some grief, some need for consolation. Sethe is unable to ask for help or consolation from the community, however, because the price for such help would be an admission of wrongdoing and a request for forgiveness—and Sethe, believing that she has done nothing wrong, requires no forgiveness. The community also believes that God or some other supernatural force will punish Sethe for her act. Thus, when Beloved appears, in both her ghostly and corporeal manifestations, several of the women believe that she is just punishment for Sethe's crime.

The division between Sethe and the community is healed only after long-held beliefs shift. Denver triggers the reconciliation when her own beliefs about the relationship between Sethe and Beloved change; Beloved, previously believed by Denver to be Sethe's victim, is now believed to be Sethe's tormenter. The newly gained belief that Sethe and eventually she herself will die if she does not obtain food for them motivates Denver to act, to gather courage to step outside the yard of 124 Bluestone to ask for help. After being asked for help, the community also experiences a change in beliefs: Beloved is no longer a God-sent punishment but the devil. With this change in perception, the community acts unhesitatingly to exorcise a source of danger not only to Sethe and Denver but to the community as a whole.

The beliefs that create and then dissolve the boundary that separates Sethe from the community in *Beloved* are convoluted and complex. They are based on the shared experience of slavery, a shared world view about relationships between the living and the dead and between God and humans, and a shared understanding of the codes and mores that bind communities. Despite this shared experience, world view, and understanding, however, Sethe's unexpected and unprecedented response to Schoolteacher's attempt to reclaim her family demonstrates that a person's beliefs are, in the end, not always the product of cultural conditioning alone but also the result of an individual and eccentric retention, rejection, and assimilation of experiences. Had Sethe not overheard Schoolteacher directing his nephews to list her animal characteristics on one side of the page and her human characteristics on the other or had she not had such success in delivering her children to safety on her first flight from slavery or had not any number of other events occurred, she might not have held the beliefs that caused her first to kill her child and then to believe in the rightness of the act and her right as a mother to commit it. The reconciliation of Sethe with the women of the community does not mean that either she or they will ever change their beliefs about Sethe's rights as a mother. The reconciliation is made possible not by a change in this central belief but by the changes in belief held by Denver and the community about Beloved's identity. As for Ts'ai Yen and the Southern Hsiung-nu, the divisive boundary between Sethe and the community is not likely to ever fully disappear; however, that boundary is weakened by the communication—the exchange of words and kindnesses—that takes place across it.

As I have argued in chapters 2 through 7, the six works examined in this book suggest that the destruction, denial, or distortion of those beliefs that define, sustain, and empower individuals and cultures can result in psychic and even physical disorder. These works also suggest, however, that beliefs create divisive boundaries and that the loss, or adaptation, of such beliefs can destroy those boundaries. Whether the loss of beliefs and the consequent destruction of boundaries are destructive or empowering depends on whether the boundaries defined by the beliefs are experienced as protective or as limiting and confining. The works suggest, then, that power derives not from blindly accepting inherited beliefs but from examining and evaluating them to determine whether the boundaries they create are those within which one is capable of living and growing. They also suggest that power derives from the ability, once those beliefs and boundaries are defined, to find a voice with which to communicate across them.

As readers of the works discussed in this book, we understand that to reach us, the voices of the storytellers must transcend boundaries imposed not only by space, time, and text but also by differences in belief and culture. Suspended by the storyteller's art, however, we overcome difference to listen to the voices, hoping to receive some gift from their stories, their lives, their worlds that is of value in our own. The gift we receive may be as tenuous as an hour's entertainment and escape or as momentous as the discovery of a new identity, a new reality, a new world. The voices of these storytellers—the narrators and characters created by Smith, Erdrich, Silko, Naylor, Morrison, and Kingston—lift from the written page, rise on a whisper of wind, and riding across the boundaries separating one culture from another, speak to all those who are willing and able to listen.

Notes

Chapter 1 Belief, Ethnicity, and Self-Definition

1. Toni Morrison, "An Interview with Toni Morrison," *Contemporary Literature* 24 (1983): 428.

2. E. Fuller Torrey, *Witchdoctors and Psychiatrists* (New York: Harper & Row, Perennial Library, 1986), p. 123.

3. Rosalind B. Reilly, "*Oral History:* The Enchanted Circle of Narrative and Dream," *Southern Literary Journal* 23 (1990): 92.

4. Paula Gunn Allen, *The Sacred Hoop: Recovering the Feminine in American Indian Traditions* (Boston: Beacon, 1986), p. 209.

5. Gloria Naylor, *Mama Day* (New York: Random House, Vintage Books, 1989), p. 49.

6. Toni Morrison, *Beloved* (New York: Knopf, 1987), p. 257.

7. For reasons discussed more fully in chapter 7, note 3, I distinguish between Kingston the author and Maxine the narrator when discussing *The Woman Warrior.*

8. Maxine Hong Kingston, *The Woman Warrior: Memoirs of a Girlhood Among Ghosts* (New York: Knopf, Borzoi Books, 1977), p. 257.

9. Dexter Fisher, *The Third Woman: Minority Women Writers of the United States* (Boston: Houghton Mifflin, 1980), p. 143.

10. Bettina Aptheker, *Tapestries of Life: Women's Work, Women's Consciousness, and the Meaning of Daily Experience* (Amherst: University of Massachusetts Press, 1989), p. 20.

11. Werner Sollors, *Beyond Ethnicity: Consent and Descent in American Culture* (New York: Oxford University Press, 1986), p. 7.

12. William Petersen, "Concepts of Ethnicity," in *Concepts of Ethnicity*, ed. Stephan Thernstrom (Cambridge, Mass.: Harvard University Press, Belknap Books, 1982), p. 1; also in *Harvard Encyclopedia of American Ethnic Groups* (Cambridge, Mass.: Harvard University Press, 1980).

13. Sollors, *Beyond Ethnicity*, p. 25.

14. Horace Kallen, *Culture and Democracy in the United States* (1924; reprint ed., New York: Arno, 1970), p. 94.

15. Michael Novak, "Pluralism in Humanistic Perspective," in Thernstrom, *Concepts of Ethnicity*, pp. 52–53; also in *Harvard Encyclopedia of American Ethnic Groups*.

16. Fredrik Barth, *Ethnic Groups and Boundaries* (Boston: Little, Brown, 1969), pp. 14, 15.

17. Toni Morrison, "Toni Morrison Now," *Essence*, October 1987, p. 36.

18. Julia Kristeva, "Women's Time," *The Kristeva Reader*, ed. Toril Moi (New York: Columbia University Press, 1986), pp. 203, 209.

19. Linda Hutcheon, *A Poetics of Postmodernism: History, Theory, Fiction* (London: Routledge, 1988), p. 68.

20. Henry Louis Gates, Jr., "The Master's Pieces: On Canon Formation and the African-American Tradition," *South Atlantic Quarterly* 89 (1990): 105.

21. Louise Erdrich, "Louise Erdrich, Partner in a Conspiracy to Write," *New York Times*, 13 October 1986, p. 17. Numbers on precontact populations of Native Americans vary tremendously. James S. Olson and Raymond Wilson, in discussing the population in the continental United States only, state that "most historians and anthropologists put the figure at approximately one million on the eve of contact, although other estimates by reputable scholars put the number considerably higher" (*Native Americans in the Twentieth Century* [Urbana: University of Illinois Press, 1984], p. 29). Dexter Fisher, however, uses numbers similar to those cited by Erdrich: "By 1910 the government estimated that 210 thousand Indians were left of the 10 to 15 million people who were natives of America when Europe first made contact with the New World at the end of the fifteenth century" (*The Third Woman*, p. 6). Even allowing for the difference in geographical areas for which the estimates are given, the discrepancy between the two estimates is quite large.

22. Louise Erdrich, "Where I Ought to Be: A Writer's Sense of Place," *New York Times Book Review*, 28 July 1985, p. 23.

23. Toni Morrison, "The Ghosts of 'Sixty Million and More,'" *Newsweek*, 28 September 1987, p. 75.

24. Jeffery Paul Chan et al., "An Introduction to Chinese-American and Japanese-American Literatures," in *Three American Literatures*, ed. Houston A. Baker, Jr., and Walter J. Ong (New York: Modern Language Association, 1982), pp. 197, 209.

25. Paula Gunn Allen, *Spider Woman's Granddaughters* (New York: Fawcett Columbine, Ballantine Books, 1989), p. 15.

26. Irene Mack Pyawasit, "'God Gave You a Big Mouth,'" in *Dignity: Lower Income Women Tell of Their Lives and Struggles*, comp. Fran Leeper Buss (Ann Arbor: University of Michigan Press, 1985), p. 153.

27. N. Scott Momaday, *House Made of Dawn* (New York: Harper & Row, Perennial Library, 1968), p. 122.

28. Joseph Campbell, *Myths to Live By* (1972; reprint ed., New York: Viking Penguin, Bantam Books, 1988), p. 89. Fortunately, however, because a few Native Americans, such as Pyawasit, succeeded in keeping their religion inside them, hidden from the destructiveness of the dominant culture, many Plains Indian religions and rituals, such as the Sun Dance, have been revivified and are practiced today.

29. Aptheker, *Tapestries of Life*, pp. 135–36.

30. Elizabeth Janeway, *Powers of the Weak* (New York: Knopf, 1980), p. 167.

31. Novak, "Pluralism in Humanistic Perspective," p. 49.

32. Ursula Le Guin, *Always Coming Home* (New York: Harper & Row, 1985), p. 29.

33. Campbell, *Myths to Live By*, p. 68.

34. Dennis A. Bagarozzi and Stephen A. Anderson, *Personal, Marital, and Family Myths: Theoretical Formulations and Clinical Strategies* (New York: Norton, 1989), p. 34.

35. As Toril Moi notes, some feminist literary theorists argue that this goal of achieving "harmonious integration" is a phallic goal, based on the desire for an autonomous, self-contained entity freed of all conflict, contradiction, and ambiguity (*Sexual/Textual Politics: Feminist Literary Theory* [London: Methuen, 1985], p. 8). The primary thesis of this book, however, is based on my own conviction that emotional, mental, and spiritual health and power depend on the recognition and acceptance of the multiple conflicting aspects of one's identity and the continuing attempt to bring those differences into some semblance of accord and cooperation. Not to do so runs the risk of the colonization of marginal selves by a dominant self, which has most likely attained dominance in accordance with or reaction against external, socially dictated beliefs about what is strong, valuable, praiseworthy.

36. Trinh T. Minh-ha, *Woman, Native, Other: Writing Postcoloniality and Feminism* (Bloomington: Indiana University Press, 1989), p. 89.

37. Rita Felski, *Beyond Feminist Aesthetics: Feminist Literature and Social Change* (Cambridge, Mass.: Harvard University Press, 1989), pp. 106, 104.

38. Sollors, *Beyond Ethnicity*, p. 171.

39. Ibid., pp. 207, 247.

40. Michael M. J. Fischer, "Ethnicity and the Post-Modern Arts of Memory," in *Writing Culture: The Poetics and Politics of Ethnography*, ed. James Clifford and George E. Marcus (Berkeley: University of California Press, 1986), pp. 196, 230.

41. Gloria Anzaldúa, *Borderlands/La Frontera, the Mestiza* (San Francisco: Spinsters/Aunt Lute, 1987), pp. 78, 77.

42. Ibid., pp. 22, 59.

Chapter 2 A Witch and Her Curse

1. Lee Smith, *Oral History* (New York: Random House, Ballantine Books, 1984), p. 93. Subsequent citations of this book are given parenthetically within the text.

2. Southern Appalachia encompasses the Appalachian Mountains, Appalachian Valley, and Allegheny Mountains as they extend from Maryland to Alabama.

3. Henry D. Shapiro, *Appalachia on Our Mind* (Chapel Hill: University of North Carolina Press, 1978).

4. Lee Smith, "An Interview with Lee Smith," *Appalachian Journal* 11 (1984): 247–48.

5. Emma Bell Miles, *The Spirit of the Mountains* (1905; reprint ed., Knoxville: University of Tennessee Press, 1975), pp. 66–67. Miles was born and raised in the mountains of Tennessee but later moved to Chattanooga, where her success as a writer and painter opened the way for her acceptance by the wealthy society of the city. Her experiences from both inside and outside Appalachia gave Miles a bicultural view that distinguishes *The Spirit of the Mountains* from similar books written by outsiders looking in at Appalachia.

6. Ibid., pp. 37–38.

7. The reader does learn near the end of Granny's own narration, however, that not all the men in Tug share her beliefs in witchcraft. Recognizing that Emmy is nothing more than "a crazy girl" (p. 49), they laugh at those who believe in and fear Emmy's supernatural powers.

8. Frank Soos, "Insiders and Outsiders: Point of View in Lee Smith's *Oral History*," *Iron Mountain Review* 3, no. 1 (1986): 21.

9. Smith has been criticized for her tendency to people her novels with beautiful women and handsome men. See, for example, Denise Giardina's review of *Oral History* in *Belles Lettres* 4, no. 3 (1989): 10. Although Smith's characters may not appear realistic and certainly do not meet modern standards for "feminist" literature, they are true to the oral tradition of Appalachia, particularly its ballads of romantic love and killing passion.

10. Smith says that on the advice of her editor at Putnam's, she omitted a section of the original manuscript that had been written from Emmy's point of view. "It was a very disjointed stream-of-consciousness thing," she says, "because she [Emmy] was crazy. My idea about Red Emmy was that she was a girl, an orphan, who had been sexually abused when she was a child, by a preacher, actually, and his wife. . . . it showed that she wasn't a witch at all, that the way she was was probably understandable, given what all she had been through" (Lee Smith and Dorothy Hill, "'Every Kind of Ritual': A Conversation," *Iron Mountain Review* 3, no. 1 [1986]: 27).

11. John C. Campbell, *The Southern Highlander and His Homeland* (1921; Lexington: University Press of Kentucky, 1969), p. 32; Cratis Dearl Williams, *The Southern Mountaineer in Fact and Fiction*, 3 vols. (Ph.D. diss., New York University, 1961; Ann Arbor, Mich.: University Microfilms, 1966), 3:130–31.

12. Horace Kephart, *Our Southern Highlanders* (1913; reprint ed., Knoxville: University of Tennessee Press, 1976), pp. 330–32.

13. Richard Burlage, whose obsession for Dory Cantrell seems to mirror Almarine's for Red Emmy, gives a clue to the cause of Almarine's physical decline. Like Almarine, Richard also loses weight, a consequence, he says, of his emotional state: "I went always, in those days, in a state of grace, or dread perhaps, a state at any rate of a kind of emotional pointillism, with each nerve quite on edge" (p. 158).

14. Christina Larner, *Witchcraft and Religion: The Politics of Popular Belief* (Oxford: Blackwell, 1984), p. 151.

15. Sally's remark has been frequently quoted by reviewers and critics as summing up the curse of the Cantrells, but their interpretations of who wants what differ. See, for example, the analyses by Rosalind B. Reilly ("*Oral History*: The Enchanted Circle of Narrative and Dream," *Southern Literary Journal* 23 [1990]: 91) and Anne G. Jones ("The Orality of *Oral History*," *Iron Mountain Review* 3, no. 1 [1986]: 16).

16. Sally does not learn that Maggie and Pearl are not Luther's children until she asks Luther whether Pearl, thrown out by her husband, can come home to live (p. 280).

17. Harriette C. Buchanan, "Lee Smith: The Storyteller's Voice," in *Southern Women Writers: The New Generation*, ed. Tonette Bond Inge (Tuscaloosa: University of Alabama Press, 1990), p. 344.

Chapter 3   Predator, Scavenger, and Trickster-Transformer

1. Louise Erdrich, *Tracks* (New York: Harper & Row, Perennial Library, 1989), p. 177. Subsequent citations of this book are given parenthetically within the text.

2. "Chippewa" and "Ojibwa" are alternate spellings for the name of a single tribe. Because Erdrich uses "Chippewa," I use that spelling except when quoting from

anthropological and religious scholars, most of whom tend to use "Ojibwa." Similarly, I use Erdrich's spelling of "Manitou" except when quoting from the scholars, who tend to use "manito."

3. Ruth Landes, *Ojibwa Religion and the Midéwiwin* (Madison: University of Wisconsin Press, 1968), p. 8.

4. Although Fleur does gather roots for curing, she does not perform that function for the community, limiting her efforts at curing to herself and her immediate family.

5. Moses is also a visionary, so extreme, in fact, that he lives as a hermit; however, because he is not central to the novel, I do not include him here. Moses apparently conducts or assists in all types of sorcery, providing both "good medicine" and "bad medicine" on request, usually for a fee.

6. Louise Erdrich, "Louise Erdrich, Partner in a Conspiracy to Write," *New York Times*, 13 October 1986, p. 17. See chapter 1, note 21, for variations in estimates of the population of precontact Native Americans.

7. Although Moses Pillager also survives, Nanapush clarifies that Moses is not descended from Old Man Pillager (p. 33). A member of the Pillager clan rather than the Old Man's family, Moses receives his powers from sources (or experiences) other than Pillager blood.

8. Christopher Vecsey, *Traditional Ojibwa Religion and Its Historical Changes* (Philadelphia: American Philosophical Society, 1983), pp. 121, 138.

9. The name of Erdrich's water monster, Misshepeshu, is adapted from the term by which the underwater panthers, lions, and lynxes were known—*micipijin,* or Missipeshu (Victor Barnouw, *Wisconsin Chippewa Myths and Tales* [Madison: University of Wisconsin Press, 1977], p. 133). The name of the lake Fleur lives on, Lake Matchimanito, is drawn from "Matchi Manito," the name given to an evil Manitou—sometimes associated with the water monster and sometimes with the cannibalistic ice skeleton, Windigo—that was the Chippewa version of the Christian devil (Vecsey, *Traditional Ojibwa Religion,* p. 82).

10. Landes, *Ojibwa Religion and the Midéwiwin,* p. 31.

11. The water monster was believed to have given copper to the Indians (Vecsey, *Traditional Ojibwa Religion,* p. 74). Victor Barnouw includes among his collection of Chippewa animal tales the story of a woman who, when attacked by a water lion, cut off its tail with her paddle. When the tail fell into her boat, she discovered that it was made of copper; she took it home to her father, who became rich (*Chippewa Myths and Tales,* pp. 132–33).

12. Landes, *Ojibwa Religion and the Midéwiwin,* pp. 195–98.

13. Vecsey, *Traditional Ojibwa Religion,* p. 148. Nanapush's story of the visitation by what might have been a spirit bear to help Fleur in the difficult birth of her first child suggests that the bear was one of her Manitous.

14. The continued existence of the water Manitou, despite its reputation for drowning children and fishermen, is important to the survival of the Chip-

pewa. As the spirit that controls the availability of land and water animals, he can withhold fish and game from enemies; alternatively, however, he can provide fish and game to friends or to those who placate him by offering tobacco and food. Thus, the retreat or death of Misshepeshu, despite the fear he evokes, would be destructive to the tribe.

15. Landes reports that a common injury inflicted by Chippewa sorcerers was the "twisted mouth," a paralysis of the facial nerves that "was visited upon women who gossiped unduly or who laughed too readily" (*Ojibwa Religion and the Midéwiwin*, p. 62). Clarence's twisted mouth is a permanent reminder that he had "laughed too readily" after cutting Margaret's hair.

16. Vecsey, *Traditional Ojibwa Religion*, pp. 140–41.

17. Landes, *Ojibwa Religion and the Midéwiwin*, p. 43.

18. Catherine Rainwater, "Reading between Worlds: Narrativity in the Fiction of Louise Erdrich," *American Literature* 62 (1990): 405–22.

19. Vecsey, *Traditional Ojibwa Religion*, p. 68. Pauline's visions, depicting an ongoing battle between Christ and Misshepeshu, merge two different myths—the Christian myth of the continuous battle between Christ and Satan and the Chippewa myth of the never-ending battle between the thunderbird Manitous and the water monster. The thunderbirds—the arctic owl, the golden eagle, and the bald eagle—are the supernaturals of the sky (Landes, *Ojibwa Religion and the Midéwiwin*, p. 22). Vecsey sees the thunderbirds, who control the game of the air (birds), as counteracting the power of the water Manitou, who controls the game of the land and water (mammals and fish) (*Traditional Ojibwa Religion*, p. 75). Thus, in Pauline's visions, which merge the two myths, Christ can be seen as a sky supernatural (characterized, however, as a crow rather than an eagle or an owl) battling the water Manitou, Misshepeshu, for control of the Chippewa.

20. Rainwater, "Reading between Worlds," p. 409.

21. Vecsey, *Traditional Ojibwa Religion*, p. 77.

22. Landes, *Ojibwa Religion and the Midéwiwin*, p. 13.

23. Rainwater, "Reading between Worlds," p. 409.

24. The spelling of the trickster-transformer's name is as varied as the versions of the stories relating his exploits. Landes, working with the Chippewa in Minnesota in the 1930s, uses "Nehnehbush" (*Ojibwa Religion and the Midéwiwin*); Barnouw, collecting tales in northern Wisconsin in the 1940s, uses "Wenebojo" (*Chippewa Myths and Tales*); Paul Radin and A. B. Reagan, working with the Chippewa of Sarnia, Ontario, in the 1910s, use "Manabozho" ("Ojibwa Myths and Tales," *Journal of American Folk-Lore* 41 [1928]: 61–146); and Vecsey, after reviewing more than forty versions of the Chippewa creation myth, uses "Nanabozho" (*Traditional Ojibwa Religion*).

25. Vecsey, *Traditional Ojibwa Religion*, pp. 89–91.

26. Ibid., pp. 92, 94.

27. Paula Gunn Allen, "Teaching American Indian Oral Literature," in *Studies in American Literature*, ed. Paula Gunn Allen (New York: Modern Language Association, 1983), p. 50.

28. Radin and Reagan, "Ojibwa Myths and Tales," pp. 61–146.

29. Vecsey, *Traditional Ojibwa Religion*, p. 99.

30. Landes, *Ojibwa Religion and the Midéwiwin*, pp. 47–49.

31. Vecsey, *Traditional Ojibwa Religion*, p. 61.

Chapter 4   Calling Tayo Back, Unraveling Coyote's Skin

1. Leslie Marmon Silko, *Ceremony* (New York: Viking, Penguin Books, 1986), p. 169. Subsequent citations of this book are given parenthetically within the text.

2. Leslie Marmon Silko, "Language and Literature from a Pueblo Indian Perspective," in *English Literature: Opening Up the Canon*, ed. Leslie A. Fiedler and Houston A. Baker, Jr. (Baltimore: Johns Hopkins University Press, 1981), pp. 54, 56, 55. The spelling of Thought Woman's name varies among writers and ethnographers, as does that of many Native American names. Silko uses a different form—Ts'its'tsi'nako, Thought-Woman—in *Ceremony* from that used in the printed version of her presentation to the English Institute—Tséitsínako, Thought Woman. Throughout this section I retain both spellings, using the spelling found in the publication that is cited.

3. Leslie Marmon Silko, "A Conversation with Leslie Marmon Silko," *Sun Tracks* 3, no. 1 (1976): 32.

4. Ibid.

5. These opening details of the story, which tell how Coyote switched skins with the hunter to trick the hunter's wife into sleeping with him, are not included in the version used by Silko in *Ceremony*. This summary is drawn from the version recorded by Father Bernard Haile, published in Leland C. Wyman's *The Red Antway of the Navajo* (Santa Fe: Museum of Navaho Ceremonial Art, 1973), pp. 129–35, and reprinted in Robert C. Bell, "Circular Design in *Ceremony*," *American Indian Quarterly* 5 (1979): 58–60.

6. Bell provides excellent background on the importance of ritual identification and recapitulation in Navajo curing ceremonies ("Circular Design in *Ceremony*," pp. 47–62). Also see Edith Swan's discussion of the use of the Ghostway Ritual, a "generic ceremonial procedure used as an antidote in treating conditions resulting from witchcraft" ("Healing via the Sunwise Cycle in Silko's *Ceremony*," *American Indian Quarterly* 12 [1988]: 321).

7. Paula Gunn Allen, *The Sacred Hoop: Recovering the Feminine in American Indian Traditions* (Boston: Beacon, 1986), p. 61.

8. Rocky is killed by his desire to be accepted by the white world just as surely as Tayo's mother was. In fact, Betonie suggests that had Rocky survived the war, he would most likely have ended up among the Indians dying in Gallup (p. 131); thus, Auntie's son ends up—and would have ended up—similarly to

Auntie's sister despite the distinction Auntie perceives in her son's and sister's relations with whites.

9. Silko, "A Conversation," pp. 29–30.

10. Silko, "Language and Literature," p. 58.

11. Ma'see'wi and Ou'yu'ye'wi, the war twins charged with "caring for the / mother corn altar," cause a drought when they desert the altar for Ck'o'yo magic (p. 46). Rocky and Tayo can also be seen as war twins, lured from the force of vitality and birth by the counter force of witchery's Ck'o'yo magic—the destruction and death of the white man's war.

12. One symptom of Tayo's illness is his distorted thinking; he forgets, for example, that both Josiah and Rocky could always find their way home, crossing the boundary between life and death, because they would have known "exactly which way to go and what to do to get there." Directions based on actual geographical landmarks are extremely important in Pueblo stories. Pueblo hunting stories, Silko explains, often "contained information of critical importance about behavior and migration patterns of mule deer. Hunting stories carefully described key landmarks and locations of fresh water. Thus a deer-hunt story might also serve as a 'map.' Lost travelers, and lost piñon-nut gatherers, have been saved by sighting a rock formation they recognize only because they once heard a hunting story describing this formation" ("Landscape, History, and the Pueblo Imagination," *Antaeus* 57 [1986]: 88). The special significance of the many landmarks, places, and directions that are so carefully identified in *Ceremony* is discussed by Robert M. Nelson ("Place and Vision: The Function of Landscape in *Ceremony*," *Journal of the Southwest* 30 [1988]: 281–316) and by Edith Swan ("Healing via the Sunwise Cycle," pp. 313–28; "Laguna Symbolic Geography and Silko's *Ceremony*," *American Indian Quarterly* 12 [1988]: 229–49).

13. LaVonne Ruoff notes that Silko's emphasis on the need to add to or change ritual derives in part from Laguna's history of cultural change and syncretism: "The Laguna pueblo became a refuge at many different times for many different groups." As a result, "there is a long tradition of incorporating into Laguna tradition what was brought in from other groups. . . . The continuing process of changing rituals is an adding to, rather than a taking away: it does not involve a sense of loss" (Kathleen M. Sands and LaVonne Ruoff, eds., "A Discussion of *Ceremony*," *American Indian Quarterly* 5 [1979]: 67–68).

14. The question of Ts'eh's identity and the nature of the relationship between Ts'eh and Tayo have received a good deal of critical attention. Robert M. Nelson believes Ts'eh to be "a 'spirit of place,' a more-than-human being who knows how Things Work and who is willing to share this knowledge with the People" ("Place and Vision," p. 285). Kenneth Lincoln sees Ts'eh both as the spirit-woman of Tse-pi'na (Mount Taylor) and as "a spirit sister of Yellow Woman, . . . whom the Laguna call 'the mother of us all,'" as do Carolyn Mitchell and Edith Swan (Kenneth Lincoln, *Native American Renaissance*

[Berkeley: University of California Press, 1983], pp. 240, 234; Carolyn Mitchell, "*Ceremony* as Ritual," *American Indian Quarterly* 5 [1979]: 33; Swan, "Laguna Symbolic Geography," p. 238). Swan also suggests that Ts'eh is a Ka't'sina because her face is described as being similar to the mask of an antelope dancer (p. 242).

The descriptions of Ts'eh and her relationship with Tayo support all these associations. As Paula Gunn Allen comments, "If you try to define who Ts'eh is, you find that she is Reed Woman, Spider Woman, Yellow Woman, on and on. . . . She has many faces . . ." (Sands and Ruoff, "A Discussion of *Ceremony*," p. 67). Ts'eh, in fact, seems to reflect, incorporate, and *continue* the other females who have touched Tayo's life in passing: Tayo's mother, Night Swan, Betonie's grandmother. Thus, in addition to eliciting associations with spiritual helpers and deities, she elicits similar associations with ancestral spirits. Ts'eh, then, is not intended as a single, clearly defined person but, rather, as a projection of ever-expanding, continuously resonating associations. Clearly, she is a spiritual helper to Tayo, whether one views her as a supernatural presence cloaked in a human skin or as a human who—like Betonie, Descheeny, and Night Swan—possesses special powers to know, see, guide, and heal. Tayo himself seems to view Ts'eh as a human endowed with special powers for, after spending the summer with her, he concludes that "like old Betonie, she could see reflections in sandrock pools of rainwater, images shifting in the flames of juniper fire; she heard voices, low and distant in the night" (p. 232).

15. Silko, "Language and Literature," p. 56.
16. As Roberta Rubenstein notes, Silko's use of the pronoun "she" rather than a specific name for the female Tayo thinks of when he crosses the river leaves the identity of the figure open, incorporating Tayo's mother, Ts'eh, the mother of the people, the earth (*Boundaries of the Self: Gender, Culture, Fiction* [Urbana: University of Illinois Press, 1987], p. 202).
17. Allen, *The Sacred Hoop*, pp. 209–10. Laguna, as Allen explains, is an ancient Keres gynocratic society, in which an individual's place within the universe is determined by clan membership, which in turn is defined by matrilineal descent. Tayo grew up in his grandmother's home and thus was fully informed about his descent; however, his aunt's stories about his mother distorted his knowledge of her. Thus, Tayo does not really "know" his mother and his relationship with her until he rediscovers her abiding love and continuous presence.

Chapter 5 Modern Rationality and the Supernatural

1. Gloria Naylor, *Mama Day* (New York: Random House, Vintage Books, 1989), p. 285. Subsequent citations of this book are given parenthetically within the text.
2. Patricia Olson, "Gloria Naylor's Unrealized Myth," review of *Mama Day*, by Gloria Naylor, *Christian Century*, 16 November 1988, p. 1047.

3. Miranda is somewhat slow, however, in recognizing the approach of the hurricane that hits Willow Springs during George and Cocoa's visit. She blames her failure to note the obvious signs, seen but not *seen* when she took George fishing off the east bluff, on her efforts to prevent George from hearing voices from Bascombe Wade's grave. Miranda also refers frequently throughout the novel to a fading or diminishment of her powers to hear, see, and remember as a result of her increasing age.

4. When Ruby later succeeds in placing a curse on Cocoa, Miranda is surprised that she has ignored her earlier threat and can only conclude that Ruby is "crazy" (p. 271) or that "Ruby don't know me. . . . she *can't* know me or she wouldna done this" (p. 265).

5. Albert J. Raboteau notes the belief among slaves that being born the seventh son of a seventh son was one source of a conjurer's power (*Slave Religion: The "Invisible Institution" in the Antebellum South* [New York: Oxford University Press, 1978], pp. 276–77). Although John-Paul himself neither inherited nor developed powers of conjuration, he recognized his eldest daughter's "gift" to heal when she was still quite young (pp. 88–89).

6. Miranda's thoughts about the extent and limitations of her control over Bernice seem to reflect Naylor's feelings about her control, as a writer, over the characters she creates. Naylor says about her relationship with Willa Prescott Nedeed in *Linden Hills*, "I created a way for her to see her own reflection in a pan of water because she had no self up until that moment. . . . I had my ending all set. But when this character who had lived with me now for two years finally discovered her face in that pan of water, she decided that she liked being what she was. . . . And I said, 'Oh, Lord, woman, don't you know what the end of this book got to be?' . . . I was angry with her for a good week—I just stopped writing and ran around the house cursing her. But then again that was *her* life and her decision. . . ." (Gloria Naylor and Toni Morrison, "A Conversation," *Southern Review* 21 [1985]: 587).

7. The growth, multiplication, and movement of lizards, snakes, scorpions, and toads inside the body was commonly believed to be one form of hoodoo death. See, for example, Zora Neale Hurston, *Mules and Men* (1935; reprint ed., New York: Negro Universities Press, 1969), p. 232; Robert Tallant, *Voodoo in New Orleans* (1946; reprint ed., New York: Collier, 1962), pp. 195–202; and Newbell Niles Puckett, *Folk Beliefs of the Southern Negro* (1926; reprint ed., Montclair, N.J.: Patterson Smith, 1968), pp. 249–55.

Chapter 6   The Ghost as Demon and Savior

1. Toni Morrison, *Beloved* (New York: Knopf, 1987), p. 257. Subsequent citations of this book are given parenthetically within the text.

2. Toni Morrison, "Rootedness: The Ancestor as Foundation," in *Black Women Writers (1950–1980): A Critical Evaluation*, ed. Mari Evans (New York: Doubleday, 1984), p. 342.

3. Middleton Harris, ed., *The Black Book* (New York: Random House, 1974), p. 10.

4. Toni Morrison, "The Site of Memory," in *Inventing the Truth: The Art and Craft of Memoir,* ed. William Zinsser (Boston: Houghton Mifflin, 1987), pp. 106–7, 109–10.

5. Karla F. C. Holloway, "*Beloved:* A Spiritual," *Callaloo* 13 (1990): 522.

6. As the street number 124 suggests, the presence of Sethe's third child is most powerfully felt because of her glaring absence from the house on Bluestone Road.

7. Melville Herskovits, in *The Myth of the Negro Past* (1941; reprint ed., Boston: Beacon, 1958), argues that certain elements of African-American religious belief and practice are African in origin. In 1963, however, E. Franklin Frazier took exception to Herskovits's claims, arguing that few, if any, elements of African culture survived slavery (*The Negro Church in America* [1963; reprint ed., New York: Schocken, 1974]). Although Frazier successfully refutes many of Herskovits's conclusions, other scholars have continued to study Africanisms in African-American culture. In 1990, for example, Joseph E. Holloway published *Africanisms in American Culture* (Bloomington: Indiana University Press), a collection of essays describing the retention of African cultural elements within the United States.

   Morrison has written about the survival of Africanisms in modern American language in several essays, and the histories she provides for several characters in *Beloved* would allow for the retention of African religious beliefs among the people living in and around 124 Bluestone during the 1870s. For example, Sixo remembers the country he came from, still speaks only broken English, and continues to slip away at night to dance his native dances. Sethe, whose mother and wet nurse came over on a slave ship, remembers the slaves at the plantation where she lived before Sweet Home dancing the antelope and speaking another language. She believes that plantation was in Louisiana or Carolina; the first location suggests extremely large plantations, and the second suggests the Gullah settlements of the Sea Islands. Both are sites at which, even Frazier admits, Africanisms could have survived (*The Negro Church,* pp. 10, 20).

8. John Mbiti, *African Religions and Philosophy* (New York: Praeger, 1969), p. 162.

9. Ibid., p. 163.

10. Ibid., p. 162.

11. "Toni Morrison, in Her New Novel, Defends Women," interview with Mervyn Rothstein, *New York Times,* 26 August 1987, p. C17.

12. Deborah Horvitz, "Nameless Ghosts: Possession and Dispossession in *Beloved,*" *Studies in American Fiction* 17 (1989): 159, 164. My reading of Beloved as a supernatural being who has absorbed a collective memory of life in Africa and the Middle Passage owes much to Horvitz's analysis of *Beloved,* particularly that of the two segments presenting Beloved's "unspoken thoughts." Horvitz sees

Beloved as "both an individual and a collective being," arguing further, however, that Sethe's mother and Sethe's dead daughter "are a conflated or combined identity represented by the ghost-child Beloved" (p. 158). I do not find this latter thrust of Horvitz's reading entirely convincing because I can find no evidence in the novel that the child on the slave ship is, as Horvitz argues, Sethe's mother. One distinction between my own reading and Horvitz's is that I see Beloved not as an individual/collective *being* but as an individual spirit (that of Sethe's daughter) who has absorbed a collective *memory* that supplements, and in some cases supplants, her own individual memory.

13. Wilfred D. Samuels and Clenora Hudson-Weems, *Toni Morrison* (Boston: Twayne, 1990), p. 104.

14. Beloved's loss of a personal identity may also be connected to the loss of her name. The name by which she was known for the first two years of her life is never used and is thus lost to her. Only "Beloved" is engraved on the dead daughter's gravestone, a name that calls up not only the spirit of Sethe's beloved daughter but also the spirits of *all* the beloved, abandoned daughters. In addition, it calls up the spirits of those African-American females who were called "beloved in the dark and bitch in the light" by white men (p. 241).

15. Morrison sees flight—"the sense of going out too far where you're not supposed to go and running toward confrontations rather than away from them" and "taking risks"—as a "masculine" tendency ("'Intimate Things in Their Place': A Conversation with Toni Morrison," in *Chant of Saints,* ed. Robert Stepto and Michael Harper [Urbana: University of Illinois Press, 1979], p. 221; also in *Massachusetts Review* 18 [1977]: 473–84). Many of her most memorable female characters incorporate and act on this tendency, becoming pariahs, such as Sula, or sustaining ancestral figures, such as Pilate. One difference is that an ancestral figure successfully balances the best of both male and female tendencies whereas the pariah tends to lose her sense of balance, allowing one aspect of self to dominate and negate the other (Morrison, "Rootedness," p. 344). Morrison believes that by combining both tendencies, black women "can combine the nest and the adventure"; they can be "both safe harbor and ship," capable of holding together and nurturing a family *and* venturing out into the world to take risks (Morrison, "Toni Morrison," in *Black Women Writers at Work,* ed. Claudia Tate [New York: Continuum, 1983], p. 122).

16. Horvitz, "Possession and Dispossession," p. 159.

17. Judith Thurman, "A House Divided," review of *Beloved,* by Toni Morrison, *The New Yorker,* 2 November 1987, p. 178.

18. Cynthia A. Davis discusses characters in Morrison's first three novels in terms of Sartrean ideas about "the Look" and "Bad Faith." "Human relations," Davis writes, "revolve around the experience of 'the Look,' for being 'seen' by another confirms one's reality and threatens one's sense of freedom. . . . the Other's look makes me see myself as an object in another's perception." Davis's analysis focuses on those characters who exhibit Bad Faith by "trying to define

themselves through the eyes of others," either through dependence on each other or through internalization of the Look of the dominant culture ("Self, Society, and Myth in Toni Morrison's Fiction," *Contemporary Literature* 23 [1982]: 324–25). Denver's dependence on Beloved's gaze is not so much an instance of Bad Faith as it is a necessary step in separating from Sethe's gaze, which never distinguishes child as separate from mother. Unlike Sethe, Beloved does not love or need Denver; as a result, she does see Denver as separate, as an object, and under that impersonal, objective gaze Denver experiences herself as separate.

19. The truly free characters in Morrison's novels are, she says, those who "express either an effort of the will or a freedom of the will. It's all about choosing. . . . If you own yourself, you can make some types of choices, take certain kinds of risks" (Morrison, "Toni Morrison," p. 125).

20. Morrison's triadic relationships among women have been discussed by several critics. Susan Willis, for example, suggests that Morrison's three-women households are social utopias because they "do not permit heterosexuality as it articulates male domination to be the determining principle for the living and working relationships of the group" ("Eruptions of Funk: Historicizing Toni Morrison," in *Specifying: Black Women Writing the American Experience* [Madison: University of Wisconsin Press, 1987], p. 106). Morrison, however, does not believe that three-women households are sufficiently "nourishing." In *Song of Solomon,* she says, Pilate's daughter Reba and granddaughter Hagar suffer "because of the absence of men in a nourishing way. . . . That is the disability we must be on guard against for the future—the female who reproduces the female who reproduces the female" ("Rootedness," p. 344). Thus, Paul D's attempt to displace Beloved to insert himself is a positive move; however, he, Sethe, and Denver must all reevaluate themselves in light of the past before the new relationship can become viable.

21. One of the things that Baby Suggs had liked about Sweet Home was that Mr. Garner "didn't stud his boys. Never brought them to her cabin with directions to 'lay down with her' . . . or rented their sex out on other farms. It surprised and pleased her, but worried her too. Would he pick women for them or what did he think was going to happen when those boys ran smack into their nature?" (p. 140). Baby Suggs recognizes that to allow the slaves no avenue of sexual release is unnatural, damaging, and potentially dangerous.

22. Paul D, like the unknown white men, is guilty of having called Beloved "beloved in the dark and bitch in the light."

23. "It was absolutely the right thing to do," Morrison says of Sethe's act, "but she had no right to do it" ("Toni Morrison Defends Women," p. C17). Sethe, of course, disagrees.

24. Sethe's self-sufficiency also causes problems for Paul D. His reaction to Sethe's successful escape from Sweet Home combines pride that she succeeded with annoyance that she succeeded without the help of Halle or himself (p. 8). The

annoyance reflects Paul D's misconceptions about what it means to be a man or to be a woman. One of the things he learns is that, to save and be saved, a person must combine both masculine and feminine tendencies, to be both the ship and the safe harbor.

25. Michael Awkward, "'The Evil of Fulfillment': Scapegoating and Narration in *The Bluest Eye*," in *Inspiriting Influences: Tradition, Revision, and Afro-American Women's Novels* (New York: Columbia University Press, 1989), pp. 74–75.

26. The black communities characterized in Morrison's novels are noted for their tolerance of evil. In response to a question by Claudia Tate concerning her feelings about the pariahs in her first three novels, Morrison says, "Black people at one time . . . thought evil had a natural place in the universe; they did not wish to eradicate it. They just wished to protect themselves from it, maybe even to manipulate it, but they never wanted to kill it" (Morrison, "Toni Morrison," p. 129). The decision of the community to drive out Beloved is apparently based, then, on a belief that she is harmful, that eradication is necessary "to protect themselves." According to Mbiti, "when spirits 'endanger' a village, there are usually formal ceremonies to drive away the notorious spirits" (Mbiti, *African Religions and Philosophies*, p. 82). Thus, the move to eradicate Beloved by women who have armed themselves not only with Christian belief but also with magic charms and potions suggests a healing ceremony to combat spirit possession.

Chapter 7 Warring with Ghosts

1. Maxine Hong Kingston, *The Woman Warrior: Memoirs of a Girlhood Among Ghosts* (New York: Knopf, Borzoi Books, 1977), pp. 83–84. All subsequent citations of this book are given parenthetically within the text.

2. Maxine Hong Kingston, "Special Eyes: The Chinese-American World of Maxine Hong Kingston," *Belles Lettres* 4, no. 2 (1989): 10.

3. In this chapter I distinguish between Kingston the author and Maxine the narrator, who are not necessarily the same even though *The Woman Warrior* is an autobiography. Although many events and feelings described in the book are undoubtedly factual, others are imaginative re-creations of the actual events and feelings. It is virtually impossible for the reader to distinguish between an actual event, Brave Orchid's imaginative re-creation of an event, Kingston's imaginative re-creation of an actual event, or Kingston's imaginative re-creation of one of Brave Orchid's imaginative re-creations. (In this way the book demonstrates the process of "talking-story," the cumulative and individual re-creations of a story over time.) The reader who is unfamiliar with Chinese mythology and with the Chinese experience in America suffers the additional handicap of not recognizing when Kingston is intentionally modifying and transforming the myths or the experiences to achieve subtleties of irony and theme. The reader is also unable to distinguish between what "Maxine" felt, believed, or understood at the time an event occurred and what Kingston

felt, believed, or understood at the time she wrote about the event. Obviously, the thematic connections among events and the continual play on words that make the book such an artistic achievement are the work of Kingston the author rather than Maxine the narrator. In fact, one senses that "Maxine" is a character developed and filled in during the process of writing and thus is, like the other women described by Kingston in the book, a ghost that is given substance and materiality as the work progresses.

4. Vivian Hsu notes that "Kingston's use of the term 'emigrant' is very apt. The first generation of Chinese in America emigrated out of China, but have not spiritually immigrated to America. They wander in a ghostlike existence, hanging on to a former reality" ("Maxine Hong Kingston as Psycho-Autobiographer and Ethnographer," *International Journal of Women's Studies* 6 [1983]: 437).

5. The tendency to identify one's own race or tribe as "human" and all other races and tribes as "nonhuman" or "the enemy" is a form of ethnocentrism inherent to most, if not all, cultures. As George Murdock points out, "a people usually calls itself by a flattering name or by a term signifying simply 'men,' 'men of men,' 'first men,' or 'people.' Aliens, on the other hand, are regarded as something less than men; they are styled 'barbarians' or are known by some derogatory term" ("Ethnocentrism," in *Encyclopedia of the Social Sciences,* ed. Edwin A. Seligman and Alvin Johnson, vol. 5 [New York: Macmillan, 1931], p. 613). David Leiwei Li explains that "the usage of 'ghost' for foreigners became a common practice probably in the late nineteenth century when Western imperial powers invaded the Chin Empire of China with guns and opium. For the first time in history the citizens of the 'Central Kingdom' were decentered and they strove to retain their centrality by defining their oppressor as the other, the 'ghost,' the 'Kuei' which takes on the meaning of 'devil' and 'demon' " ("The Naming of a Chinese American 'I': Cross-Cultural Sign/ifications in *The Woman Warrior,*" *Criticism* 30 [1988]: 508).

6. Shih-Shan Henry Tsai cites the Chinese population in Stockton in 1940 as 1,052 compared to a native population of 54,714 (*The Chinese Experience in America* [Bloomington: Indiana University Press, 1986], p. 107).

7. Maxine Hong Kingston, "Eccentric Memories: A Conversation with Maxine Hong Kingston," *Michigan Quarterly Review* 26 (1987): 178.

8. Ibid.

9. Kingston herself has been criticized, primarily by the Chinese-American writer Frank Chin, of having misrepresented the Chinese in her works to gain the acceptance of American (western) readers and publishers. What I attempt to demonstrate in this chapter is that Maxine/Kingston creates an individual, eccentric identity based on her personal experience of what it means to be Chinese-American.

10. Joanne S. Frye, "*The Woman Warrior:* Claiming Narrative Power, Recreating Selfhood," in *Faith of a (Woman) Writer,* ed. Alice Kessler-Harris and William

McBrien, Contribution in Women's Studies 86 (New York: Greenwood, 1987), p. 295.

11. In an interview with Arturo Islas, Kingston says, "Part of sanity is to be able to understand the language of other people, and . . . even when people aren't mad, sometimes when you hear two people speaking in another language, you get a little bit of paranoia. 'Are they saying something about me?' . . . So, when Moon Orchid goes over the edge, . . . I am hinting that perhaps if she spoke the language, it might have saved her" (*Women Writers of the West Coast*, ed. Marilyn Yalom [Santa Barbara: Capra Press, 1983], p. 17).

12. King-Kok Cheung, " 'Don't Tell': Imposed Silences in *The Color Purple* and *The Woman Warrior*," *Publications of the Modern Language Association* 103 (1988): 164.

13. Tsai, describing the reactions of Chinese females emigrating to America after 1965, says that "they discovered a society that seemed to them more of a matriarchy than a patriarchy. . . . they envied the freedom and property rights enjoyed by their American counterparts. In particular, they liked the American concept of love and marriage. Acculturated Chinese women began to insist on the right to fall in love and to be married without parental arrangement" (*Chinese Experience in America*, p. 158). Maxine's spiritual well-being depends, in part, on her ability to stretch her mind sufficiently to allow for the paradox that the "barbaric" Americans treat women more humanely than do the "civilized" Chinese.

14. "The Ballad of Mulan," written in the fifth century, is a 62-line poem telling the story of a young woman who, dressing in men's clothing, takes her father's place in a ten-year war to save China from foreign domination. In the original poem, then, Mulan is neither a rebel nor a leader of armies. She is merely one of many warriors who "in ten years had won their rest" and who, in reward for their service and loyalty, "saw the Emperor's face" and received "lordships," "lands," and "prize money." (Mulan asks only for a camel to carry her home.) Mulan's fame, then, is founded on the exemplary filiality displayed by a female rather than on exceptional military exploits and victories; in fact, the poem's description of the ten years of battle, limited to less than ten lines, is sparse and bare (Arthur Waley, trans., *The Temple and Other Poems* [New York: Knopf, 1923], n.p.). All the rich detail of Fa Mu Lan's battles is a product of Maxine's own imagination, which merges other stories of battle with Sunday-afternoon movies seen at the Confucius Church to create her own individual "mind-movies" (pp. 19, 203). Just as Maxine transforms her nameless aunt into an individual with solidity and substance, so does she transform Fa Mu Lan. In both cases, the resulting figure reflects ambivalent aspects of Maxine's own spirit and personality.

15. Kingston's description of Fa Mu Lan seems to parody two early types of the modern "feminist" that emerged during the 1960s and 1970s: (1) the woman who succeeds in a man's world by transforming herself into a "man," imitating

male behavior, values, and appearance, and (2) the "superwoman," who is a "man" in the office and a perfect wife and mother in the home. Thus, Kingston's portrayal of Fa Mu Lan calls into question the whole concept of a "successful female" in a world that is dominated by male standards of success. On the other hand, the "witch amazons" may be a parody of those radical feminists who see the elimination of males as the only way to construct a world acceptable to women. Kingston, then, apparently sees problems with both of the first two phases of feminism, as does Julia Kristeva in her 1979 essay "Women's Time" (*The Kristeva Reader*, ed. Toril Moi [New York: Columbia University Press, 1986], p. 203).

16. The training on the mountain is not a part of "The Ballad of Mulan." This portion of Kingston's treatment of the Fa Mu Lan legend presumably derives from the movies she watched as a child. Speaking of the entire "White Tigers" chapter, Kingston says that it "is not a Chinese myth but one transformed by America, a sort of kung fu movie parody." American readers' preference for this chapter, she says, demonstrates the stubbornness with which they cling to their beliefs in what is actually "oriental fantasy"; her placement of the chapter early in the text was intended "to show that the childish myth is past, not the climax we wish for" ("Cultural Mis-readings by American Reviewers," in *Asian and Western Writers in Dialogue: New Cultural Identities*, ed. Guy Amirthanayagam [London: Macmillan, 1982], p. 57). Nevertheless, several lessons Fa Mu Lan learns on the mountain, even though the sequence does mock American "oriental fantasy," guide Maxine's journey from girlhood to womanhood and are clearly important enough to Kingston that she develops them thematically throughout the text.

For a discussion of the ways in which Kingston rewrites Chinese myth in *The Woman Warrior* and *China Men*, see Cheung ("'Don't Tell,'" pp. 162–74); Li ("Naming of a Chinese American," pp. 497–515; "*China Men:* Maxine Hong Kingston and the American Canon," *American Literary History* 2 [1990]: 482–502); and Leslie W. Rabine ("No Lost Paradise: Social Gender and Symbolic Gender in the Writings of Maxine Hong Kingston," *Signs* 12 [1987]: 471–92).

17. According to Kingston, "To live a true human life today, we have to imagine what goes on when we turn on the machines. 'The Brother in Vietnam' [in *China Men*] warns about how easy it is to operate an instrument panel and not see the people far away dying horribly. . . . The yearning for beauty can prettify reality, and sometimes imagination has to restore us to terror" (Kingston, "Imagined Life," *Michigan Quarterly Review* 22 [1983]: 566). Whereas Fa Mu Lan "prettif[ies] reality," Maxine imagines so much terror around her that she must learn to apply logic to rid her world of ghosts.

18. As Li notes, the name "Brave Orchid" itself suggests the paradox of the woman: "'Brave Orchid' can hardly be a Chinese name given its inherent contradiction in terms. 'Bravery' is a masculine quality. . . . 'Orchid,' with its tender floweriness, however, is a conventional equivalent of femininity. . . . Nevertheless,

the name becomes fictionally viable and even convincing because Brave Orchid turns out to be a living exemplifier of the paradoxical appellation. She is at once a female vanguard of the self-reliant rugged individual and a version of traditional motherhood" ("Naming of a Chinese American," p. 502). Also see Roberta Rubenstein's discussion of Maxine's experience of Brave Orchid as a paradox (*Boundaries of the Self: Gender, Culture, Fiction* [Urbana: University of Illinois Press, 1987], pp. 172–76).

19. *The Oxford English Dictionary*, s.v. "nightmare."

20. Maxine depicts Brave Orchid, as well as the other students at To Keung School, as being poised between the modern and the traditional. The women are modern in their desire to break out of the traditional roles for Chinese women as well as in their goal of learning and applying modern medicine to heal their patients. The fact that many of their future patients will retain traditional views—both of the roles of women and of the most effective methods of healing—means that Brave Orchid and the other students will discover, as Maxine does several years later, that their feet are still wrapped in "double binds" (p. 48). Brave Orchid's dual world view, blending the modern with the traditional, confuses and frustrates Maxine. Nevertheless, this dual view ultimately proves beneficial because, while Brave Orchid's traditional views threaten to entrap Maxine, her modern views enable Maxine to fight against entrapment. Thus, Maxine, when she "modernizes" traditional Chinese myths to aid her in her individuation as a Chinese-American female, is merely moving another step forward in the direction—from traditional to modern to, perhaps, postmodern—already established by her mother.

21. Rubenstein, *Boundaries of the Self*, p. 174.

22. Kingston's depiction of the suffering caused by separation from home, family, and civilization (Han customs, thought, food, and drink)—a suffering that is compounded by Ts'ai Yen's lack of someone to talk to—is true to the fourth lament of Ts'ai Yen's original poem, as translated by Rewi Alley in *The Eighteen Laments by Tsai Wen-chi* (Peking: New World, 1963). What Kingston omits from her summary of the poet's experience, however, is the terrible separation and grief Ts'ai Yen later experiences when, having been ransomed by her family after twelve years of captivity, she is forced to abandon the two children she bore to her "barbarian" husband. As a result, she finds herself torn by conflicting desires—the desire to go home and the desire to stay with her children. In the twelfth lament Ts'ai Yen says,

to go back home,
to stay on here, those two opposites
I cannot hold together in my heart.

By the fifteenth lament, her confusion is replaced with anger and bitterness that a mother must be separated from her children, "living apart / yet under the same sky" (Alley, *Eighteen Laments*, n.p.). Thus, the portion of Ts'ai Yen's story omitted by Kingston, yet known to Chinese readers, tells of mothers and children forever separated, as Brave Orchid and Maxine are separated, by both geographical boundaries and "boundaries not delineated in space."

Chapter 8 Boundaries and Belief

1. Bettina Aptheker, *Tapestries of Life: Women's Work, Women's Consciousness, and the Meaning of Daily Expression* (Amherst: University of Massachusetts Press, 1989), p. 20.

2. Rewi Alley, *The Eighteen Laments by Tsai Wen-chi* (Peking: New World, 1963), n.p. Although my discussion of Ts'ai Yen in this chapter is based on details provided in Alley's translation of the original poem as well as those provided by Kingston in *The Woman Warrior*, it is strongly colored by my own interpretation of Ts'ai Yen's story as an analogue to Maxine's experience growing up in America.

3. Maxine Hong Kingston, *The Woman Warrior: Memoirs of a Girlhood Among Ghosts* (New York: Knopf, Borzoi Books, 1977), pp. 11, 87.

4. Maxine Hong Kingston, "Special Eyes: The Chinese-American World of Maxine Hong Kingston," *Belles Lettres* 4, no. 2 (1989): 10.

5. I have been encouraged by several readers, both of my dissertation drafts and my manuscript, to clarify my own position on the question of whether ethnicity is sociobiologically inherited or whether it is constructed. I find that I am unable, however, to position myself on either side of a question that I do not see as having an either/or answer. My personal belief is that each individual is the product of complex and unpredictable interactions among genetic inheritance, cultural and social influences, individual experiences during all stages of development (not just childhood), and the choice/will of the individual to encourage, rebel against, or modify biologically or socially inherited tendencies. Any developmental theory that attributes differences among individuals or among groups to a single phenomenon (genetic inheritance, cultural conditioning, or boundary creation) or to a single component of one's total makeup (race, gender, or class), although helpful in explaining the causes of difference, is far too limiting to be realistic. Furthermore, I believe that the word "construction" has recently assumed more negative connotations than I attribute to it; for me all beliefs—all realities—are sociocultural constructs. Inherited beliefs gain credibility and power when experiences substantiate them. When new experiences discredit those beliefs, the beliefs change; they are reconfigured, or reconstructed, to accommodate the new experiences. As beliefs are reconstructed, so are the differences—the boundaries—that distinguish and separate individuals and groups. The fact that beliefs can be constructed, however, does not mean that many people do not, unfortunately, simply inherit beliefs.

6. Lee Smith, *Oral History* (New York: Random House, Ballantine Books, 1984), p. 134.

7. Toni Morrison, *Beloved* (New York: Knopf, 1987), p. 42.

Index

Belief in self, 31, 32, 64, 65, 104, 110, 112, 114, 116, 118, 120–21, 123–25, 127, 128, 187

Belief in supernatural: among Africans, 133–34, 205n.26; among Appalachians, 7, 10–11, 28–30, 43–45; among Chinese, 155, 158; among Chippewa, 7, 53–54, 58–66, 68, 71, 79–81, 196nn.9, 11, 196–97n.14, 197nn.15, 19, 24; as constructive, 6, 7, 8, 10, 28–30, 32–33, 45, 50–51, 83, 87–88, 89, 114–15, 116, 120, 128, 129–30, 154, 155, 175, 184, 187, 189; destruction of, by dominant culture, 5, 7, 19, 20, 64, 81; as destructive, 6, 7, 8, 10, 28, 30, 32–33, 44, 51, 61, 62, 87–88, 116–17, 120, 128, 129–30, 154, 184, 186, 189; as ignorance, 43–44; among Pueblo, 83–84, 85–87, 89–91, 94, 96, 199n.11; relation of, to expectation, 35–36, 117–18, 150; validation of, through experience, 4–5, 30–31, 35, 89–90, 96, 184, 188. See also Power

Bell, Robert C., 198n.6

Beloved (Morrison), 6, 8, 129–53, 154, 185, 187–89, 190

Beyond Ethnicity (Sollors), 12, 14–15

Bicultural experience, 9, 24, 93–94, 156, 161–62, 166–68, 178–80, 181–84, 206n.4, 207n.11. See also Dual heritage; Multicultural experience

Black Book, The, 131

Boundary: of Appalachia, 27, 45–50; choice of positioning oneself in relation to, 25; between classes, 47–48, 186; communication across, 9, 179–80, 182, 189–90; as confinement, 6, 9, 28, 46–51, 141, 142–43, 155, 186, 189; consequences of crossing, 5–6, 7, 15, 52–53, 81, 85, 87–89, 94, 98, 102, 108, 109, 130, 145,

154–55, 160, 164–65, 167, 174–75, 179–80, 183–84, 188, 209–10n.22; construction of, and power of definition, 15; as exclusion, 9, 15, 28, 45–47, 130, 155, 186; between individual and dominant culture, 5; between individual and group, 5, 45–46, 50, 130; as protection, 16, 82, 142–43, 180, 189; and relation to belief, 6, 16, 181–90, 210n.5; removal of, 53, 81, 103, 124, 130, 182, 183, 184, 188; response to, 92. See also Community, and nonconforming individual; Conflicting world views

Buchanan, Harriette C., 49

Cahan, Abraham, The Rise of David Levinsky, 24

Campbell, John C., 37

Campbell, Joseph, 19, 22

Carabi, Angeles, 155

Catholicism, 67, 74, 97

Ceremony (Silko), 6, 7, 82–108, 109, 129, 184, 185, 190

Chan, Jeffery Paul, 18

Chesnutt, Charles, 10

Cheung, King-Kok, 168

Chicanos, 15; response to biculturalism, 24–25. See also Mexican

Chin, Frank, 206n.9

Chinese, 154–80, 182–83, 185, 206nn.4, 9, 207n.13, 208n.18, 209n.20. See also Women, Chinese

Chinese American, 10–11, 154–80, 183, 185, 206n.9. See also Asian American

Chippewa, 7, 53–81, 184, 196–97. See also Belief in the supernatural; Manitou; Shaman; Trickster; Visionary Experience; Windigo

Christ, 66, 68, 69, 71, 72–75, 197n.19

Coatlicue, 24–25

Colonization: of American ethnics, 18–21; process of, 20

Community: and evil, 81, 152–53; failure of, 151–52; guilt of, 152; isolation from, 56, 71, 130, 138, 141, 187; and nonconforming individual, 21, 28, 60, 71, 130, 138, 140, 150–51, 159, 160, 164, 186, 187–88; as nurturer, 140, 145, 151; as oppressor, 21; regard of, for healer, 31–32; and relation with spirit world, 124, 130, 133–34; representation of, by women writers

Conflicting world views: between Chippewa and Christians, 52–53, 66–75; consequences of, 7, 94, 183; within cultures, 8, 45–46, 138, 150, 186–88; between modern rationality and supernatural, 4–5, 8, 109–10, 112, 116, 120–21, 122–25, 128, 187; between Native Americans and European Americans, 7–8, 52–53, 66–75, 82–83, 85, 87–91, 92, 94, 95–96, 99, 100, 184–85; reconciliation of, 7–8, 83, 108, 110, 112, 116, 124–25, 127–28, 131, 183, 188–90; between witchery and creativity, 84–85, 87, 106

Conjure woman, 110, 201 n. 5; relation of, to community, 115–16, 117

Cultural annihilation, 5, 18, 55–56, 184

Curse, 6, 46–47, 49, 96–97, 103, 104, 195 n. 15; invention of, 41–45

Davis, Cynthia A., 203–4 n. 18

Deicide, 19

Devil, 28, 30, 33, 44, 50, 66, 69, 70, 73, 74–75, 130, 196 n. 9, 197 n. 19, 206 n. 5

Difference: ambivalence toward, 23; assertion of, 5, 10, 11, 15–16, 181–82; and conflict, 9; and desire for acceptance, 67, 69, 97–99, 162; desire to eliminate, 9, 11, 16, 67, 69, 73–74, 91–92, 121, 162, 164, 167, 182, 183; fear of, 92, 93–94; of individual from community, 33, 39–40, 50; as strength, 89, 91, 94, 101–2. *See also* Community, and nonconforming individual; Ethnicity

Dislocation, 56, 112, 126, 157, 163–66, 168, 178–80

Dual heritage, response to, 9, 22–23, 66–75, 85, 88, 93–94, 101–2, 121–22, 164. *See also* Bicultural experience; Multicultural experience

Eccentricity, 41, 60, 160, 161, 163–64, 165, 183, 185, 189, 206 n. 9

Eighteen Laments by Tsai Wen-chi, The, 209–10 n. 22

Erdrich, Louise, 12; *The Beet Queen*, 65; on cultural annihilation, 18, 55; *Love Medicine*, 55, 56, 74–75; on survival, 55; *Tracks*, 6, 7, 52–81, 82–83, 129, 184–85, 190

Ethnicity: and belief, 16, 185; definition of, 12–13; as difference, 13; and individuality, 21; and marginality, 13, 16; as product of artificially constructed boundaries, 13, 14–15, 210 n. 5; as sociobiological force, 12–15, 210 n. 5

Ethnic literature: and assertion of difference, 5, 10; and concern with confrontation between cultures, 11–12; and concern with individual, 5, 21; definitions of, 12; differences in, between male and female writers, 11–12; and feminist literature, 16; as realistic representation, 10–11; as source of role models, 21; and treatment of alternative belief systems, 5; and treatment of empowerment through self-definition, 10, 20

Ethnic writer, definition of, 16. *See also* Ethnic literature

Ethnocentrism, 206 n. 5

European American, 7, 15, 26, 56, 82, 85, 133, 184

Felski, Rita, 23–24

Female madness, 131, 163–68, 179–80; and internal conflict, 55, 66, 68–69, 71–75; and sexual repression, 42–43, 68, 69–71, 72

Feminist literature, 16

Fischer, Michael M. J., 24

Fisher, Dexter, 11, 192 n. 21

Frazier, E. Franklin, 202 n. 7

Frye, Joanne S., 161–62

Gates, Henry Louis, Jr., 17–18

Ghosts, 8, 28, 29, 61, 155–56; as aliens or barbarians, 139, 156, 166, 206 n. 5; communication with, 59, 79, 109, 110, 111, 112–13, 122, 123, 128, 129, 134, 139, 178; confrontation with, 8–9, 154, 155, 157, 173, 175, 176–77; as embodiment of past, 9, 28, 133, 135, 146, 151, 152–53; exorcism of, 9, 151, 173, 175, 180, 188; as nightmare, 174–77; as reflection of other, 8, 132, 133, 136–37, 140, 142, 143, 146, 150, 152; resistance against joining, 71, 79–80; solidification of, 9, 154, 159, 160, 162, 171–72, 180, 206 n. 3, 207 n. 14

Giardina, Denise, 194 n. 9

God, Judaeo-Christian, 3–4, 28, 34, 43–45, 68, 112, 114–15, 121, 124, 150

Haley, Alex, 11

Healer, 31–32, 34, 113–14, 115–20, 175, 209 n. 20. *See also* Conjure woman; Medicine man; Shaman

Herskovits, Melville, 202 n. 7

Holloway, Joseph E., 202 n. 7

Holloway, Karla F.C., 133

Home, 8, 109–10, 126, 127, 157. *See also* Loss, of home

Hoodoo, 110, 115, 116, 117, 121–23, 187, 201 n. 7. *See also* Voodoo

Hopi, 87

Horvitz, Deborah, 135, 140, 202–3 n. 12

Hsu, Vivian, 206 n. 4

Hudson-Weems, Clenora, 136

Hurston, Zora Neale, 10

Hutcheon, Linda, 17–18

Identity: acquired through vision, 58, 67–68; choice of, 15, 24–25, 74, 107, 185; construction of new, 6, 8, 21, 24–25, 35, 68–69, 73–74, 81, 110, 125, 127–28, 154–55, 159, 183, 185; dismissal of, by contemporary theorists, 17–18, 21; importance of, to ethnics and feminists, 17–18, 21; imposed from within, 7, 52; imposed from without, 6, 7, 21, 33–40, 50, 93, 98, 132, 133, 148–49, 150; lack of, 130, 132, 136, 137; loss of, 53, 64, 81, 88, 102, 126, 156, 168, 203 n. 14; restoration of, 87, 88, 102–3, 107; search for, 23–24. *See also* Self; Self-definition

Imagination, 109, 110, 126, 142–43, 154, 155, 158, 159, 160, 164, 167–68, 169, 171–72, 207 n. 14

Individuation. *See* Self-definition

Internal conflict, 5, 7, 8, 9, 15, 55, 65–75, 83, 85, 87–88, 92, 89–94, 99, 100–104, 108, 130, 136, 140, 141–42, 161–63, 165–68, 170, 174, 176–77, 183, 209–10 n. 22. *See also* Self-definition

Intuitive knowledge, 114

Janeway, Elizabeth, *Powers of the Weak*, 20

Japanese, 95–96, 99, 107

Johnson, James Weldon, *The Autobiography of an Ex-Colored Man,* 24

Kallen, Horace, 13–14

Kephart, Horace, 38, 49

Keres, 107–8

Kingston, Maxine Hong, 12; on dissociation from terror of war, 208n.17; on ghosts, 155, 159; on oriental fantasy, 208n.16; and parodies of feminism, 207–8n.15; on past, 158; on sanity and ability to speak dominant language, 207n.11; *The Woman Warrior: Memoirs of a Girlhood Among Ghosts,* 6, 9, 154–80, 182–83, 185, 190

Kiowa, 19

Kristeva, Julia, "Women's Time," 17, 207–8n.15

Laguna Pueblo, 85, 87, 88, 90, 91, 95, 96, 97, 100, 104, 105, 107–8, 184, 199n.13. *See also* Pueblo

Land: connection with, 84, 91, 103, 104–5; separation from, 97, 104. *See also* Loss of land

Landes, Ruth, 53, 58, 72, 78, 197nn.15, 19, 24

La Virgen de Guadalupe, 24–25

Le Guin, Ursula, *Always Coming Home,* 22

Li, David Leiwei, 206n.5, 208–9n.18

Lincoln, Kenneth, 199n.14

Living-dead, 133–34

Loss: of connection with deceased, 79–80; of family, 56, 59, 63, 65, 71, 79, 92, 95, 97, 98, 127, 138, 157–58, 161, 163; of home, 65, 158, 163, 178–80; of land, 56–57, 59, 64–65, 98–100, 103; of mother, 92, 95, 97, 104, 105; of self, 97, 108, 126, 157; of spirit, 156–57, 158, 163–65, 168;

of supernatural guardians, 61, 65, 73, 80; terror of, 105; of way of life, 27–28

Madness, 59, 72, 75, 96, 156–57, 163, 207n.11. *See also* Female madness

Mama Day (Naylor), 6, 8, 109–28, 129, 185, 186–87, 190

Manito. *See* Manitou

Manitou, 53–54, 58, 61, 63, 64, 65, 67, 68, 70, 72, 73, 80, 196nn.9, 13, 196–97n.14, 197n.19

Matriarchy, 100, 107–8

Mbiti, John, *African Religions and Philosophy,* 133–34, 205n.26

Medicine man, 85, 86, 88, 89, 91, 95–96, 98, 99, 100–101, 198n.6. *See also* Healer; Shaman

Memory, 134–35, 140, 142, 144, 151; collective, 132, 135, 139, 148, 202–3n.12

Menominee, 19

Mexican, 89, 90–91, 93–94, 101, 180. *See also* Chicanos

Middle Passage, 135, 153, 202n.12

Miles, Emma Bell, 194n.5; on endurance of Appalachian women, 28, 49–50; on female elders of Appalachia, 31, 32; *The Spirit of the Mountains,* 28–29

Minh-ha, Trinh T., 23

Mitchell, Carolyn, 199n.14

Moi, Toril, 193n.35

Momaday, N. Scott, 11; *House Made of Dawn,* 19

Morrison, Toni, 12; *Beloved,* 6, 8, 129–53, 154, 185, 187–89, 190; on *Beloved,* 135, 204n.23; *The Bluest Eye,* 152; on choice of identity, 15; on collective African-American past, 135; on community response to evil, 205n.26; on effort of will, 204n.19; on male and female tendencies,

Pueblo, 7, 82, 83, 92, 102, 108, 184, 198, 199n.12. *See also* Laguna Pueblo

Pyawasit, Irene Mack, 19

Rabinowitz, Paula, 158, 159
Raboteau, Albert J., 201n.5
Radin, Paul, 77, 197n.24
Rainwater, Catherine, 67, 68, 74
Reagan, A. B., 77, 197n.24
Reilly, Rosalind B., 7
Ritual, 116, 118–19, 123, 198n.6
Rubenstein, Roberta, 176, 200n.16, 208–9n.18
Ruoff, LaVonne, 199n.13

Samuels, Wilfred D., 136
Satan. *See* Devil
Self: lack of, 136, 143, 201n.6; loss of, 108, 126, 144; as object of gaze, 143–44, 203–4n.18. *See also* Identity; Self-definition
Self-definition: and belief in supernatural, 6, 9, 28, 154–55; failure of, 50, 68–69; and health, 6, 8, 16, 83, 88, 102–3, 107–8, 130; and power, 6–10, 17–25, 52, 55, 56, 74, 83, 88, 108, 137, 145, 150, 153, 159, 177, 183, 185; and resolution of conflict, 22, 168, 209n.20; and search for authentic self, 23–24; and separation from family, 22, 126–27, 145, 168, 177, 183. *See also* Identity; Self
Separation. *See* Self-definition, and separation from family
Sexuality, 32–33, 36–40, 41–43, 46, 47, 68, 69–71, 77, 138, 146, 147–48, 149, 204n.21
Shakespeare, William, *The Tempest,* 110
Shaman, 54–55, 63, 67, 77–78, 80, 173, 175. *See also* Healer; Medicine man; Witch

Shame: experienced by Native Americans, 18, 97–100, 103; of mixed heritage, 93, 121
Shapiro, Henry D., *Appalachia on Our Mind,* 27
Silence. *See* Voicelessness
Silko, Leslie Marmon, 12; *Ceremony,* 6, 7, 82–108, 109, 129, 184, 185, 190; on Pueblo narrative, 83, 106, 107, 199n.12; on role of storytelling, 93; on witchery, 84, 85
Slavery, 5, 18, 112, 131, 132, 135, 137–41, 146–49, 150, 153, 167, 169, 170, 174–75, 178, 179, 187, 188, 204n.21
Smith, Lee, 12; *Oral History,* 6–7, 26–51, 52, 53, 129, 185, 186, 190; on Red Emmy, 195n.10
Sollors, Werner, *Beyond Ethnicity,* 12, 14–15, 24
Soos, Frank, 32
Speech: consequences of, 168; power of, 162–63, 168, 172, 174, 177, 178, 179, 189. *See also* Storytelling; Voice; Voicelessness
Spirits. *See* Ghosts
Spiritual connection, 105, 107–8, 109, 120, 128, 130, 133–35
Storytelling, power of, 29, 30–33, 41, 42–44, 60, 65, 79, 89–94, 95, 96, 100, 106–7, 144–45, 156, 189–90. *See also* Speech; Voice; Voicelessness
Sun Dance, 19, 78, 193n.28
Survival, 7, 49, 53, 56–58, 89, 110, 141, 150; through adaptation, 88, 90, 101; and assertion of difference, 181–82; costs of, 55–56, 75, 79; impulse toward, 149–50; responsibility of, 55, 57, 63–64, 80; and self-definition, 6, 56, 83, 88, 89. *See also* Transformation and survival
Swan, Edith, 198n.6, 199n.12, 199–200n.14

Talking-story, 205 n. 3

Tempest, The (Shakespeare), 110

Thurman, Judith, 142

Torrey, E. Fuller, 4–5

Tracks (Erdrich), 6, 7, 52–81, 82–83, 129, 184–85, 190

Transformation: from Asian to Caucasian, 164; from benign spirit to evil ghost, 130, 133, 150–61, 188; from Chippewa to Christian, 74; from ghost to human, 9; from human to animal, 60, 67, 85–87, 88, 148–49, 167; from human to ghost, 171–72; from human to witch, 60, 88, 99–100; from Indian to American, 98; from self to stranger, 8, 82, 109, 112, 125, 126; and survival, 65, 75, 76, 80; of trickster-transformer, 76–77

Transformation ceremony, 87, 88, 89, 102

Triadic relationship, 142, 145, 204 n. 20

Trickster, 75–80, 197 n. 24

Tsai, Shih-Shan Henry, 206 n. 6, 207 n. 13

Vecsey, Christopher, 58, 60, 64, 68, 76, 196 n. 9, 197 nn. 19, 24

Visionary experience, 53–54, 58, 59, 66–68, 171

Voice, disembodied, 29, 110–11, 112–13, 126; location of, 9, 10, 24–25, 155, 168, 169, 178, 179–80, 182. *See also* Speech; Storytelling; Voicelessness

Voicelessness, 17, 137, 141, 144, 159, 160–63, 164–68, 171–72, 176, 178, 179, 182. *See also* Speech; Storytelling; Voice

Voodoo, 10. *See also* Hoodoo

Walker, Margaret, 10

Williams, Cratis Dearl, 37

Willis, Susan, 204 n. 20

Wilson, Raymond, 192 n. 21

Windigo, 71–72, 81, 196 n. 9

Witch: Appalachian beliefs about, 28, 30, 33–36, 37; Chippewa beliefs about, 7, 60, 62, 65–66; Hopi beliefs about, 87; and independent woman, 40–41, 59–60, 170–71; invention of, 32, 33–41; power of, as function of belief, 7, 60–61, 62; relation of, to community, 7, 54, 60–62, 186; and sexuality, 32–33, 36–40, 146. *See also* Conjure woman; Shaman

Witchery, 35, 84–89, 94–95, 99–100, 101, 102, 105–6

Woman warrior, 158, 168–73, 175–76, 178, 207 n. 14

Woman Warrior: Memoirs of a Girlhood Among Ghosts, The (Kingston), 6, 9, 154–80, 182–83, 185, 190

Women: Appalachian, 6, 38–39, 49–51, 186; Chinese, 158, 160, 166–68, 170, 183, 207 n. 13, 209 n. 20; negative response to self-sufficient, 40–41, 59–60, 150, 151, 205–6 n. 24

"Women's Time" (Kristeva), 17, 207–8 n. 15